Leaving Certificate
Higher Level

English Revision for Leaving Certificate Higher Level

THIRD EDITION
FOR EXAMINATIONS IN 2003 AND 2004

Anne Gormley

GILL & MACMILLAN

Gill & Macmillan Ltd
Hume Avenue
Park West
Dublin 12
with associated companies throughout the world

© Anne Gormley 2001 and 2002
0 7171 3468 7

Print origination in Ireland by
O'K Graphic Design, Dublin

> Note: The texts, films and poems in this book are prescribed for the Higher level Leaving Certificate examinations in June 2003 and June 2004.

The paper used in this book is made from the wood pulp of managed forests. For every tree felled, at least one tree is planted, thereby renewing natural resources.

All rights reserved.
No part of this publication may be reproduced, copied or transmitted in any form or by any means without written permission of the publishers or else under the terms of any licence permitting limited copying issued by the Irish Copyright Licensing Agency, Irish Writers' Centre, Parnell Square, Dublin 1.

Contents

Acknowledgments	viii
Preface	ix
1. Revision Techniques	1

Paper I

2. Examination Techniques in Paper I	2
3. Comprehension	3
Characteristics of comprehension passages	3
Types of prose writing	3
Structure and form of comprehension passages	7
The language of comprehension	13
Characteristics of well-written answers in comprehension	14
Comprehension vocabulary	17
Exercises on style	22
4. Composition	25
General notes on writing	25
Problems and pitfalls	26
Preparation	28
Planning	30
The paragraph	32
Check-list for writing compositions	41
5. The Language Genres	42
The language of narration	42
The language of argument	50
The language of information	61
The language of persuasion	75
The aesthetic use of language	88
6. Samples of Paper I with Model Answers	96
Structure of paper I	96
First sample paper: culture and trends	97
Second sample paper: violence and destruction	102
Third sample paper: communication	110
Fourth sample paper: life-styles	115
Fifth sample paper: home and identity	122
Model answers to comprehension questions	128

Paper II

7. Examination Technique in Paper II ... 151
   - Prescribed texts for examination in 2003 ... 151
   - Prescribed texts for examination in 2004 ... 153
   - Examination technique in paper II ... 155
   - Answering literature questions ... 155
8. The Study of a Single Text ... 158
   - How to answer a question on the study of a single text ... 158
   - Sample draft answers ... 159
   - *Amongst Women* (2003 and 2004 exams) ... 159
   - *Wuthering Heights* (2003 and 2004 exams) ... 160
   - *The Remains of the Day* (2003 exam only) ... 161
   - Sample complete answers ... 163
   - *Macbeth* (2003 and 2004 exams) ... 163
   - *Silas Marner* (2004 exam only) ... 166
   - Possible types of questions for the study of a single text ... 168
9. The Comparative Study of Texts ... 170
   - What is a comparative study? ... 170
   - Answering a question on the comparative study of texts ... 171
   - Draft questions and sample answers ... 172
   - Possible types of questions on the comparative study of texts ... 179
10. Notes on Some Prescribed Texts ... 181
    - *Wuthering Heights* (2003 and 2004 exams) ... 181
    - *Amongst Women* (2003 and 2004 exams) ... 184
    - *Silas Marner* (2004 exam only) ... 186
    - *The Remains of the Day* (2003 exam only) ... 188
    - *Death of a Salesman* (2003 exam only) ... 190
    - *A Doll's House* (2004 exam only) ... 192
11. Notes on Shakespeare Drama ... 195
    - Tragedy in Shakespeare ... 195
    - *Macbeth* (2003 and 2004 exams) ... 197
    - *Othello* (2003 exam: comparative studies only) ... 200
    - *King Lear* (2004 exam: comparative studies only) ... 210
12. Notes on Films ... 223
    - Characteristics of films ... 223
    - *The Third Man* (2003 exam only) ... 224
    - *My Left Foot* (2003 exam only) ... 228
    - *A Room with a View* (2004 exam only) ... 231
    - *The Dead* (2004 exam only) ... 236
    - *Cinema Paradiso* (2003 and 2004 exams) ... 238
    - *Strictly Ballroom* (2003 and 2004 exams) ... 241
    - *On the Waterfront* (2003 and 2004 exams) ... 243
    - *Richard III* (2003 and 2004 exams) ... 245
13. Unseen Poetry ... 249

Approaching the unseen poem	249
Method of answering questions on an unseen poem	256
Questions and sample answers	256
14. Prescribed Poetry	265
Approaching the question	265
Questions and sample answers	266
Possible types of questions on prescribed poetry	272
15. Answers	273
16. Past Examination Papers	275

Acknowledgments

For permission to reproduce copyright material in this book, grateful acknowledgment is made to the following:

Harper Collins for extracts from *Wild Swans* by Jung Chang;

John Murray (Publishers) Ltd for an extract from *Wheels Within Wheels* by Dervla Murphy;

Peters Fraser Dunlop for an extract from 'The Reaping Race' by Liam O'Flaherty (© Liam O'Flaherty);

Random House Group Ltd for an extract from *An Evil Cradling* by Brian Keenan, published by Hutchinson (© Brian Keenan 1992) and for an extract from *In Patagonia* by Bruce Chatwin, published by Jonathan Cape (© Bruce Chatwin 1977);

Faber and Faber Ltd for an extract from *Lord of the Flies* by William Golding, an extract from *Murder in the Cathedral*, 'The Hippopotamus' and an extract from 'The Waste Land' from *Collected Poems, 1909–1962* by T. S. Eliot, 'Epitaph on a Tyrant' from *Collected Shorter Poems* by W. H. Auden, and 'You're' from *Collected Poems* by Sylvia Plath;

Curtis Brown for an extract from 'Summer Night' from *Look at all those Roses* by Elizabeth Bowen;

Extracts from newspaper articles are from the *Irish Times, Irish Independent, Sunday Business Post, Daily Telegraph,* and *Guardian.*

Photos: The Kobal Collection; *Irish Times*; Gamma; Frank Spooner Pictures.

The publishers have made every effort to trace copyright holders, but if they have inadvertently overlooked any they will be pleased to make the necessary arrangements at the first opportunity.

Preface

In this revision book, guidelines are set out clearly that will enable you to revise for the Leaving Certificate course at Higher level. The book gives a series of practical guidelines on how to tackle both paper I and paper II. There are notes on the different language genres, together with sample material and commentary, which will help you in dealing with questions on paper I. There are also a number of samples of paper I. These follow the same form—that is, comprehension and composition—as the examination on paper I.

The book also deals with paper II. There are guidelines on how to prepare for the question on both the single study of a text and the comparative study of texts. The notes on all texts are specifically designed for Higher level. There are also notes on Shakespeare plays, a compulsory question at Higher level.

Guidelines are also given on answering questions on both the prescribed and the unseen poetry. The method of answering poetry questions in both the prescribed and the unseen section is clearly outlined. In addition there are sample answers on both unseen poetry and some of the prescribed poetry on the course.

I hope the practical approach adopted throughout this book will enable you to prepare in an efficient and focused manner for all aspects of this course.

Revision Techniques

1. Make sure you are completely familiar with the syllabus and the requirements for Higher level. Know exactly how many questions you have to answer on each paper and how much time you have for answering each one. Know what sections or questions are compulsory.
2. Prepare yourself for paper I, which covers *comprehension* and *composition,* by reading material on topics you are interested in. Gather ideas on these topics and perhaps write them up in a notebook.
3. Study unseen passages for the comprehension section, and practise writing answers to these. Many times it can help to compare your own answers with some of the sample answers already done in this book.
4. Practise writing answers on the writing assignments in the different language genres. Make sure your expression is original and striking.
5. Identify clearly what text—whether a play or a novel—you will choose for the detailed question in paper II, as you will need to know this more thoroughly. Practise writing essays on both the detailed study of a text and the comparative section. Give yourself the same amount of time that you will have in the examination.
6. Establish clearly which three texts you are studying for the comparative question on paper II. Remember that you can study a film for this question. If you do take a film, watch it several times, and try to familiarise yourself with the central issues and the techniques.
7. Know your texts, whether book or play, very well. You cannot read your texts often enough. There is no substitute for your own intimate interaction with the text. Understand what you are reading; follow what is happening. If you miss a connection in the story, you will find yourself increasingly puzzled as you read on. Ask yourself the following questions: Why are the characters behaving in this way? How is the plot constructed? Study key passages and sections in great detail. Take note of important quotations, and familiarise yourself with the plot and the main features of the characters.
8. In the Shakespeare play, take note of key scenes and soliloquies. Study these in relation to the development of character and the plot.
9. You have two questions to answer on the poetry, so remember to prepare a question on one of the prescribed poets and one on how to answer an unseen poem.

Paper I

2
Examination Techniques in Paper I

1. The total number of marks for this paper is 200, or half the total for the examination. There are 100 marks for the comprehension and 100 marks for the composition assignment.
2. Four comprehension texts are given, each followed by two questions (question A and question B). You must answer *two* questions: question A on *any text* and question B on *any other text*. You cannot answer two questions on the same text.
3. In addition, you must answer one question on a composition or writing assignment.
4. The time limit for this paper is $2\frac{1}{2}$ hours.
5. Spend 75 minutes on the comprehension and 75 minutes on the writing assignment.
6. Give yourself approximately 35 minutes on each comprehension question.
7. Answer the comprehension questions first, since they demand less effort at creative thinking. Both the passage and the questions are clearly laid out.

3
Comprehension

CHARACTERISTICS OF COMPREHENSION PASSAGES

In the comprehension passage, always look for the following:
theme—this is the subject matter of the writing;
tone—this is the relationship between the writer and the reader, *how* the writer is saying what is in the passage;
intention or purpose—this is the reason why the writer wrote the passage.

All three features are related. If a writer's intention is to condemn violence, the theme will reflect that intention. A writer may wish to tell a story, so the subject matter will be presented in the form of a narrative. Another writer may wish to persuade the reader about something and will therefore use a persuasive style of writing.

TYPES OF PROSE WRITING

- Autobiography
- Argument
- Information
- Narration
- Persuasion
- Description

Autobiographical writing

In this kind of writing we get an insight into the mind of the writer. The use of the subjective 'I' is a feature of autobiographical writing.

Example

> In May 1953 my mother went into hospital to have her third child, who was born on 23 May—a boy called Jinming. It was the missionary hospital where she had stayed when she was pregnant with me, but the missionaries had now been expelled, as had happened all over China. My mother had just been given a promotion to head of the Public Affairs Department for the city of Yibin, still working under Mrs Ting, who had risen to be party

secretary for the city. At the time my grandmother was also in the hospital with severe asthma. And so was I, with a navel infection; my wet-nurse was staying with me in the hospital. We were being given good treatment, which was free, as we belonged to a family 'in the revolution'.

(Jung Chang, Wild Swans)

Comment
This is an example of autobiographical writing, in which the writer recounts some details about her life and events in her family during the 'Cultural Revolution'.

Argument writing
In writing that is based on argument, the information is presented in a logical and organised manner. The method of the writer here is detached and factual.

Example
> Humankind is under an obligation to preserve its physical health and well-being and to avoid anything that might endanger it. It is wrong to take alcohol in volumes that affect the rightful use of reason and one's consciousness.
>
> Drug addiction, apart from being an offence against the individual human person, is also a destabilising factor in society as a whole. The relationship between rising crime and drug abuse is evident. For that reason, the state has a duty, in the interests of the common good, to make all forms of drug-taking illegal, not to speak of trafficking in them. It would abdicate responsibility if it permissively tolerated any form of so-called 'soft' drugs.

Comment
The style of writing here is based on argument. The tone is clear and factual. The argument here is based on the dangers of drug abuse. The writer establishes his argument here on a fact: the need to preserve one's physical well-being. The effects of drug addiction are clearly stated in the parallel between rising crime and drug abuse.

Informative writing
The purpose of this type of writing is to inform or to convey certain facts in a clear and terse manner.

Example
> Pope John Paul has signed a decree recognising a miracle by Pope John XXIII, which will allow for his beatification. He also recognised a miracle attributed to the Dublin-born Benedictine priest Dom Columba Marmion, who died in 1923. Elected to the papacy on the death of Pope Pius XII in 1958, Pope John was already elderly. He was to become the most radical and the best-loved Pope of the century. The miracle is based on a vision of Pope John by Sister Caterina Capitani at Naples in 1966. Then twenty-two, she was dying of acute peritonitis. She had received the last rites when, on 25 May 1966, she said Pope John appeared and told her he had answered her prayers. Her recovery was immediate. Still alive, she is now nursing in Sicily.

Comment
This extract is taken from a newspaper report. It is a clear example of informative writing, as it gives the reader information and facts about the beginnings of the process of beatification of Pope John XXIII.

Narrative writing
In narrative writing the writer is telling a story. There is a definite arrangement of ideas or sequence of events. Narrative prose puts an emphasis on description: describing people, actions and events in detail.

Example
> One sunny frosty December morning I set out to cycle to the foot of the Knockmealdown Mountains, some eight miles north of Lismore. I took a picnic and ate it by a lively brown stream, and then thought it would be fun to climb to the top of Knockmealdown—an easy little mountain of just under 3,000 feet.
>
> I had been up several times before, with my father and Pappa and sundry guests, and was familiar with the easiest route. But somehow the climb took longer than expected, and as I approached the top the weather began to change. The air lost its crispness and the Galtees to the north-west disappeared as clouds came rolling south over the plain of Tipperary. Before I was half way down both the clouds and the dusk had overtaken me. But I was too inexperienced to be immediately afraid. For ten or fifteen minutes it all seemed a glorious adventure and I never doubted that I would soon hear the stream and feel the road beneath my feet. Not until darkness came, and the mist turned to rain, and a wind began to moan, did panic threaten. Then I stumbled into an old turf-cutting that should not have been on my route, and burst into tears.
>
> (Dervla Murphy, *Wheels Within Wheels*)

Comment
This is an example of narrative writing, which has a strong personal flavour and pays a lively attention to small details. The writer recounts in a vivid and intimate manner an incident that affected her deeply. She uses an **anecdote** here, which is a feature of narrative writing: a single incident is told in the form of a story. This incident almost always contains a definite point. Through the incident where the writer got lost in the mountains we learn how unpredictable and dangerous the weather can be.

Persuasive writing
The purpose of persuasive writing is to sway the reader towards a certain viewpoint on the strength of feeling and emotion.

Example
> In the current debate on street violence, I have to say I'm amazed at the very cursory mention of alcohol. The truth is that alcohol is responsible for a very substantial number of violent attacks.
>
> I don't drink, and sometimes when I walk home at night through Temple Bar I wonder

whether I've stepped into some bizarre alternative Dublin. Between the fresh vomit, the streams of urine, the shouting yobs, the general air of disorder and the occasional acts of violence, the easy availability of alcohol has to be blamed.

All my friends drink, and I don't object to people drinking. But I do object to the acceptance of an atmosphere in which drink-related civil disorder is accepted as unavoidable, and the Gardaí just have to contain it as best they can.

Secondly, I don't accept the age-old belief that someone who misbehaves under the influence is socially cleared of responsibility. No-one is forced to drink.

So what to do? Prohibition isn't an option, politically or practically. But a tough line on public drunkenness, under-age drinking and drinking in public streets should be enforced. Heavy fines should be imposed, and in particular, bars that serve under-age drinkers or people obviously drunk should have their night's takings confiscated.

I'm twenty-seven years old, I'm not a reactionary, but I'm appalled at seeing the city I was born and live in deteriorate into a yobbos' paradise. Am I on my own in feeling this?

Comment
This is taken from a letter written to a daily newspaper and is an example of persuasive writing. The writer makes use of colourful analogies, such as 'some bizarre alternative Dublin' and 'a yobbos' paradise', to illustrate his points about drinking. He concludes on a rhetorical question, which is a feature of persuasive writing.

Descriptive writing

Where narrative writing tells us what people and things *do,* descriptive writing tells us what people or things *are like.* Joseph Conrad said that descriptive writing, 'by the power of the written word, makes you hear, makes you feel; before all makes you see.'

This type of writing illustrates the power of the imagination to create unusual images or to juxtapose exciting and dynamic ideas. It differs from factual or argument writing in that it links ideas through word repetition and image association rather than through logic. There is a strong emphasis on drawing descriptions of things or people.

Descriptive writing
- gives a clear picture
- selects details with great care
- uses precise vocabulary and avoids exaggeration.

Example
As soon as the sun was down, the air was full of bats, cruising as noiselessly as cars upon asphalt; the nighthawk swept past too—the bird that sits on the road and in the eyes of which the lights of your car gleam red a moment before he flutters up vertically in front of your wheels. The little spring hares were out on the roads, moving in their own way, sitting down suddenly and jumping along to a rhythm, like miniature kangaroos. The cicadas sing an endless song in the long grass, smells run along the earth, and falling stars run over the sky, like tears over a cheek.

A few miles out, in the Maasai reserve, the zebra are now changing their pasture, the flocks wander over the grey plain like lighter stripes upon it, the buffalo are out grazing on the long slopes of the hills. My young men of the farm would come by, two or three together, walking one after the other like narrow dark shadows on the lawn.

(Karen Blixen, *Out of Africa*)

Comment
This is a splendid example of the use of detailed and vivid description. In this passage the writer sharply focuses on small details, which is a striking feature of good descriptive writing. Note, for example, the comparison between the cars and asphalt. The use of similes in writing can lend a richness and immediacy to description.

Note
Some comprehension passages will contain a mixture of styles. The intention of the writer will largely dictate what style they will use. A writer may decide to attack corruption in the political sphere: so, for example, they could use argument and an ironic tone. Another writer may wish to tell a story, so they could make use of the anecdote to illustrate a point more effectively.

STRUCTURE AND FORM OF COMPREHENSION PASSAGES

A comprehension passage is made up of

- paragraphs
- sentences
- words.

The **structure** is the layout of the writing, whether it is written as one continuous piece of prose, or structured in paragraphs, or is simply a series of sentences.

Paragraphs

A paragraph consists of one main sentence, usually called the **topic sentence**. The rest of the paragraph consists of support for that topic sentence. In a comprehension passage, the paragraphs may be clearly outlined, or the passage may simply be one independent piece of writing. When you are studying paragraphs for comprehension, examine

- the topic sentence: try to find where exactly in the paragraph it comes. Usually topic sentences come at the beginning or end of a paragraph
- the linking devices used by the writer to tie up the different ideas in each paragraph.

Sentences

A sentence may be defined as a group of words that makes complete sense. Sentences may be classified according to

- their purpose
- their syntax
- their form.

Purpose
According to its mood or purpose, a sentence may be
declarative—a statement or an assertion:

> John's wife died of cancer.
> Mary broke the vase.
> It's a lovely sunny day.

interrogative—asking a question:

> Have you seen him?
> Where's the cat?

imperative—giving a command:

> Please stop talking.
> Don't burn the toast.
> Close your books.

exclamatory—expressing surprise or shock:

> 'Oh, what a rogue and peasant slave am I!'
> My mother won the lottery!
> Imagine that!

Syntax
According to its syntax, a sentence may be
simple—made up of one subject and one object:

> The typist made an error.

compound—just two simple sentences connected by a conjunction:

> The typist made an error, and then she spilt the coffee.

complex—a simple statement followed by one or two qualifying clauses:

> Computers require a particular set of aptitudes, and if these aptitudes are missing, little can be done, and misery is guaranteed to millions of people.

Form
According to form, a sentence may be
periodic—with the main idea coming at the end:

> Spectacular though the parade was, it passed by largely unnoticed.
> Surprised and excited, the scientists who witnessed the event found themselves wondering, is this how life got started?

loose—the main point coming at the beginning:

> The parade was spectacular, but it passed by largely unnoticed.
> We can make impersonal places, like offices and factories, bear the imprint of our personality: pin-ups on the wall behind the workbench, trendy executive toys, gold pens, silver-mounted portraits on the executive's desk (or, equally revealing, nothing at all).

balanced—having a similarity of thought and a similarity of structure. The purpose can be to create dramatic effect. Balanced sentences can also show that a writer is drawing on different aspects of the subject matter to drive home the point:

> To be a woman writer long meant, may still mean, belonging to a literary movement apart from, but hardly subordinate to, the mainstream: an undercurrent, rapid and powerful.
>
> The true gentleman is too clear-headed to be unjust; he is as simple as he is forceful, and as brief as he is decisive.

inverted—with the subject of the sentence coming in the middle or at the end:

> Seeing a bullfight in Valencia, I understood why people can find it such a fascinating thing.
>
> Now in this dawn, how or why he did not know, his brain, without help or knowledge, had made that leap and combined with impeccable logic those two simple but momentous propositions.

antithetical—creating an **antithesis**, which could be described as similar to a balanced sentence but with the balance created by opposing ideas:

> The husband is a ruthless businessman, while his wife is a docile and humble woman.
>
> The farmer is a just and loyal employer, while his employees are dishonest and unfaithful.
>
> That girl is strong and powerful in her manner, while her brother is weak and cowardly.

The way writers construct sentences can reveal certain attitudes they may have towards the subject. A series of terse sentences can contribute to the flow of thought in a passage:

> The performance came to an end with two choruses, the second more subtle in its harmonies. The choir stood still and let their voices resonate around the small German church. There was no applause. No-one moved. The conductor did not move. There was a sort of stunned silence, but it was deliberate. It lasted one minute, perhaps more. And then there was a shuffling of papers, but no coughs or whispers. The performers remained still. No-one spoke. People began to move quietly from their seats.

Simple sentences anchor a writer's thoughts securely. However, a series of too many simple sentences can cause the writing to be jerky and monotonous. Examine the following opening, on the subject of success, which is made up of a series of simple sentences:

> Swallowing, then inhaling deeply, I plunged forward. 'How could you, after all I have told you? What are you trying to do? What right have you to disfigure such a beautiful area?'
>
> Beneath my steadfast gaze he slowly transformed into a tall, cruel, bellowing devil. 'Vanessa, my dear, I've won. It's all over. Construction is going ahead. All your exaggerated stabbings and jibes didn't work. Who

cares about wildlife? Today the only thing that counts is money, and, along with genius, I've a lot of that.'

The sentence's structure here makes the piece of writing incoherent and jerky. The following sentence structure would be more effective:

> As I plunged forward, I inhaled deeply. I began to cry out as I directed my gaze in his direction. 'How could you do this, after all I told you? What are you trying to do? Who gave you the right to devastate and disfigure the whole area, which is so beautiful?'
>
> As I looked at him he slowly changed and began to look like a tall and cruel devil-like figure. With a slow, measured voice he bellowed: 'Vanessa, my dear, it's all over. I've won. The construction is going ahead, in spite of all your jibes and criticism. In this world, the only thing that counts is money, and, as well as genius, I've got lots of that. So who cares about wildlife?'

Words

It is important to understand clearly how words are used in writing. The same word can be used to persuade, to argue, or to describe something. A writer can also use words to draw pictures or images of certain things.

There are different kinds of words. *Pictorial* words draw an image or picture of something. *Concrete* words give a specific idea about something, for example a heavy man, a round table, a tall girl, a circular motion, an oval face, a hollow cheek, a gaunt child, a green, ripe apple.

Abstract is the opposite of concrete. It means something that is not specific or tangible, for example goodness, loyalty, whiteness, truth.

The context of words

Examine the context of certain words. Both the *context* and the *connotations* of words can affect the message or purpose of the writer. The same word or set of words can be used to provoke a totally different type of reaction in the reader, depending on its context.

(1) Bombshell from Brazil explodes onto catwalk.

(2) He dropped a bombshell in the department when he announced that he was resigning.

The first sentence is a headline taken from a magazine. The second is an informal and casual use of language, taken from a personal letter.

(1) Torrid time for retailers.

(2) Retailers will have to audit their accounts before the next budget.

(3) He works as a retailer.

The first sentence is a headline from a newspaper, written in a sensational way in order to attract attention. It is an example of an emotive statement. The second is simply a factual account of how retailers will have to organise their accounts before the next budget, and it could feature in a newspaper article. The third is a simple assertion or statement that can also be spoken.

(1) Pets find their patch in star-studded glory.

(2) Pets are usually familiar with their own patch in the garden.

(3) She was mending the patch when the pets wandered over to her.

The first sentence is a headline from a newspaper. The second is taken from a book on gardening and deals with the peculiar habits of pets. The third is a statement taken from a story.

So we can see that the context of words can affect their meaning in a sentence.

The connotation of words

The connotation of a word is the emotive impact it may have on a reader—the associations, whether positive or negative, it conjures up in the mind. Word connotations all suggest certain attitudes to an idea. Examine the following words, and consider the various connotations that spring to mind when you read them:

> cool
> upbeat
> traditional
> soap opera
> obese
> foolish
> raw

Word connotations can be achieved in different ways: through

- syntax
- alliteration
- assonance
- cacophony
- sibilance
- repetition.

SYNTAX

Syntax can be defined as the order of words a writer uses when constructing sentences. The syntax can play a large part in the communication of certain ideas to the reader and in controlling or manipulating the reader's responses.

ALLITERATION

This is the repetition of consonant sounds, especially the initial consonants of words. Through the alliteration of certain consonants, different moods or emotions can be conveyed.

> He feared he would go mad or fall ill, yet if he once let go, the elaborate scaffolding he had so painfully erected would fall asunder.

The repetition of the *f* sound here is an example of alliteration and serves the function of underlining the emotion of fear within this man.

> I realised I had looked my last on youth and little more,

> For they are not made whole that reach the age of Christ.

The *l* sound here emphasises the sense of loss experienced by the writer.

Assonance

This is the repetition of vowel sounds, which conveys a musical or sensuous impact or a sense of harmony. Look at the following lines of poetry, all of which are examples of the use of assonance, each with a different effect or a different connotation:

> only a man harrowing clods …
> with an old horse that stumbles and nods …

The repetition of the *o* sound here emphasises the sense of isolation in the lines.

> Fall, gall themselves, and gash gold-vermilion.

Repetition of the *a* and *o* sounds here depicts a sense of richness.

> … Nor does long our small
> Durance deal with that steep or deep. Here creep …

There is assonance in the repetition of the *e* sound, and it emphasises a profound sense of disorientation and confusion in the writer.

Cacophony

Cacophony or *dissonance* is the opposite of assonance: it consists of the repetition of 'hard' sounds, such as *k,* to suggest a harsh or grating mood.

> Blight and famine, plague and earthquake, roaring deeps and fiery sands
> Clanging fights and flaming towns and sinking ships
> and preying hands.

The connotations underlying the use of cacophony in these lines suggest destruction and devastation.

Sibilance

This is the repetition of *s* and *z* sounds, and its use in writing serves the function of appealing to the senses. The following lines, from two different poems, contain some striking examples of the use of sibilance:

> starlight lit my lonesomeness
> when I set out for Lyonesse …

> turning the silver out of dark grasses
> where the skylark had lain …

Repetition

A writer can repeat the same word or set of words for purposes of emphasis. This type of emphatic repetition underlines different points more effectively for a writer:

> the beating down of the wise,
> and great Art beaten down.

he knew he was on the point of breaking through—he knew it …

no development has provoked more religious awe, more contentious debate, more lyrical speculation …

Word connotations can also be achieved by means of
- irony
- simile
- metaphor.

The combined use of these different techniques can add up to what is termed the *figurative use* of language.

THE LANGUAGE OF COMPREHENSION

Style

'Style' is the ability to present a subject in a way that is best suited to achieving the writer's aim. It is important when understanding a passage to know how to 'read between the lines', to understand how language and imagery both work to create a certain tone or mood, and how they all add up to a coherent style.

Note the difference between 'tone' and 'mood'. **Tone** is the relationship a writer establishes with the reader: how the writer is saying what is in the passage. **Mood** is the atmosphere of the piece of writing.

Imagery

Words can also be combined to form images or 'word pictures'. (The use of imagery will form an essential part of the section called the 'language of aesthetics'.)

When you see imagery in comprehension pieces or writing, ask yourself the following questions:
- What does it say?
- Why is it used?
- How well does it work in the passage?
- Has it 'sound effects' or certain connotations?

There are different kinds of imagery:

simple:

Easter Island is the loneliest inhabited place in the world. The nearest solid land the inhabitants can see is in the firmament, the moon and the planets.

original:

His instincts threw up their defences against the scandalous notion of being creative.

In some cathedrals you can see demonic winged creatures referring diplomatically to the majesties of political power. The cathedral therefore can be seen as an awesome engine of communication.

Copies of the molecule began to evolve, and it began to perform new and unexpected chemical tricks.

vivid or clear:

>The matador, gorgeous in green and gold, skipped with unbelievable nimbleness and daring in front of the bull, varying his blows with caresses on the soft nose and deft little side-kicks on the jaws.

exotic:

>A hedge of hibiscus bordered the airport buildings. Sunbirds glittering with green and blue iridescence played around it, darting from one scarlet blossom to another, hanging on beating wings as they probed for nectar. I noticed a chameleon motionless except for its goggling eyes, which swivelled to follow every passing insect.

startling:

>The calves sang to my horn, the foxes on the hill barked clear and cold …

>Fury had shrieked 'No lingering! Let me be fell: force I must be brief.'

>O the mind, mind has mountains cliffs of fall
>Frightful, sheer no-man fathomed.

Images can be used for different reasons in writing:

to illustrate a point:

>He is nearly as tall as a Dublin policeman, and preaching literature, he stood on the hearthrug, his feet set close together. Lifting his arms above his head (the very movement that Raphael gives to Paul when preaching at Athens)...

to provoke atmosphere:

>The edge of a colossal jungle, so dark-green as to be almost black, fringed with white surf, ran straight, like a ruled line, far, far away along a blue sea whose glitter was blurred by a creeping mist.

to provoke an emotional impact (the following lines are from an advertisement for perfume):

>Each woman should have her own subtle fragrance—one that will suit her style and that is a true expression of her personality. Each must use it as much to denote what kind of woman she is, her emotions and her aspirations, as to enhance her outward appearance.

Remember, imagery is effective when it conveys what a writer intends in a vivid and economical way. The use of imagery can also help a writer to achieve originality of expression in writing.

CHARACTERISTICS OF WELL-WRITTEN ANSWERS IN COMPREHENSION

1. Your answers must reflect a clear understanding of the content of the passage.
2. Organise your thoughts clearly. Focus on exactly what you are asked. Avoid padding or introducing irrelevant points.
3. Have a thorough grasp of the writer's intention in writing. Be able to understand whether the writing is persuasion, argument, or narration.

4. Develop the ability to follow a line of argument and to evaluate the points objectively.
5. Your answers must show a basic knowledge of the constituent elements of writing: how to structure sentences and paragraphs, how to use and understand tone and imagery.
6. Use clear, correct English and lucid argument to support your statements.
7. Answers must be
   - clear
   - logical
   - factual
   - precise
   - simple, and not ambiguous or awkward.

Common errors in comprehension answers
1. Misunderstanding the content of the passage.
2. Using incorrect facts or information in answers.
3. Misunderstanding the questions. Distinguish between such terms as
   'How does the writer reach the conclusion …?'
   'Why does the writer claim that this is the case …?'
   'Demonstrate from your own experience …'
4. Not giving reasons for answers when asked to do so.
5. Badly structured answers, where the main point is ignored and irrelevancies are introduced and developed.
6. Badly written answers, with faulty grammar, weak expression, and poor punctuation.
7. Not answering the question asked but rambling and going off the point.

Method of tackling comprehension questions
1. Remember, you have *two* questions to answer on comprehension. These must be taken *from two different texts*.
2. Spend 35 minutes approximately on each question.
3. Read the passage through several times, in order to grasp the gist or general idea of what it is about. Try to examine what the primary purpose of the passage is: is it informative, narrative, or persuasive?
4. Scan quickly the layout of the passage. If the text is divided by sub-headings, many times these headings can provide you with an idea of what the passage is about and how the points are developed.
5. Sometimes it can help to write out one sentence or phrase on the main idea of the passage. This can help to focus your mind and keep to the point.
6. If the passage uses *imagery*, examine why it is used and what point is being made by it.
7. Does the writer intrude in the text, and can you see why?
8. In a passage that is factual or based on argument, know how to distinguish facts from opinions. See whether there is evidence to support the points made.

9. Before beginning to write your answers, work on a rough draft—getting your points down in note form—for each question.
10. Tackle every aspect of your question. Keep control of time. Stop when your allotted time is up.
11. Use your own words as much as possible.
12. When reading back, read your answers with a purpose. Check the question and then your answer. Have you answered the question asked? Have you used examples that are relevant and useful? Is your answer clear and logical, or is it repetitive and long-winded?

The summary

A summary tests your ability to
- condense material, choose the main points from a piece of writing and express them in appropriate and clear language
- organise material in a coherent and logical manner.

Method of writing a summary

1. Grasp the general gist or message of the writing.
2. Write down the main points in the form of a rough draft.
3. Rewrite the summary in the form of one main paragraph.
4. Include all dates, numbers, or statistics.
5. Write your summary in the past tense.

Read the following article (from a 'healthy living' newspaper), then study the sample summary that follows.

Threat to natural health supplements

Today you can walk into any health shop and buy safe health-supporting supplements of your choice at reasonable prices—just as you have been able to do for the last twenty years or so. You can select your vitamins, your garlic or evening primrose oil or other natural remedies from the vast array that is available. You can also discuss your purchase with the sales assistant to make sure it is the right one for you.

But all this could change. In May this year the Irish Medicines Board issued a document entitled *Guide to the Definition of a Medicinal Product*. Without question, this document threatens the rights of health-conscious consumers to buy effective and safe supplements of their choice. If the proposals in this document become law, many safe and popular products could disappear from the shelves, simply because the IMB has decided to reclassify them as medicines and not food supplements. Enforcement of the proposals would require most products to have a medicinal licence, which, even if it were possible to obtain one, would cost thousands of pounds and take several years of clinical trials and scientific work for each product. Of necessity, these costs would be passed on to the consumer.

The IMB claim this is an issue of safety; but reclassifying supplements would not make them safer. Products at present produced under food law have to be 100 per cent safe; medicines do not.

As you would expect, consumers are extremely unhappy with this situation and are asking why the IMB has decided to pre-empt legislation, which is expected towards the end of this year, by bringing out their own guidelines.

Sample summary

Safe health supplements of your choice can be got at reasonable prices from any health shop. You can select vitamins, garlic, evening primrose oil or other natural remedies that are available. This could change. In May this year the Irish Medicines Board issued a document entitled *Guide to the Definition of a Medicinal Product*. If its proposals become law, many products could be reclassified as medicines rather than food supplements. The enforcement of these proposals would require that these products have a medicinal licence. This would cost thousands of pounds, which would have to be paid for by the consumer.

The IMB claim this is an issue of safety. Products now covered by food law have to be 100 per cent safe; medicines do not. Consumers are unhappy with this situation and are questioning the IMB's decision to pre-empt legislation by issuing their own guidelines.

Remember, in comprehension a good Honours pupil must be able to ask and answer the following questions:
1. What was the writer's intention in writing this passage?
2. Who is the intended audience for this passage? Are the techniques used suitable for this audience? Explain why.
3. Is the writing structured clearly in paragraphs; and if so, does each paragraph fit into the scheme of the writing as a whole?
4. Is the writer appealing to our emotions or to our intellect? Why is this so?
5. Does the nature of the subject justify the use of the emotions employed? Remember that emotion must be restrained in writing if it is to achieve the desired effect.
6. If the writing is based on argument, do you find the arguments convincing? If so, why?
7. Is the style uniform, or does it vary? If so, why is this? Does the style suit the subject, or is it too dull, or too ornate?
8. What do the style and the subject matter tell us about the writer?
9. Look at the writer's choice of words to see whether they are relevant, excessive, appropriate, precise ...

COMPREHENSION VOCABULARY

You should know the difference between the following words:

analyse: 'take apart' an idea or a statement in order to consider all its aspects
compare: show the similarities or the differences between things ('compare with': make a comparison; 'compare to': suggest a similarity)
contrast: show the differences between things
criticise: point out mistakes and weaknesses in a balanced way

define: give the precise meaning of a concept
discuss: explain a passage and give details, with examples
disprove: produce arguments that show something to be false
evaluate: discuss, but go on to judge for and against
explain: offer a detailed and exact explanation of an idea or principle
illustrate: give examples that demonstrate and prove a point
justify: give the reasons for a position
prove: give answers that demonstrate the logical position
state: express the points briefly and clearly
summarise/outline: give only the main points—not details
trace: give a description in logical or chronological order of the stages of a process

Study the meaning of the following literary terms
alliteration: repetition of the same initial consonant:
> the beating of the baton
> leafy with love

allusion: a reference; allusions can be
—scientific:
> Newton's laws in physics

—literary:
> the poetry of Heaney is rich in symbolism

—historical:
> the Wild Geese fled

ambiguity: the use of an expression or word that has a number of possible meanings in such a way that it is difficult to tell which meaning is intended:
> love is blind

analogy: a comparison that points out a relationship or similarity between two things
aphorism: a short, powerful maxim: a concise statement of truth:
> brevity is the soul of wit
> borrowing dulls the edge of husbandry

archaism: a term that is obsolete or no longer in use:
> perchance
> methinks
> thou

assonance: the rhyming of vowel sounds within words:
> thought her too proud
> watery hazes of the hazel

atmosphere: the feelings or emotions evoked by nature or a piece of music, art, etc.
balance: placing two parts of a sentence, or words within a sentence, in such a way as to be in opposition to one another:
> People who are powerful renounce coercive power but not the power that rests on persuasion
> Fools step in where angels fear to tread

bias: a prejudice: favouring one side in an argument
cadence: the rhythmical rising and falling of language in writing or speech
caricature: the portrayal of a person in which certain characteristics are exaggerated so that the person appears ridiculous
cliché: a hackneyed expression so overused as to have lost its impact:
> slowly but surely
> up for grabs

climax: the culminating moment in a play, poem, or piece of prose
colloquial: belonging to common or ordinary speech: informal language
connotations: reverberations, or what is implied by a word
diction: the writer's choice of words
digression: turning aside from the main subject
ellipsis: the omission of words, usually indicated by *omission points* (…)
emotive: tending to arouse emotion or feelings
empathy: the complete association of the self with another being
epigram: a short sentence expressing a witty thought or shrewd comment
euphemism: a mild expression in place of a harsh one
figurative language: language that contains many figures of speech, such as metaphors or similes
hyperbole: exaggeration to achieve a certain effect
idiom: an expression peculiar to a certain language
image: a word-picture
implication: something that is hinted at or suggested rather than stated explicitly
inference: a judgment or conclusion derived from a statement
invective: wordy abuse or denunciation
irony: an incongruous contrast between the words used and their implication
lucid: vivid or clear
lyrical: literally, like a song; figuratively, full of praise:
> he waxed lyrical about her talents

maxim: an adage: an established principle or truth expressed in a concise form:
> Present fears are less than horrible imaginings
> Brevity is the soul of wit

metaphor: a comparison between two things without using 'like' or 'as'
mood: the feeling or atmosphere created by a piece of writing
moral: concerned with the good or bad of human behaviour
oratorical: eloquent
paradox: a statement that is apparently contradictory but might be true in a way
parenthesis: an aside
pathos: pity, sadness or tenderness created by a writer
personification: investing inanimate things with human qualities
platitude: a trite or commonplace remark
polemics: the art of controversial discussion
precis: a summary

pun: a play on words that are similar in sound but different in meaning
quip: a sharp retort
rhetoric: persuasive and impressive speech or writing
sarcasm: bitter or wounding remarks made at the expense of another person
satire: exposing folly by means of ridicule
simile: the comparison of two things, using the words 'like' or 'as':

> as plain and as unadorned as the unclouded sky—and about as beautiful

slang: extremely informal expressions that are fashionable for a time but usually go stale very quickly
syntax: the grammatical arrangement of words in the form of sentences
tone: the voice of the writer or speaker
verbosity: wordiness: using more words than necessary, especially pompous ones:

> we would labour with all the wit of us, all the strength of us, to reach our goal [we would try with all our strength and intelligence to reach our goal]
> on a six-monthly basis [every six months]

Common vocabulary errors

Be aware of the difference in meaning between the following sets of words.

advance: progress, going forward:

> the advance of medicine, the advance of old age, the advance of time

advancement: promotion, or helping forward:

> The Government is working for the advancement of education

affect (a verb): This word has different meanings:
(*a*) to produce an effect on:

> The climate affected his health

(*b*) to move or influence:

> The news affected relations with Japan
> The film affected me deeply

(*c*) to pretend something, to pretend to feel:

> He affected shock at the news

effect (a noun): the result or consequence of an action:

> The effects of the nuclear fall-out were disastrous

When used as a verb it means to cause or bring about:

> The prisoners tried to effect an escape

agree with: to regard something with approval:

> I agree with the minister's new proposal

agree to: to give consent:

> They were forced to agree to the plans for the new building, though they did not like them

allusion: an indirect reference:
> She drew on several literary allusions in her lecture

illusion: a false image:
> He has illusions of greatness

delusion: a false belief, with no basis in fact:
> He suffers from delusions ever since the accident
> She is under the delusion that she can write well

anecdote: a short story
antidote: a medicine used to counteract the effects of a poison or disease

approve: to give consent to:
> The committee has approved the budget

approve of: to think well of, to regard with favour:
> He did not approve of the plan to build an extension to the house

artful: cunning or deceitful:
> He is an artful planner when it comes to getting more money

artless: natural, innocent:
> She is a simple, artless girl

assent/consent: Both words mean 'agree to', and both take the preposition 'to'. Assent is immediate agreement; consent is agreement after some consideration.

cancel: to put off altogether
postpone: to put off until later

censor: to examine books, films or plays with the intention of suppressing anything offensive.
censure: to criticise strongly:
> The teacher censured the pupil for cheating in the examination

compare to: to state a resemblance between two things:
> Shakespeare compared the world to a stage and men and women to players

compare with: to place side by side and note the resemblances but mainly the differences:
> Most working people are better off compared with how they were in the fifties

credible: believable:
> a credible story

creditable: deserving of merit:

a creditable achievement

credulous: ready to believe anything

defective: faulty:
> The computer is defective

deficient: lacking in something:
> You're deficient in vitamin C

definite: certain:
> a definite offer

definitive: final, complete:
> a definitive explanation

disinterested: detached, not emotionally involved, objective
uninterested: not interested, not paying attention:
> A judge should be disinterested in a case, but not uninterested

instantaneous: immediate, over in an instant:
> an instantaneous reaction
> death was instantaneous

simultaneous: happening at the same time:
> simultaneous translation

its (a possessive adjective):
> The cat is licking its paw
> The world is using up its resources

it's: a contraction of 'it is' (a pronoun and a verb):
> It's a fine day

lose (a verb):
> I lose my keys frequently
> I've lost my confidence in the Government

loose (an adjective):
> The door-handle is loose

stationery (a noun):
> The stationery shop is on the corner

stationary (an adjective): at a standstill:
> The car is stationary

EXERCISES ON STYLE

Examine the following sentences, then rewrite them correctly. (You can compare your answers with those on page 272.)

1. Shorten and increase the vigour of the following sentences:
   (a) Looking at the house from the outside I would imagine there to be about twenty rooms in the house.
   (b) The writer uses short to the point sentences with humour and sarcasm to keep the reader interested in the passage.
   (c) Boyle full of self delusion sees himself as the man of the house.
   (d) Many of these sort of teenagers result from homes where parents are unable to control them properly or the mother is at work and has no time for her children.
   (e) I would be delighted if you could please write back to me and tell me if and when you are available to do it for me.
   (f) What he means by this is that wherever there is a place it is made a place by people being there.
2. Criticise the following sentences under the headings repetition, punctuation, use of clichés:
   (a) When he states his points of arguments he doesn't condemn himself to one side he tries to incorporate the other side too.
   (b) You could find it in a magazine which rich people buy, you wouldn't find it in a newspaper because there are too many pictures.
   (c) The house is enormous and is not the usual type of house, it appears to be an old house that has been restored.
   (d) The environment where a person lives can tell you a lot about that person, if for instance you were in an untidy house you would presume that the owner was a laid back easy going character.
   (e) The image I get from Oprah on her programme tells me what type of person she is and her way of life, and I think her home would be the best way to tell me about her.
   (f) This would indicate to me that this is a family which leads a classy life-style by the mirror and the picture of the woman with the pearls.
3. Rewrite the following sentences by eliminating the repetition and improving the grammar:
   (a) The play is filled with jealousy and betrayal one sign of this is Iago.
   (b) In university students consistently analyse their actions with great scrutiny feverishly fearing that they may unwaveringly upset a fellow peer or teacher.
   (c) I am writing this letter to you to let you know what type of images and photographs I want included in my photo gallery.
   (d) The surplus between cost and selling price arose.
   (e) Trade fairs are a commercial feature today many being in new exporting markets.
   (f) I believe the writer puts across his argument very well and he also perceives human tendencies and exposes them in his argument very well.
4. Rewrite the following sentences and eliminate ambiguity:
   (a) I find myself grappling to maintain my popular personage.

(b) The application of time and motion study to this section will, of course, result in appreciable improvement from the production standpoint.
(c) Regrettably I'm stuck steadfast in this tedious unwelcoming claustrophobic condition where no-one knows the despair filled plight I must participate in every day and the lonesome state I am in.
(d) Re your order for Boxhead golf clubs of 15 ult., we beg to advise that these are out of stock.
(e) During the winter the 15:20 train (which during the summer runs on weekdays but not on Sundays) will not run on Sundays.
(f) To these people they soldier on, perhaps living on very little for many years struggling in their quest for success.

4 Composition

GENERAL NOTES ON WRITING

How to write effectively

Good, effective writing is a craft that can be acquired with a good deal of hard work and a knowledge of the basics. Successful writing involves taking into account a number of different things. It means
- knowing how to construct sentences so that they form effective and clear paragraphs
- the ability to construct paragraphs and to link them together to achieve a coherent unity and structure
- selecting the appropriate style for your reader
- mastering the conventions of spelling and punctuation
- polishing and revising what you have written.

Every form of written communication must take into account the following elements:
- a writer
- an audience or 'receiver'
- the purpose of the communication.

Before you start writing, establish clearly
- what the purpose of your communication is
- what your subject matter is
- the type of reader, and what expectations they have.

Effective writing means that what you have written is both relevant and appropriate to the situation. For effective writing, therefore, bear in mind the following elements:
- purpose
- topic or subject

- context
- audience
- language or techniques.

Genres of writing

The prose composition should be an attempt to present a reasonable and logical interpretation of the topic you chose. The Leaving Certificate course offers you the opportunity to write in a variety of genres. These include

- the language of narration
- the language of argument
- the language of information
- the language of persuasion
- the aesthetic use of language.

As we have already seen in the section on comprehension, none of these methods is completely clear-cut. In other words, a piece of informative writing will involve some amount of persuasive techniques, while writing an argument means that you must communicate information in a certain way.

The art of writing a composition can be mastered with time and effort. It is essential in writing a composition that you take into account certain things, such as pre-composition writing and the different features of the language genres, together with some basic knowledge of how sentences work to form paragraphs and how paragraphs are constructed to form a full composition.

Your composition must be your own individual response to the subject. It is important, therefore, not to regurgitate material or to learn compositions off by heart. Nor is it advisable to write a composition simply 'off the top of your head', without any preparation. It can be useful to use fifth year and perhaps some holiday time to read and prepare material on different styles of compositions. Remember, the best compositions are written on topics that you enjoy. Learn, therefore, to identify your own style, and to work at cultivating various interests.

PROBLEMS AND PITFALLS

Content

One of the main problems is in knowing what exactly to write. The fact of having to write on an unseen topic at Higher level can be confusing and unsettling for many people. The content in compositions must reflect a certain maturity of approach and a balance of judgment, particularly when writing on factual topics. Avoid digression or introducing irrelevant information. Avoid repetition of ideas.

The language genres

The different language genres or styles for the English course have certain distinctive features. It is important to be aware of these aspects and to know how to use them.

Writer's block and exam paralysis
Overcoming exam paralysis and starting to put pen to paper is another problem.

Lack of unity and structure
There is also the difficulty of organising ideas, of knowing exactly how to construct a paragraph and how to select relevant information and to discard useless ideas. Sometimes pupils have problems in writing a suitable opening paragraph.

Poor timing
Time and time management can be a further problem.

Faulty style
Faulty style can be shown in many different ways: excessive repetition, poor spelling, and bad grammar.

Misinterpreting the question or the title
This can occur from a careless reading of the titles.

Solving these problems

1. Gather ideas from newspapers or magazines that deal with current affairs, and keep a notebook in which you can jot down ideas. Identify your style of writing and what genres appeal to you. The advice from your teacher can be invaluable here. For the most part you write best on subjects that you enjoy or feel strongly about.
2. Study the guidelines in this section on how to write in the different language genres (page 42). Know exactly what is required for each genre. Also, study the sample material provided for each genre and in particular the commentary after each one.
3. The main thing in overcoming exam paralysis is to put pen to paper and simply to write until your thoughts become coherent.
4. Some of the pre-writing strategies, such as 'brainstorming' and writing a rough outline, can help you to structure your ideas and to organise your thoughts more clearly. The section on paragraphing, and especially on opening paragraphs, offers some guidelines and sample material to help you construct opening paragraphs.
5. Set deadlines for yourself when writing throughout the year. Remember, you have approximately 75 minutes in the exam to write the composition.
6. Pay attention to such details as spelling, handwriting, and grammar. Correct all spelling errors, and check that every word you use is the right one. Read your work aloud if possible: this can alert you to all repetition, not only of words but also of ideas. Study the section on style (page 13), and learn how to eliminate common errors in both grammar and spelling.
7. Read the questions and titles slowly, and take account of every word and the possibilities or connotations of each word.

Preparation

Pre-writing activities

The success of a finished product depends to a great extent on the preparation that has gone into making it what it is. This applies also to a piece of writing. Some of the more important pre-writing activities include
- brainstorming
- clustering
- outlines
- free writing.

Brainstorming

This is the process of throwing your imagination into high gear and trying to trigger off as many ideas as possible on the topic. It can be useful to use such techniques as 'trigger questions' (why? how? where? what? when?) to generate ideas on the topic.

Look at the following samples of how you can brainstorm a topic.

Topic 1: The modern magazine
What exactly is a magazine?
What qualifies it as modern?
What is the difference between a modern magazine and an old-fashioned one?
Who decides that a particular magazine is modern or not?

Topic 2: The place of colour in life
What exactly is colour?
Why are there different kinds of colours?
What place has colour in life?
How does colour affect us?

Clustering

Draw together all the points you have generated from your brainstorming. Begin by 'clustering' your ideas or assembling them into groups. For example, look at the brainstorming above on the topic 'The modern magazine'. Answer some of the questions, then cluster these answers.

For example, you can discuss the different types of magazines today. You may go on to discuss whatever is modern or popular: clothes, beauty tips, love, favourite types of food or holidays. You could also contrast today's publications and trends with those of the past. When you group these ideas together you will have the basis for an outline.

Outlines

Outlines form another part of pre-writing activities. The use of outlines can be very helpful when you are planning a writing activity and in particular a composition. Outlines are the result of brainstorming and drawing up clusters of ideas before you set about the process of writing. Outlines have the following advantages:

- They organise your thoughts.
- They clarify exactly where you are going in the composition.
- They help to provide a direction for a flow of ideas in the composition.
- They help to overcome exam paralysis. Staring at a blank page can be a daunting experience, and the rough outline can be a life-saver here.
- They help you to organise and structure paragraphs.

Rough outlines help you to organise your thoughts; they show what needs to be emphasised and what needs to be eliminated, where repetition occurs, etc. Many common errors can be eliminated through the outline, such as
- gaps in the logical development of ideas
- excessive repetition
- omission of central ideas and information on the subject
- going off the point
- insufficient evidence and examples.

The following is an example of brainstorming a topic, then clustering the ideas together and finally drawing up an outline. Examine the method closely, and try to follow it in your writing assignments.

Topic
Compose a persuasive composition that seeks to establish the need for a greater awareness of sex stereotyping.

Sample brainstorm
Use trigger questions on the topic:
- What is sex stereotyping?
- How is this created?
- Where is this situation most in evidence?
- What can be done to remedy it?

Sample clustering of ideas
Answer the questions from your brainstorming session, then cluster or gather together these answers; for example:

> The problem consists of stereotyping people because of their sex.
> Sex stereotyping can be seen in certain types of advertisements: the helpless woman, the resourceful man.
> Some television serials stereotype male and female characters: the slim, tall women, the strong men in fast cars.
> There needs to be a more balanced presentation of male and female roles in the media.

Sample outline
Establish greater awareness of stereotyping in society.

Opening paragraph
The images of Mother cooking a meal, Father watching television on Saturday evening. Father objecting to slogan in advertisement on television: So simple even he can do it.

Paragraph 2
Images of chaos when Father runs the house. Order and harmony with the presence of Mother. The recognition of this type of stereotyping in advertising.

Paragraph 3
Discuss how some areas of professional life limit and isolate people. 'Female jobs': secretaries, cleaners, nurses. 'Male jobs': technicians, drivers.

Paragraph 4
The media constantly consolidate these images: for example in 'The Simpsons', the intelligent and resourceful mother and daughter nevertheless do the housework.

Paragraph 5
The effects of this on society. Friction between men and women as pressures to conform intensify. The typical image that women mechanics or bus drivers have to be resilient and tough to survive.

Concluding paragraph
The need to tackle this issue: men and women to deal with their limitations and transcend the pressures coming from the media. Television programmes need to broaden the outlook of people on this issue.

Study this composition (which is given in full on page 86), and read the commentary.

Free writing
Free writing is a helpful method of warming up before you begin the process of writing in a formal and coherent manner. The main idea underlying this activity is to put pen to paper and to get going on the writing process immediately. Simply write about anything you choose and in whatever way you like, not caring about punctuation, spelling, or structure. Write without stopping. Don't stop to plan, organise, or edit. It can help to concentrate on some topic and to set yourself a time limit. The main idea is to generate as many words as possible on the paper.

PLANNING

1. Be decisive with regard to selecting what topic or question you are going to write about.

2. Rephrase the title as a question (if it is not already in the form of a question); this will help to generate ideas on the subject.
3. Brainstorm the topic by using trigger questions such as who? why? how?
4. Cluster ideas that are related. Be clear about what direction your essay is taking. Don't introduce irrelevant material or go off the point.
5. Select material for paragraphs. Write out fully the topic sentence of each paragraph.
6. Your composition must have a general unity of impression. This will be shown in a clear, conclusive and satisfactory ending and in a logical development of thought between the paragraphs.

Ten basic hints on writing a composition
1. Write every day. Write a paragraph on any topic in order to improve your expression and your flow of thought.
2. Cultivate your own ideas on current events. You can do this by having a notebook in which to collect ideas throughout the year.
3. Understand the topic fully; otherwise don't write on it.
4. Always engage in some of the pre-writing activities—brainstorming, clustering, free writing, and drawing up outlines—before writing seriously on the topic.
5. Avoid errors made in previous writing work by learning spellings and correcting mistakes in grammar.
6. Identify your strengths and weaknesses in writing. Work at eliminating the weaknesses and at improving the strong points.
7. Write simply. Choose a simple word instead of a more obscure expression. Avoid using clichés: 'few and far between', 'in the heel of the hunt', 'to tell you the truth'.
8. Work at writing interesting and arresting openings.
9. Draw up your own list of quotations and clever phrases and use them in written work.
10. Don't make general or global statements without supporting them with clear and specific examples and evidence.

Ten do's
1. Write a paragraph every day, on any topic. Leave it to 'cool', then come back later and correct it.
2. Always brainstorm your title, and always write rough drafts.
3. Organise your paragraphs, putting the most important ideas first.
4. Write interesting and exciting opening paragraphs.
5. Make your composition a reasonable length: three to four pages of standard paper is usually sufficient.
6. Make sure the ideas you use are relevant. Use your own ideas.
7. Make your conclusion clear, fairly substantial, and non-repetitive.
8. Vary the length and structure of your sentences.
9. Link your literature course to your composition; weave in quotations or ideas naturally and fluidly.
10. Read your composition aloud in order to hear your mistakes.

Ten don'ts
1. Don't go off the point: stick to the topic.
2. Don't use direct speech unless it is necessary.
3. Don't use two different ideas in one paragraph.
4. Avoid self-conscious expressions: 'I hope to prove …' or 'I feel that I have shown …'
5. Avoid the use of clichés and repetitive phrases.
6. Don't use quotation marks unless you are quoting.
7. Avoid the use of a definition in your opening paragraph.
8. Don't conclude your composition in mid-air.
9. Don't conclude on one sentence.
10. Don't reproduce compositions that have been learnt off by heart.

THE PARAGRAPH

Every piece of prose composition is based on knowing how to build sentences to form an effective paragraph. A paragraph is like a miniature composition: it should have a clear beginning, a middle, and a conclusion.

Each paragraph deals with one section of your subject. Each paragraph has one main idea or topic sentence, together with support or examples. The paragraph must have a unity: all ideas, examples, statistics or illustrations must be related to the main idea.

Paragraphs can be connected by linking or transitional devices such as 'nevertheless'. 'furthermore', 'however', 'if', 'or', 'so'. Paragraphs can be of any length; however, avoid extremes, that is, writing a paragraph that is either very long or very short. Generally speaking, there should be a variety in the construction of paragraphs within the composition.

Features of paragraphs
- Clarity
- Unity
- Emphasis
- Coherence
- Transitional or linking devices between paragraphs

Clarity
Good writing aims at communicating effectively to your readers, not merely impressing them. The main idea must be clear to your reader. Generally speaking, the topic sentence usually comes either at the beginning or end of a paragraph.

The following paragraph is an example of clear writing:

> When the Black and Tan lorry left the strand road to swing instead towards the centre of the town, the Dummy was lounging at the corner house. All evening he had stood there in the mild warmth of the October sunlight, and though he was startled he did not move.

But when the lorry passed close to him, his eyes narrowed and his head inclined slightly towards the wide strand on his left. He counted the turns. The engine slowed, revved, dropped again. It was going towards Freddie's house. By the time it stopped completely he was hammering loudly at one of the small cottages which faced the strand.

(James Plunkett, *The Web*)

Comment

The main or topic sentence is clearly set out in the opening sentence of this dramatic piece of writing. The remaining sentences demonstrate the reaction of the character to the arrival of the Black-and-Tan lorry in the town.

Unity

Unity occurs in a paragraph when the main idea is clearly stated and all examples or supporting material are related to that main idea.

> So great and deep a cave, of course, had to be dark. But it was even darker than François had expected when he crawled through the narrow entrance. Then he could tell from the feel of the sand underneath his hands that he was inside it in depth. He looked carefully all round him but could see nothing to indicate the presence of Xhabbo, Nuin-Tara, and Nonnie. Were it not for Hintza, who, as always, unless ordered away, was close to him, he could easily have thought himself to be alone. The darkness indeed was so dense that it was almost tangible, and as he stood up, silently and slowly, his left hand brushed the air in front of his face as if to clear the black matter from his eyes. It was a most unpleasant feeling, as if this profound darkness around him had found an ally within, inflicted on them all by the tragic events of the day. The whole was not just a sensation conveyed by the senses but a powerful emotion arguing with the voice of despair that the last light was about to be extracted from life on earth.
>
> (Laurens van der Post, *A Far-Off Place*)

Comment

The theme or main point of this paragraph is the extreme state of darkness within the cave. Every sentence relates to the opening sentence here. The writer draws some vivid images of the effects internally and externally on the characters.

Emphasis

Emphasis comes from the position of the key sentence within the paragraph. This sentence can occur anywhere in the paragraph.

The following two paragraphs show the effect of placing the topic sentence in a distinctive position within the paragraph.

> Colour tends to be a subconscious element in films. The use of colour in films is strongly emotional in its appeal, expressive and atmospheric rather than conspicuous or intellectual. Psychologists have discovered that most people actively attempt to interpret the lines of a composition, but they tend to accept colour passively, permitting it to

suggest moods rather than objects. Lines are associated with nouns, colour with adjectives. Line is sometimes thought to be masculine; colour feminine. Both lines and colour suggest meanings, then, but in somewhat different ways.

COMMENT
The opening sentence here is the topic or main sentence. Every other sentence is developed from this main sentence and illustrates an example of how colour is accepted as a subconscious element of films.

Coherence
Coherence means the logical flow of thought between ideas. All the sentences in a paragraph must relate to the topic sentence and to one another. There must be a link between one sentence and another in such a way that the reader will see clearly a logical progress and development in thought within the paragraph.

There are different ways of achieving coherence within a paragraph. A writer can use linking or transitional words, such as 'moreover', 'but', 'furthermore'. The writer may also use the repetition of the same word, phrase or sentence to link the ideas within the paragraph. The following paragraph is an example of the smooth and logical flow of thought from one idea to another.

> Michael Gill and his wife came last. Gill had begun to reap with the slow methodic movements of a machine driven at low pressure. He continued at exactly the same pace, never changing, never looking up to see where his opponents were. His long lean hands moved noiselessly, and only the sharp crunching rush of the teeth of his reaping-hook through the yellow stalks of the rye could be heard. His long drooping eyelashes were always directed towards the point where his hook was cutting. He never looked behind to see had he enough for a sheaf before beginning another. All his movements were calculated beforehand, calm, monotonous, deadly accurate. Even his breathing was light, and came through his nose like one who sleeps healthily. His wife moved behind him in the same manner, tying each sheaf daintily, without exertion.
>
> (Liam O'Flaherty, *The Reaping Race*)

COMMENT
This is an example of a coherent and fluid stream of thought between one idea and another. The writer cleverly registers each movement of Gill as he carries out the task of reaping the sheaves of rye. Each sentence is linked to the preceding one, and each flows effortlessly and fluidly along to give a striking image of two people caught up in a reaping competition.

Remember, in order to achieve coherence within a paragraph:
1. Establish clearly your topic sentence.
2. Do not introduce two topic sentences or two different ideas in one paragraph.
3. Make sure that every point made in the paragraph has some relation to this topic idea.

4. Every sentence must develop or advance the preceding ideas or build up to a climax if the topic sentence comes at the conclusion of the paragraph.
5. Do not digress or introduce irrelevant statements into the paragraph.
6. Use linking devices to help provide a smooth and logical continuity within the paragraph.

Linking devices

The use of transitional words or phrases can not only serve the function of linking ideas within the same paragraph but can also serve as a link between the different paragraphs. Linking devices can elaborate and develop a writer's argument.

Look at the following examples of how linking devices can be used in different ways:

TO SHOW CONTRAST BETWEEN IDEAS
    But,
    Nevertheless,
    Still,
    Although,
    Conversely,
    Yet,
    On the contrary,

TO EMPHASISE A POINT
    For example,
    For instance,
    In fact,
    Indeed,

TO SHOW CAUSE AND EFFECT OR THE CONSEQUENCES OF SOMETHING
    Therefore,
    Thus,
    As a result,
    Accordingly,

TO SHOW RELATIONS OF TIME AND SEQUENCE
    Then,
    Later,
    Afterwards,
    Next,
    Meanwhile,
    Soon,

TO SUM UP OR CONCLUDE
    In conclusion,
    Finally,
    To sum up,

Examine the following two extracts, which are on different subjects and have clear linking or transitional devices, both within and between them. Then study the commentary carefully.

Passage 1
Dare to be dangerous by embracing the hottest colour of the season—red—in shades veering from poppy to plum. On the catwalk, red mixed boldly with tamer neutral tones to create a sophisticated look. Even Prada, the most minimalist of designers, included a bold red knee-length coat in the autumn-winter collection. For those without diminatrix tendencies there was a more subtle offering from Valentino, who showed a beautifully delicate yet stunning bodice-style dress that fell just above the ankle.

If you're wary of red, then embrace it with caution. This season leather is one of fashion's most basic allies, because it never goes out of vogue. If leather does not appeal to you, because you think it requires too much attitude to wear it, then think again.

The main thing to keep in mind is contrast. Match it with cool jerseys or delicately soft wools for maximum appeal. For most of us, the only thing standing in our way of going hell for leather is cost. If you want to get a leather effect without getting into ferocious debt, then the only way to do it is with PVC.

COMMENT
This extract is from a newspaper account of the latest colours and style in clothes. It is written for a general audience and, obviously, for women. Note how the linking word 'if' is used to offer an alternative to the colours and styles that are mentioned. Also, such terms as 'For those' and 'For most of us' are clearly persuasive and designed to win the reader around to accepting the idea that is being expressed.

Passage 2
Watching Irish politics over the last fifteen years has been like practising deep-space astronomy. It used to be that astronomers watched the skies and noted what they could see. Now, trying to work out what is going on in the wider universe, they pay as much attention to what they cannot see. By observing the motions of heavenly bodies they guess at the forces that must be operating on them. From the way known objects behave, they can be pretty sure that bodies they cannot yet see are affecting them. Eventually, as they look harder, they get clear images of where those bodies are buried.

So it has been with political life. It's been obvious to anybody looking at it with half an eye that invisible forces have influenced its movements. Decisions have been made, actions taken that are simply inexplicable unless we assume the presence of some unseen force, some hidden pull.

We have to conjecture that this force is corruption. But, until the McCracken Tribunal, we couldn't see it with the naked eye, name or place it.

Even now we haven't got the clear, sharp images of our political universe that would allow us to understand exactly how it has worked. However, we still have to work on the assumption that there are many black holes, uncharted but discernible by their effects.

COMMENT

In this article several clear transitional devices are used to signal a relation between the different ideas. The writer proceeds to develop the argument by using certain linking terms, such as 'It used to be', 'By observing', and 'Now it is'. The use of certain words and phrases, such as 'Eventually' and 'So it has', shows the reader what the results of such findings have been. The writer draws a contrast between the ideas by using the linking words 'but' and 'however' and the phrase 'even now we haven't got'.

The introductory paragraph

The introductory and the concluding paragraphs are the two most important paragraphs in your composition.

The introductory paragraph has two main functions:
- to capture the attention of your reader
- to introduce your material and demonstrate your stance or approach to the subject.

The opening paragraph of your composition must be interesting and arresting for your reader. Avoid openings that are predictable and dull, for example definition-style openings:

> Fashion may be defined as …
> This technological age may be seen as …
> 'This great stage of fools' is a saying that is true because it is all round us …

Make sure your opening paragraph is original or takes an original slant on the topic. It can help to use an anecdote or a quotation, or a surprising statistic. Look at the following paragraph:

> **The new youth**
>
> If the whole point of each fresh generation is to moult, revolt and supplant its parents, to crash through the creaky barriers of the establishment—quite simply, to inherit the earth —then it must be disconcerting to be young right now. The old battles are over. And the new ones, whatever they might be, have not yet taken shape—aside from the sense of helplessness that the very earth the young are inheriting is increasingly damaged. There is no world war; there is no cold one either. For many people in their twenties that good fortune is offset by a yawning lack of common purpose: even the horrors of the Balkan wars did not generate the solidarity of common conflicts. And so the battle cry of the young, 'Do it yourself, for yourself', sounds suspiciously like a Nike ad.

COMMENT

This paragraph takes an interesting and original angle on the subject. A variety of sentence structure and vocabulary is used, and the images used are relevant and punchy.

Now study the following paragraphs (taken from pupils' actual work), and examine the commentary following each one.

Hairstyles
I glance at the mirror illuminated by tiny white lights which make you look frighteningly pale and pudgy and just as quickly averted my eyes. This mirror does absolutely nothing for one's appearance, I thought grimly. My hair dripping wet was stuck to my face and there was a big white patch on my forehead where my make-up used to be until some over-eager employer decided to herself that I didn't need make-up on that part of my anatomy. This is too humiliating. I decide that I'll do it myself in future. The future always turns into the next time, though. Vanity and pressure from my friends prevail. It's unfashionably long, look at your split ends, and don't you know that rubber bands break your hair? were constantly being hurled at me, so after one particularly spirit-crushing evening of abuse I made an appointment at the hairdresser's. The 'Guillotine'. How appropriate, I think, as I make the phone call with a certain amount of dread.

COMMENT
This is an example of a weak opening. No real statement is made, and no topic sentence is established. The sentence structure is too long and confusing. The writer here seems to be unpacking the contents of her mind onto paper in a disorderly and confusing manner. There is no clear topic sentence, and there is poor organisation of thought within the paragraph.

REWRITTEN VERSION

I glanced at the mirror, illuminated by tiny white lights, which make one look frightfully pale and pudgy. I quickly averted my eyes. I began to think grimly: This mirror does absolutely nothing for one's appearance. I stood before the mirror. My hair, which was dripping wet, stuck to my face. There was a big patch on my forehead where my make-up had smudged. I felt humiliated, and decided to do it myself next time. But personal vanity, combined with pressure from my friends, prevailed over everything. Comments such as 'It's unfashionably long,' 'Look at your split ends' and 'Don't you know that rubber bands break your hair?' had been hurled at me repeatedly. So, after one of these sessions of abuse from my friends, I made an appointment with a hairdresser called the 'Guillotine'. How appropriate, I thought, as I made the phone call, not without a certain amount of dread.

The advertising jungle
The world in which we live today seems intent on bombarding us with images of ultra-shining cars that are so clean you can see yourself in them.
   Image after image jumps off our television screens out of our radios in through our car windscreen, off roadside hoardings, in a desperate attempt to force us into buying products we don't need and if we really thought about it don't even want. Tempting us to part with our hard earned money so that we can build up more and more material goods which will in turn make us all much better people, because don't forget the more we have and the more we own the better we are, forget about the man down the road who has no money for food.

COMMENT

There is no clear direction in this paragraph. The punctuation is weak, and the paragraph has no clear topic sentence. The writer uses excessive repetition. The words 'advertising' and 'jungle' are not even mentioned.

REWRITTEN VERSION

> Today's world of advertising seems to bombard us at all angles with numerous images, from those of ultra-shining cars to the latest trends in clothes or that super-modern gadget for your kitchen. Images assault us from every place, whether the television screen, the radio, or on hoardings. All are united in the fact that they represent an attempt to manipulate us into buying products we do not need or even want. These images are designed to tempt us to part with our hard-earned money in order to accumulate more material goods. Furthermore, we are enticed into buying more, under the illusion that the more we have the happier and more fulfilled we will be. Of course these advertisements do little for the man down the road who has not even got the money for food.

The concluding paragraph

Your concluding paragraph is your final statement on the topic of your composition. It is the last impression left on your reader, and therefore it is vitally important.

A good conclusion has two purposes:
- to round off the main points or ideas in your composition satisfactorily;
- to provide a general unity of impression.

Avoid conclusions that repeat the main ideas of your composition in the same words. On the other hand, you should avoid going to the other extreme by introducing a different approach or new ideas in your conclusion, which will only serve to frustrate your reader. One happy medium between the two extremes is referring back to the introductory paragraph and developing the anecdote or statistic or simply the point that was made there. This method can ensure that there is a unity in your composition. If, for example, a composition on 'European Union: where to go to from here?' begins like this:

> Ever since the term 'European' was first used, in the time of Charlemagne, its interpretation has been disputed. What does it mean to be European today? For those in other continents it means simply the people who live in this one. And there are an awful lot of people living here, from Austrian farmers to Norwegian taxi-drivers, who don't identify themselves as European …

the conclusion could consist of the following:

> A European Union in the future would be a world mode of what I call 'liberal order'. By this I mean an order without a single dominant power, flexibly open to different alliances of states on different issues and ultimately committed to the peaceful resolution of all conflicts between its members. It is only in this way, I believe, that the hopes and fears of

the three different kinds of Europeans will possibly be reconciled in a way that has never been achieved since the days of Charlemagne. This is the Europe we need, and this is the Europe I urge on my fellow-Europeans.

Examine the concluding paragraph of the following composition on 'Isn't it time to limit the use of private cars?'

Until the time when responsibility is taken for this problem, the situation will only continue to worsen. Those who sit alone each morning in their cars and complain about the traffic must realise that they play a role in creating the problem itself. The public transport services too, while complaining about the difficulties they face, must realise that the inadequacy of their systems also contributes to this problem. If the problem is left unaddressed we may reach the time when limiting the use of private cars will be necessary. To avoid this situation, we must take co-operative action now and eliminate 'urban gridlock'.

COMMENT
This is an example of a concluding paragraph that makes a clear statement on the issues raised in the title. The writer here ties up certain ideas and presents some solutions in a clear and vigorous manner.

Remember that your conclusion must show that you have complete control over your subject.

Rules for a good style

1. *Write to communicate, not to impress.* Know exactly what you want to say, then go ahead and say it.
2. Put your statements in a positive form. Make your statements or ideas clear and definite.
3. Choose a specific and concrete word. Avoid the use of vague or abstract expressions.
4. Use an active verb rather than a passive one. Your writing is more effective and forceful when you use active verbs.
5. Avoid repeating yourself in the same words. Repetition has to be used correctly, otherwise it can weaken the writing.
6. Vary the length and structure of your sentences.
7. Every sentence must have a subject, a verb, and an object.
8. Always consult a dictionary when you are not sure how to spell a word, or to check the meaning of a word.
9. Get used to writing and rewriting.
10. Learn the basic rules of correct punctuation thoroughly.
11. Know how to link your paragraphs correctly. The section on paragraphs (page 32) gives examples of transitional or linking devices and how to use them correctly.

CHECK-LIST FOR WRITING COMPOSITIONS

Before you begin writing compositions, consider the following questions.

Content
- Are you presenting original and interesting ideas?
- If you are writing in the 'language of argument', have you presented the arguments in a balanced way and supported all statements made with sufficient evidence?
- Have you commented on the significance of quotations or examples in the development of your argument?
- Have you arrived at your own conclusions, or relied too heavily on the interpretations of other people?

Organisation
- Does your introduction give a clear idea of what your composition is about?
- Does each paragraph fit into the pattern of your composition and advance the main point, or are there gaps in the development of ideas, or digressions that sidetrack your points?
- Are the transitions between the paragraphs effective? Do they unify a paragraph and provide a logical development of thought between each paragraph?
- Does your conclusion link to your opening and tie in all the ideas in an interesting way? Is the conclusion positive? Is there a strong unity of impression from your conclusion?

Language
- Is the language used appropriate to the subject?
- Have you used the exact word to convey the precise meaning?
- Have you used language that is clear and comprehensible and avoided ambiguous expressions?
- Have you avoided slang and jargon?
- Are your sentences varied in length?
- Are the tenses of verbs consistent throughout?

Mechanics
- Have you avoided grammatical errors?
- Is your composition properly punctuated?
- Are all words correctly spelt?
- Are quotations or dialogue introduced correctly?
- Is there any unnecessary repetition of ideas, words, or phrases?

5
The Language Genres

Study the notes below on the different language genres. In each section there are notes and guidelines on how to understand and write in the different genres; use these to guide you through the exercises.

THE LANGUAGE OF NARRATION

In the language of narration, or *narrative writing,* the writer is telling a story.

Narrative writing is to be found in novels and short stories, plays, poems, histories, letters, some expository essays, and reviews. Non-fictional narrative includes biography, autobiography, and travel literature.

In an autobiography the writer narrates an account of his or her own life and experiences. Generally these events are narrated in chronological sequence. A biography is the study of one person's life and achievements written by another person.

Travel literature records details of journeys and the writer's impressions of places visited in a way that lends a distinctive shape to the narrative.

Features of the language of narration
1. The ability to tell a story that has an effective narrative shape, with a beginning, a middle and a conclusion that are all clearly defined. There must be a distinct arrangement in the sequence of events presented.
2. The story must have a fairly definite location and context.
3. The story should be interesting and original. Clichés and stereotyping are avoided.
4. In a good narrative the writer introduces some personal commitment or experience.
5. All description must be both vivid and realistic.
6. Sometimes an anecdote can be used as part of a narrative. Here a single incident is told in the form of a short story. The incident almost always contains a definite point.
7. The characters presented must be realistic.
8. The story must have atmosphere. There has to be a certain setting; this can be a country, or a certain type of house, or a distinct period in history.

Sample passages

I lived in Portstewart, one of the small villages on the coast. I rented a small room at the top of an old dank two-storey Victorian terrace house. The house was the last one in the terrace, and from its window I could look out on the grey, ever-restless ocean. I can still remember the view from the window and the constant changes in the sea. The weather in that part of the north of Ireland was never the kindest, though when the summer came, the landscape round us, the easy access to Donegal and to the remoter parts of the North gave the area its own particular delight.

An old retired couple who owned the house lived in two rooms on the ground floor. Mr Paul was in his eighties, and I remember him going for his nightly walk accompanied by his walking-stick and his small mongrel dog. His bent figure would brave even Portstewart's weather as he walked along the sea front. I never saw the old man at any other time apart from these walks. I heard him occasionally in his own room. His wife, his second, would sit quietly in the kitchen beside the old range, constantly knitting and offering us cups of tea as we came in from the pub or back from studying. She never bothered us much, was always friendly, and enjoyed a cup of tea with those of us who would sit and chat with her.

Mr Paul became ill very suddenly. We were not surprised, aware even then that age can be cruel. But what moved me most was his rapid decline, the fact that I never saw him walking bent double against the wind, and the sight of his walking-stick always lying in the hall. It became a strange kind of symbol. Late into the night I could hear him coughing and throwing up. The fact that we were only aware of this man's illness through his rasping cough and his wife's ministrations lent the house a kind of ominous gloom.

One evening I came in from the cold and straight to the kitchen to heat myself at the range. Mrs Paul sat alone. There was a silence I couldn't understand. I recall now that her knitting-needles were for once not in evidence. There was no steam coming out of the old kettle normally kept simmering on the hot plate. Her face was very still. It took her some time to look up, to acknowledge me coming into the room. 'Would you like a cup of tea?' I asked. She looked up slowly, and I remember her old, lined but still quite beautiful face as she said calmly and without emotion: 'My husband is dead.'

(Brian Keenan, *An Evil Cradling*)

COMMENT

An Evil Cradling describes Brian Keenan's experience as a hostage in Lebanon. This extract recounts an incident in his life, and it is written in an autobiographical and narrative style. The passage is built around a series of small, effective devices, all of which are a hallmark of good narrative writing. The use of the autobiographical 'I' adds an air of realism to the writing. The imagery and language are precise and homely, and this quality of simplicity lends an arresting impact to the writing.

Question A
1. Show how the writer builds up atmosphere in the passage.

2. Identify several details that contribute to drawing vivid descriptions in the passage.

Question B
Write a short narrative description of some experience that affected you greatly. In your description concentrate on drawing some realistic details of character.

> When the news of my birth reached Dr Xia he said: 'Ah, another wild swan is born.' I was given the name Erhong, which means 'second wild swan'.
>
> Giving me my name was almost the last act in Dr Xia's long life. Four days after I was born he died, at the age of eighty-two. He was leaning back in bed drinking a glass of milk. My grandmother went out of the room for a minute, and when she came back to get the glass she saw that the milk had spilled and the glass had fallen to the floor. He had died instantly and painlessly.
>
> Funerals were very important events in China. Ordinary people would often bankrupt themselves to lay on a grand ceremony—and my grandmother loved Dr Xia and wanted to do him proud. There were three things she absolutely insisted on: first, a good coffin; second, that the coffin must be carried by pallbearers and not pulled on a cart; and third, to have Buddhist monks to chant the *sutras* for the dead and musicians to play the *suona*, a piercing woodwind instrument traditionally used at funerals. My father agreed to the first and second requests but vetoed the third. The communists regarded any extravagant ceremony as wasteful and 'feudal'.
>
> Traditionally only very lowly people were buried quietly. Noise-making was considered important at a funeral, to make it a public affair: this brought 'face' and also showed respect for the dead. My father insisted that there could be no *suona* or monks. My grandmother had a blazing row with him. For her, these were essentials, which she just had to have. In the middle of the altercation she fainted from anger and grief. She was also wrought up because she was all alone at the saddest moment of her life. She had not told my mother what had happened, for fear of upsetting her; and the fact that my mother was in the hospital meant that my grandmother had to deal directly with my father. After the funeral she had a nervous breakdown and had to be hospitalised for almost two months.
>
> (Jung Chang, *The Wild Swans*)

COMMENT
One of the features of good narrative is describing a specific time and location. Here the writer concentrates on certain significant events that occurred when she was born, how her grandfather died, and the small details about the funeral ceremony. We also learn about her communist background and about certain customs in China.

Question A

1. Sum up in your own words the main points you have gathered about the tradition of funeral ceremonies in China.
2. What is the tone of the extract? Support your answer by reference to the passage.

Question B
Rewrite the passage in the form of a dialogue. In writing your dialogue concentrate on registering some striking features of the characters represented.

Writing in the language of narration
The skills of good narrative composition come from practice. Writing a narrative composition requires essentially the ability to write a short story. The story should have one point of view, and there should be a definite arrangement of ideas. A story must be original and interesting for your reader. A good story springs from your own experience.

How to write a narrative composition

1. Tell the story in one tense; the past tense is generally best.
2. It can help to put your own experience into the narrative: personal experience authenticates the flavour of a narrative.
3. The structure of your story can be straightforward and in chronological sequence, or it can be told in flashback. Remember, your story must have a shape: a clear beginning, middle, and conclusion.
4. Use the third-person narrator to tell your story. Avoid the use of too much dialogue, as it can break up the flow of thought. Remember, dialogue needs to be written very well in order to read well.
5. Understand the terms 'plot', 'character' and 'dialogue' when writing a narrative composition, and know how to use them correctly.

Plot
A plot can be defined as the series of events that go to make up a story.

- The plot must move forward towards a definite conclusion.
- The plot must include some element of change. The situation depicted at the beginning of the story must change as the story unfolds.
- All events of the plot must carry the narrative forward.
- There has to be a pace in the plot. Balance your beginning, middle and conclusion carefully to give your story a shape.

   Remember when planning your plot to have

- change in the story
- pace and movement in the narrative
- general shape at the conclusion.

Characters
Because stories are about people, your characters must be real, recognisable figures. Your readers must be able to recognise the characters in your story; if not, they will not arouse any interest. You can reveal the true nature of your characters through dialogue

and description. Concentrate on one or two significant features of a character when describing them, rather than on several points.

When you are describing a character, don't tell everything at once. Instead use implication or suggestion. Look, for example, at the following descriptions:

> The sister, Catherine, was a slender worldly girl of about thirty, with a solid, sticky bob of red hair, and a complexion powdered milky white. Her eyebrows had been plucked and then drawn on again at a more rakish angle, but the efforts of nature towards the restoration of the old alignment gave a blurred air to her face. When she moved about there was an incessant clicking as innumerable pottery bracelets jingled up and down upon her arms. She came in with such a proprietary haste, and looked around so possessively at the furniture that I wondered if she lived there.
>
> (F. Scott Fitzgerald, *The Great Gatsby*)

COMMENT

Here the writer concentrates on registering some small details in the picture given to us of this character. Note how the writer describes the woman's hair as a 'sticky bob of red hair'. The image of the bracelets jangling up and down her arms is vivid and clear.

Look at the effect achieved in the following description of a character:

> Mrs Reed was a woman of robust frame, square-shouldered and strong limbed, not tall, and though stout, not obese: she had a somewhat large face, the under-jaw being much developed and very solid; her brow was low, her chin large and prominent, mouth and nose sufficiently regular; her skin was dark and opaque, her hair nearly flaxen; her constitution was sound as a bell, illness never came near her; she was an exact clever manager, her household and tenantry were thoroughly under her control.
>
> (Charlotte Brontë, *Jane Eyre*)

COMMENT

The writer concentrates on drawing a clear and animated image of a certain type of person. The physical appearance of the woman is registered vividly through a striking series of small and precise points, such as her robust frame, and the fact that she is strong-limbed but not obese. Remember: good description concentrates on making the reader see clearly what is being drawn.

Dialogue

Learn to master the art of writing effective dialogue before beginning a narrative composition. The function of dialogue is to reproduce live speech. Never allow dialogue simply to slip into a conversation: it must have a purpose. Remember that one of the main features of effective dialogue is the ability to convey conflict in a realistic manner. Conversation or good dialogue can add pace and variety to an otherwise dull story.

Learn how to punctuate dialogue correctly. Use quotation marks at the beginning and end of each section of direct speech. Separate the dialogue from the narrative by means of commas. The first word in every piece of direct speech begins with a capital letter. Use a new paragraph each time there is a change of speaker.

Study the following examples of the use of dialogue in composition, then read the commentary:

'How would you like to go to school then, child Alexander, hey?'

The question took me completely by surprise, but anyway my mother answered for me. 'Frederick.' Her voice had a warning in it.

He smiled briefly in her direction. 'Hey then, my boy?'

'I hadn't really thought about it, Father.'

'Well, think about it. Now's the time. Meet a few chaps of your own age. Broaden. Polish you up a bit. Games,' he said, without any enormous conviction. 'Pass the celery, please. And things.'

I passed him the celery.

'Mr Bingham is more than adequate.' Her voice was north-north-east cold.

'Perhaps a widening of outlook would do no harm. There are other subjects which Mr Bingham …'

'He is delicate, Frederick. You must not put his health at risk.'

'In your eyes he is delicate, my dear. I see few signs of it. He has just eaten a most remarkable lunch.'

'Dr Desmond …'

'Dr Desmond is an ass.'

'Frederick, *pas devant* …'

'My dear good woman, you know perfectly well that Dr Desmond will say anything you want him to say.'

(Jennifer Johnston, *How Many Miles to Babylon*)

COMMENT

This extract depicts the strain in the relationship between husband and wife. The dialogue conveys in a strikingly terse manner the primary features of these two characters.

Mood and atmosphere

Note the difference between the terms 'mood' and 'atmosphere'. Mood is the way the writer feels; atmosphere is how the place and setting are described.

Every story needs an atmosphere. Atmosphere is created in a narrative by a careful blending of people, events, and setting. Your atmosphere must help to draw your reader into your story. While the use of imagination can help to build up an atmosphere, remember that the imagination must be controlled in writing. This is necessary in order to make your writing more realistic and authentic.

Sample composition

The following composition is written in the language of narration. It is taken from actual pupils' work and is graded according to the standards required at Higher level. Study it carefully, and pay particular attention to the commentary that follows.

The exercise was: 'Write on some experience that left a deep impression on you. Use a narrative or imaginative style in your composition.'

Awakenings

Even now, thirty years after experiencing the bullfight at San María, my pulse still races when it calls to mind
The rippling lengths of bleached canvas overhead
The golden glimmering bullring far below.
I presumed that by sitting half way up the crowded amphitheatre we would be safe,
To a certain extent removed from it all,
Protected from the ferocious intensity below.
We were not.

That summer Pat, Kilty, John Drennan and myself were enjoying a cycling tour of the Iberian Peninsula. Three young students; none older than twenty. We had been in the country for three weeks and had not yet succeeded in understanding the Spanish mindset. All we had ascertained was that they were tanned, aloof, beautiful, and gibbering.

The breakthrough came on a bright Sunday afternoon in late July. It so happened that my bicycle became punctured a few miles outside a modest uphill village called San María. Because of the severity of the puncture we had to venture into the town for an unscheduled stop.

The wife of the local garage owner—an olive, leathery-skinned woman—explained to us that he was at the bullfight, of course. Glad of a temporary respite, we all wheeled our bicycles to the stadium. We were all country boys and therefore had gone hare-coursing and hunting at home. Our voices grew to an animated pitch of feverish excitement as we neared the giant theatre.

Nearly all the seats had been taken half an hour before the event began. Luckily we managed to find three seats half way up the bustling amphitheatre.

Our hungry eyes and ears scanned the onlookers. There were people of all ages and both sexes, delight and excitement clearly visible on their faces. The hushed, reverential noise of the crowd was unlike anything I had previously experienced at hurling matches at home. It was strange and unsettling.

Only when the bull entered did I understand the reason: the close, undeniable presence of death among us. I was in no way prepared for my utter dread of the bull—a gruesome, malevolent presence. He lashed out at the crowd in general, thundering left and right. His red nostrils flared, and the muscles of his silky sweat-covered trunk contracted uncontrollably into spasms.

To my left a samba band announced the arrival of *el matador*. He was a man of twenty-two years—only slightly older than us, a local from a neighbouring upland village. As usual, his father was also a matador before him. It was said that he was a fine fighter, already in a few short years having exceeded the skill, grace and creativity of his father.

To my unaccustomed eye he was short and of slight build. Yet his puny presence had already managed to dissipate some of the bull's choking and stifling sense of menace.

The matador walked towards the bull, the crowd fell quiet, he stopped. Beast and matador silently studied each other. The bull seemed to recognise who exactly he encountered, both the purpose and significance of the encounter. This mutual appraisal lasted no more than fifteen seconds. The bull charged.

Closer and closer the ton and a half of agitating muscle charged. The matador remained motionless. His guttural growl grew to fever pitch. The matador clicked the heels of the delicate dust-covered shoes, recognising a distant face in the crowd.

Then at the last possible instant the matador stepped sideways, totally unconcerned. The crowd erupted.

Amidst the dizzying heat and deafening roars of 'Toro, toro,' a strange thing happened. Choked with fear, I experienced the most potent sense of humanity that I to this day have ever felt. Every sinew in my body pulsed with an immense feeling of pride of race. Every deft little side kick and neat little blow increased my pride in belonging to the human race.

The matador's complete superiority over the bull held me spellbound. Like everybody else, I was far too caught up in the celebration of the matador's prowess even to notice the brutish suffering of this animal. That was it. The breakthrough.

It all now made sense to me. The scenario before me had framed the idea: who exactly these people were. At first I had been horrified by the Spaniards and how lightly they weighed the life of an animal, too cosmopolitan and blasé to care for the suffering of a simple beast. I had missed the point entirely. They understood death more than I. They recognised their own place within nature as humans. They moved within nature, a powerful force with a profound understanding and respect for her.

When the time came to leave and seek out the mechanic, my whole body shook with a vibrancy and energy. It lasted for days, but the lesson learnt returned with me to Ireland, the brutal lesson that I had learnt amid the heat and bleached canvas, a lesson that eroded my prejudices and gave me a deeper insight into my humanity and even my own soul.

COMMENT
Grade B1

This composition has an effective narrative shape. It has a clear beginning, middle, and conclusion. Furthermore, the narrative is given a distinct location and time. Both the language and description used are original and vivid. The story has a dramatic immediacy. There is a wide variety of sentence structure. The terse sentence structure conveys an energy and pace to the narrative. The loose and informal paragraph structure contributes to the flow of the narrative. There is a strong sense of unity in the viewpoint.

The writer is perhaps trying to do too much in too short a space. He wishes to convey the powerful impact on him of having experienced a bullfight and to draw the conclusion that it has left a mark on him for ever. However, this is not achieved in enough detail or depth. The conclusion is somewhat abrupt. The characters in the narrative need to be developed in greater detail.

The first page is too formal. Perhaps the writer is trying too hard to impress. Phrases such as 'because of the severity of the puncture', 'I presumed' and 'having ascertained' are awkward and stiff. The use of the term 'gibbering' to describe a language the writer does not understand is offensive. However, the style of the narrative begins to flow steadily as the story develops.

Exercises on writing in the language of narration

1. Write a suitable conclusion to the following paragraph, which is written in a narrative style: 'The village to which our family had come was a scattering of some twenty or thirty houses down the south-east slope of a valley. The valley was narrow, steep, and almost entirely cut off; it was also a funnel for winds, a channel for the floods, and a bird-crammed, insect-hopping sun-trap whenever there happened to be any sun. The sides of the valley were rich in pasture and the crests heavily covered in beechwoods.'
2. Write a narrative composition on the experience of being a refugee.
3. Write on one of the following topics, using a narrative style:
   'A new millennium'
   'My first job'
   'Fragile Earth'
   'My experience of visiting the home of a pop star'.
4. Take each of these opening sentences and write a narrative-style composition:
   'They began to move up just at dusk, and by the time night fell and the first flares became visible ...'
   'His hat had rolled a few yards away, and his clothes were smeared with the filth and ooze of the floor on which he had lain ...'

THE LANGUAGE OF ARGUMENT

Argument is a form of rational persuasion. The 'language of argument' attempts to prove a particular point by using logic or evidence.

It is important to understand the difference between argument and persuasion. Argument assumes that a reader is objective, is able to follow a logical train of thought, to weigh up evidence, and will not be prevented by emotion from accepting the conclusions to which the logic or the evidence points. Argument differs from persuasion in that it appeals to the reason and to logic rather than to emotion or feelings.

Writing that uses the language of argument includes legal documents, scientific and medical journals, and newspaper reports.

Features of the language of argument

1. In a well-constructed argument, claims must always be supported. A claim is a statement that is arguable. Claims can be supported
   - by providing data or evidence
   - by facts
   - by examples
   - by statistics, where information is presented in the form of numbers.
2. Good argument must be supported by evidence that is valid. An argument is valid when the conclusion follows logically from the premise or the preceding statements. To test the validity of an argument,
   - assess the truth of the premise
   - assess the truth of each argument
   - assess the truth of each sub-argument.
3. Argument is effective when evidence and reasoning are both presented in a persuasive manner so as to convince the reader that certain opinions are preferable to others.
4. In understanding the language of argument it is important to distinguish between a fact and an opinion. A fact is something that really exists or occurs: it can be verified or proved by an objective or detached observer. The process of confirming that a statement is true is known as verification.

A fact differs from an opinion because facts can be *verified,* whereas opinions must be *supported.* An opinion is a judgment or a belief regarding something that is held by a person. It can be based on a logical inference from the facts. The following statements are examples of facts:

> The weather has got warmer over the last few years.
> The Leaving Certificate examination brings with it a great deal of pressure on pupils.

We can add some opinions to these facts; for example:

> The weather has got warmer over the last few years, and therefore we need to do something about global warming.
> The Leaving Certificate examination brings with it a great deal of pressure on pupils, and so perhaps it should be abolished.

To test factual statements we must examine the evidence. To test statements of opinion we must

- examine the evidence of fact
- examine the inferences drawn from it.

An inference is an interpretation of a fact: it is the product of a subjective reasoning process. We make inferences about things many times without realising it. For example, we meet someone we know very well, but they don't greet us, so we may infer that we have done something wrong, or that they are in bad humour. The reality may be quite different: they may simply be distracted, or tired.

The following example will illustrate more clearly the difference between a fact (or argument), an opinion, and an inference:

Fact
All the planets in the solar system are spheres.

Inference
As the planets in the solar system are spheres, the Earth must be a sphere.

Opinion
All the planets in the solar system are wonderful.

COMMENT
The first statement is a fact. The second statement is an inference that proceeds from the first one, and in this case it is true. The third statement is merely an opinion: not all people will agree with it.

The processes or stages of argument
There are different processes or stages of reasoning in argument:

- deductive reasoning
- inductive reasoning
- a priori reasoning
- a posteriori reasoning.

Deductive reasoning
Deductive reasoning begins with a general law and moves to a particular case.

> All the planets in the solar system are spheres.
> The Earth is a planet in the solar system.
> Therefore the Earth is a sphere.

The first two statements are called *premises*. They lead to the conclusion in the third statement. These three statements add up to a logical structure, which is called a *syllogism*. However, not all deductive arguments are true.

> All tigers are cats.
> Our pet is a cat.
> Therefore our pet is a tiger.

Though the first two premises are true, the concluding premise is false, and therefore the argument is false. For an argument to be valid, all premises or statements must be true.

Inductive reasoning
Inductive reasoning begins with observing individual phenomena and from them arriving at a general law.

John is a man.
John is mortal.
Therefore all men are mortal.

The structure of inductive reasoning is based on establishing certain evidence about something and then drawing a conclusion. Inductive argument can be false; for example:

Joan is a woman.
Joan is a teacher.
Therefore all women are teachers.

A priori reasoning

A priori ('from the former') reasoning goes from known causes to imaginary effects; it is a form of deductive reasoning.

They have been working all day, so they must be tired.
He crashed his car, so therefore he will buy a new one.

A posteriori reasoning

A posteriori ('from the latter') reasoning moves from known facts to probable causes.

She suffers from migraine, so she must be stressed.
The meat is not cooked, so the oven must be broken.

Fallacies in argument

A fallacy is faulty reasoning or a false or misleading argument. It is important to recognise unsound ways of reasoning or fallacies in argument, such as the following:

- faulty generalisation
- 'glittering generalities'
- begging the question
- ignoring the question
- false dilemma
- non sequitur
- emotional appeals.

Faulty generalisations

These occur through drawing the wrong conclusions from certain information. Such generalisations can be unqualified. In most cases the statement 'Killing is wrong' can be considered true; however, killing in self-defence may be justifiable, and so this statement could be considered an example of an unqualified generalisation.

Hasty generalisations or jumping to conclusions is another example of a faulty generalisation. For example, an article that claimed that most rock stars commit suicide would be an example of a hasty generalisation.

Generalisations about things involve reaching a conclusion on the grounds of certain facts or evidence. If, for example, pollution causes certain animal and plant life to die, then scientists could draw up a valid or true generalisation about the evil effects of pollution.

Glittering generalities
This is a method of obscuring an argument by deliberately keeping it vague. Glittering generalities usually involve making sweeping statements or extravagant claims about something. Some examples can be the use of certain phrases or expressions:

> The best you can get
> Tremendous value
> For tens of thousands of pupils, exams are approached with total apprehension.

Statements of this type are vague and abstract. Examine what the facts are here: what is the writer saying?

Begging the question
Begging the question means taking for granted the point that is being disputed: using the claim to support itself. In this type of argument a statement or idea is presented in such a way that presumes to be true what still has to be proved.

> We must believe that God exists, because it says so in the Bible, which is the word of God.

Here proof for the existence of God is based on an assumption of his existence and so amounts to no proof at all.

> We have to accept change, because without change there is no progress.

This statement presupposes that change and progress are synonymous, something that is not necessarily true.

Ignoring the question
In this type of argument the question or issue being discussed is ignored altogether.

Non sequitur
A *non sequitur* (Latin, 'it does not follow') is a conclusion that cannot validly be inferred from the premise or assertion.

> All rats eat rice.
> All rice is good.
> Therefore all rats are good.
> John is an Irishman.
> All Irish people are rich.
> Therefore John is rich.

The conclusions here are examples of generalisations, and they do not follow from the preceding statements.

False dilemma
This offers a choice between only two answers or two courses of action, ignoring alternative possibilities.

> The Taoiseach should abandon the budget or else resign.
> Either you welcome all immigrants to Ireland or you're a racist.

Emotional appeals
Emotional appeals include name-calling, labelling, and using loaded terms:

> They're very traditional in their beliefs.
> She's fanatical about politics.
> He's a red.

Emotional appeals invariably lead to non-sequiturs.

Sample passages

Study the following article, which makes use of the language of argument.

> 'It was like something straight out of *The Godfather*,' said the taxi-driver, appalled at the circumstances in which Sergeant Andy Callanan died in Tallaght this week. And so it was: horrible almost beyond belief, the kind of thing we thought could happen only in a film.
>
> Now we know different. And the taxi-driver's comment is sickeningly relevant, given the belief, firmly held in some quarters, that our cinema and television screens are awash with mindless violence, and that this has dreadful social implications.
>
> And the awful manner in which the garda lost his life again raises questions about our culture, how and why it is being influenced by fictional images of violence, and the links between screen violence and violence in real life. This is made all the more real by suggestions that the perpetrator of the appalling incident in Tallaght may have been influenced by a recent episode of the television series 'The Bill', featuring a scene in which a policeman was doused with petrol by someone who had a grudge against the force.
>
> The questions and the debate about them are not new. In the United States—the home of Hollywood—the director Oliver Stone is still embroiled in controversy over his film *Natural-Born Killers*. The best-selling novelist John Grisham (author of *The Firm* and *The Pelican Brief*), one of whose friends was shot by a couple claiming they had been inspired to carry out the shooting by *Natural-Born Killers,* insists that Stone should bear some of the responsibility.
>
> Are films, television plays and videos capable of influencing people to carry out acts of violence? The debate has been joined on this side of the Atlantic by Audrey Conlon, the deputy film censor, who outlined her thinking in a television interview yesterday. 'People tend to have very strong views on censorship and classification. And very often you find yourself in a corner—perhaps not trying to defend your situation but certainly trying to explain what your job is about.'
>
> So what is the most criticism a film censor gets? Do people think the censors today are too lenient, or too tough? 'Both. In one corner you can have someone saying, "You can

see anything now in the cinema; you can watch anything on video." And then the next day you'll meet someone who'll ask, "Why do we need censorship? Given that the whole media environment has changed so much, are you relevant?" The fact is that it is an area that a lot of people are interested in, particularly parents, who are concerned about what children are viewing.'

When the Video Recordings Act (1989) was introduced it meant that extra staff had to be appointed to the Film Censor's office to deal with video classification, and Ms Conlon was appointed by the Minister for Justice, Máire Geoghegan Quinn. Ms Conlon says she didn't have particularly strong views about films before becoming a censor. 'But I was always very interested in media. I'm a bit of a media junkie. When I go to a hotel somewhere the first thing I do is click on the television to see what's on CNN, and I've always been a reader of newspapers.'

In an age in which technological developments in broadcasting will very soon give us all access to two or three hundred television channels, is there still a role for the censor and a place for censorship? 'Yes. But I would prefer not to use the word censorship. People's ideas and perceptions of censorship were probably formed by what they heard about what happened here in the nineteen-forties and fifties. That's not the way the system operates at the moment. Censorship now works with a fairly light hand. Very few mainstream films are banned; but there very definitely is a need for censorship, and it's a need supported by over forty years of research.'

In other words, even in the nineteen-nineties there's a need, in Ms Conlon's opinion, to regulate in some way the material that we as a society view, and, most especially, to regulate the material that our children view. 'What the censor's office now is essentially doing is classifying material.' Which of course means that a lot of the control and responsibility is being handed back to the home. 'Certainly in the home the responsibility is being handed to the parents; but what we are giving them through the classification system is good guidelines—good consumer advice. And we're saying to them that in our opinion, based on our experience, if we classify this as 12 we are encouraging you not to let your six-year-old see it.'

Apart from the awful business in Dublin, that concern was reinforced by reports this week that two boys were motivated to try to murder a friend as a result of watching the horror film *Scream*. Little wonder that Ms Conlon would say that violence is now the main concern of the censorship office, with particular concern for its potential effects on younger people. 'This concern is not just something that we concocted ourselves. It is supported by about forty years of research, and it's research that has been done all over the world. And the conclusion is—and there will always be dissenting voices—that the mass media do bear some responsibility for contributing to violence. That's it in a nutshell.'

Does this exclude real events, like war coverage? 'No. What we see on our screens—all mediated images of violence—all contribute.'

So are we becoming desensitised to violence? Yes, the research would certainly suggest that we are. And this conclusion appears to have the support of serious researchers, meaning in the end that we are all in danger of being desensitised. 'It drips into our culture. And it appears to have done so this week with horrific consequences.'

Question A
1. What devices has the writer used to support his arguments? Refer to anecdotal evidence, factual information, classification and possible use of statistics in your answer.
2. Are the points made in this article convincing? Has the writer made use of personal opinion, or invalid or unsubstantiated claims? If so, give examples.

Question B
Write an article for a local newspaper commenting on some violent videos that you believe have a harmful effect on young people. In your article make some suggestions about how to remedy this situation.

Writing in the language of argument

When you are writing in the language of argument, the emphasis is on being able to write in a discursive manner: presenting facts and argument on a certain topic and arriving at a conclusion. In this type of writing you are trying to convince your reader that your argument is valid.

- Take a definite stance on the topic, For example in a composition on 'Spare the rod and spoil the child', you may decide to agree or disagree. The important thing is to

establish clearly, both to yourself and to your reader, what your own stance on this issue is.
- Identify your audience, whether you are writing for a group of young people, or educated professionals, or a class of schoolchildren.
- Establish what tone or point of view you will use.
- Draft an outline of the main ideas for each paragraph, and put the most important ideas first.
- Write in a balanced way. Avoid giving a one-sided presentation.
- Support every fact you make with evidence.

Remember, good argument writing is clear and concise. It is structured on original ideas, organised thought, and a balanced and logical presentation of facts. For that reason,
- use language that is formal and precise
- express ideas in a logical manner
- use transitional words to link your ideas
- anticipate the reader's opposing views
- defend your own ideas in a forceful and clear way
- avoid the use of clichés, repetition, emotional or offensive language, euphemisms, and double-speak.

Sample composition

The following composition is written in the language of argument. It is taken from actual pupils' work and is graded according to the standards required at Higher level. Study it carefully, and pay special attention to the commentary that follows. The task was to write an article for a serious journal in which you challenge or support the statement 'There are actually people who take pride in their race. This is stupid.'

> As we celebrate the end of an era and the approach of a new century, the desire to reflect on our history and actions is at a peak. This is a unique time to learn from our mistakes and take pride in our achievements. In the twentieth century the human race has advanced in some areas more than it has in the entire course of its history. However, for all our vast and wonderful achievements, the dark and destructive stain of racism remains as a reminder that in some ways we still remain almost at the same level of civilisation as the animals. This inhumanity and injustice to our fellow-humans overshadows our greatest achievements and reminds us too clearly of the savage and primitive state that remains latent within.
>
> The idea that a particular race of people could be superior to others is an absurd belief. In the words of Kofi Annan, Secretary-General of the United Nations, 'we may have different religions, different languages, different-coloured skin, but we all belong to the one human race. We all share the same basic human values.' Undoubtedly there are many things that we can take pride in: the first landing on the moon, or the first transatlantic voyage. Yet is it possible that such events can compensate for the brutal reality of two world wars, and the mindless violence perpetrated in places such as Africa and Europe,

and all carried out in the name of racism? Indeed, the few moments of glory in humankind's achievements are nothing compared with some of the grave atrocities that have been committed on our fellow-humans.

Undoubtedly racism today takes on many different aspects, from antagonising a group of travellers at their halting-site to barring someone from entry to a club because of their social status, or depriving people of educational or welfare benefits due to them.

We may ask the question, what is it that makes a person believe they are superior to another race? We are all cast from the same mould, though decorated differently. Perhaps this mistaken belief in one's superiority could stem from our past, when competition was fierce and indeed competition was the name of the game. The survival of the fittest may still survive in our subconscious thoughts today. If this is the case, then we differ little from our savage ancestors in lacking the spirit of open-mindedness to see the human race in its entirety.

While racism has been a blot on the pages of history for decades, it was only during the colonial years, when thousands of African slaves were traded like cattle between the white settlers of America, that the topic came to the forefront. To this day a rift divides the two cultures, and it has seen the growth of terror groups such as the Ku Klux Klan. Up to the sixties African-Americans had little or no rights and were still slaves to society. However, through the painstaking efforts of such people as Martin Luther King, enormous developments and inroads have been made. All this bitter hatred and animosity could have been avoided, however. It is totally unjustifiable and incomprehensible to believe that a person should consider themselves to be superior because of the colour of their skin. In fact it defies logic.

Extremist views pose the greatest problem in this particular area. Pride in one's achievements becomes converted into a brutal and radical form of racism, and in turn this is translated into profound hatred for different ways, whether the difference is manifested in religion, culture, background, or beliefs. Underlying this intransigent attitude is fear— fear of whatever is different. This fear becomes channelled into hatred and can be seen most strikingly in groups such as Combat 18 and neo-Nazism.

In these cases, violence and intimidation become the only method of communication. Diplomacy is non-existent. The results generated by such regimes are devastating. Humankind must learn that violence and injustice produce only suffering and sterility.

Adolf Hitler is an example of one such extremist. The name itself is enough to send a shiver along the spine of any humane individual. Yet he is worshipped as a god for many others. Hitler managed to find a scapegoat for the problems he confronted, both personal and political, in just about anybody, from Jews to communists. Under his brutal 'final solution', six million Jews and up to twenty million Russians became victims of Nazi concentration camps and were butchered and slaughtered by the malignant SS. His vision of an all-dominant 'Aryan' race that would triumph over humankind and last for centuries ultimately failed. Hitler has earned the unique title of having carried out more murders than any other being in history, all in the name of pride and a wilful blindness to the supposed superiority of one's race.

Racism today is deeply entrenched in the heart of our society. It is evident in all walks of life, from international politics to the area of the media. The recent move to elect Jörg Haider—a well-known master wordsmith for racism and xenophobia—in Austria sent a chill reminder across the world. It may be an interesting irony that Hitler himself was born in the same place. Many people began to fear that history would repeat itself, having borne witness to Haider's strong adherence to Hitler's views. Some people began to fear the consequences of Hitler's legacy in the wake of such political manoeuvring. In the light of this fact, Austria was politically isolated around the world. Public opinion made the statement that his beliefs are not acceptable at the start of a new century, since we know exactly what they led to in the thirties and forties. It is vitally important that a marker be put down, that when extremism is mainstreamed, something profound is happening in Europe today.

As we look back on our past we begin to realise how racism and the belief in one's superiority over another person have proved to be a disastrous combination. We are all members of the same human race. We are all entitled to the same rights and treatment because of our status as human beings. Basic unwillingness and an inability to accept this point inevitably causes conflict and war. The bloodstained history books are a colourful enough reminder of the utter pointlessness of racist beliefs. It is only when we undertake to unite and combat the various limitations within our own nature and within life in general that we can truly begin to become masters first of all of ourselves, and then perhaps we will attain some form of control over this world of ours.

COMMENT
Grade A2
This composition on the topic of racism is written in the form of an argument. It is structured clearly into a series of paragraphs, all of which deal with the subject in a factual and logical manner. The material used in the article has been well researched, and the examples and supporting evidence are both relevant and topical. The points that are made are clearly supported with evidence. Remember, good argument requires evidence and support to sustain it. The conclusion is effective, and there is a distinct unity of thought throughout the composition.

POINTS FOR DEVELOPMENT
The topic of racism has been broadened to include many other types of discrimination. The tendency to blur the meaning of 'racism' by using it as an all-purpose term for prejudice is reflected in its use here to describe discrimination against travelling people and even discrimination on grounds of social class, while the references to the slave trade and the causes of two world wars reflect an unawareness of colonialism, as distinct from racism. The scope chosen by the writer is very wide, and it may not be possible to treat all of it in sufficient depth.

Perhaps the language and style could have more energy, contrast, and colour. Some of the sentences are a little too weighty, and the argument lacks clarity at times. Always remember that good writing is clear writing.

Writing exercises
1. Write a speech for a group of business people on how you consider they could help eradicate some of the injustices in 'Third World' countries.
2. Write the speech you would give at a seminar entitled 'The power of the media'. Describe clearly your views on how the media have been either a positive or a negative influence on society.
3. Write an article for a magazine using the language of argument on the topic 'The greatest of evils and the worst of crimes is ignorance.'
4. Write a letter to a local newspaper using the language of argument on both the positive and the negative changes you have seen in Ireland over the last few years.

THE LANGUAGE OF INFORMATION

The objectives of this type of language can be
- to convey information in a succinct or terse manner
- to give instructions or make requests
- to persuade or influence the reader to adopt an attitude or act on a certain issue or matter.

The language of information is to be found in reports, journalism (newspaper, television, and radio), instructions, memos and letters, summaries, bulletins, forms, and questionnaires. Each of these forms has different objectives. Reports give a factual account of some situation or set of circumstances. Media accounts usually give a report of events in a clear and factual manner. Instructions offer a clear and terse explanation of how to do something. Memos are short messages written in an informal style. Summaries give a condensed account of information. Forms and questionnaires request information in a clear, compact manner.

Features of the language of information
1. There is clear organisation of information. All arguments and information must be presented in a logical and coherent manner.
2. The content is relevant. Do not digress from the main point in what you are writing; avoid introducing useless or irrelevant information.
3. Use an appropriate style and expression. In general, the style required for functional writing is clear and factual. Avoid the use of colourful language and images, such as:

    Performance has plummeted unexpectedly and with increasing force, because of a catastrophic lack of in-service training of staff in this area.

    Use simple factual language instead, for example:

    The lack of in-service training for staff has caused performance to fall greatly.
4. Use short sentences. Convey the information in as terse a way as possible.
5. Use the precise number of words. Avoid verbose or long-winded statements.
6. Use concrete words rather than abstract ones.

7. Use each word in a way that illustrates clearly its meaning. For example, look at the following sentences.

Check L's report.

Does this mean check the report that L has completed, or check the report on L? What does 'check' mean anyway?

Record sales figures for last year.

Does it mean write down the sales figures for last year, or that the sales figures for last year exceeded those of other years?

8. Avoid the use of slang, jargon, buzzwords, and commercialese. *Slang* is very informal language. *Jargon* is the inappropriate use of the terminology of a specialised profession. *Buzzwords* are fashionable terms often used in advertising or informal conversation. *Commercialese* consists of dated or stereotyped formulas of a kind once popular in business correspondence:

Enclosed herewith [I enclose]
Your letter is to hand [I have received your letter]
With reference to same [With regard to …]
I trust this will meet your expectations [I hope this is agreeable]

In addition, good informative writing has the following features:
- It must be simple, clear, and concise.
- The information presented must be comprehensive: it must deal with all aspects of the subject.
- It must be appropriate for the intended audience.
- The tone of the language must be objective.

In this section we will examine the different features of reports, instructions, letters and memos, etc., and study how to write them for examination purposes.

Reports
Reports, as we have seen, give a factual account of some situation. The main function of a report is to study or analyse material or information and to present this in a clear and standard form. Report-writing can have different objectives, for example:
- to inform the reader about something or to research information
- to evaluate or explain a situation or a set of circumstances
- to provoke debate on an issue.

THE LAYOUT OF A REPORT
Some of the following headings may be used in a report. Not all reports demand such detailed layout; however, it is good to be familiar with these terms in order to know how to use them.

terms of reference: the instructions that are given to those writing the report about what they have to investigate. For example, a report could have the following terms of reference: 'To report on the number of school-leavers who emigrate and work abroad.'

introduction: this sets out fully
- the main details of the report
- the questions under investigation
- the time limits
- the material or methods used.

work carried out: This section will contain detailed information on what has been done to find out information, for example any statistics that have been gathered.

findings: Under this heading comes the main body of information gathered. The material in this section must be organised carefully, and any irrelevant points must be discarded: only information bearing on the issue must be included in this section.

conclusions: These are based on the terms of reference and the findings. They should flow naturally from all the evidence and findings and should be clear, simple, and objective.

recommendations: These will include your own interpretations of any improvements or points that can be taken into account as a result of your findings. Present these simply and if possible in the form of a list.

summary: a condensed version of the report. Summaries provide a short, succinct account of both findings and conclusions. A good summary should concentrate on giving an outline of the main points and in particular the conclusions and recommendations.

acknowledgments: a list of those people and organisations that helped in any way during the research of the report.

references: any publications or other publicly available material that was used; these also should be acknowledged.

appendixes: subsidiary material gathered together at the end of the report, usually numbered. Make use of headings and sub-headings.

SAMPLE REPORT
This is an example of a report using some of the headings described above.

Report on television viewing by pupils aged between 15 and 18

Introduction
At the request of the Minister for Education and Science, a report on television viewing by young people has been authorised. The number of hours and the types of programmes watched will be studied. A list of recommendations will be drawn up.

Procedures
A detailed questionnaire on the amount of time spent watching television and on the type of programmes watched was issued to all secondary schools in the country. This questionnaire was aimed at the 15–18 age group.

Findings
Pupils generally watched between ten and twenty hours of television a week. Among the more popular type of programmes were serials, such as 'Friends', 'Neighbours', and 'Home and Away'. Boys generally watched more sports programmes than girls. Boys also spent more time on the internet than watching television.

Conclusions
Very few pupils engaged in selective viewing of television programmes. More than 80 per cent of viewing has little educational content. Many of the programmes watched were sentimental serials with little or no substance. The literary ability of pupils in this group has declined, perhaps in part because of the smaller amount of time spent reading and writing.

Recommendations
1. More programmes with an educational or informed content should be broadcast in the evenings.
2. Parents should take a more decisive part in monitoring television viewing.
3. Local libraries should provide more video and internet facilities, to stimulate young people to carry out research, to read, and to study.

COMMENTARY
A good title helps to provide a clear focus on what the report is about. The introduction sums up all aspects of the report: the reasons why the report is being undertaken, time limits, details of those carrying out the report, and who authorised it.

Remember that the style of report-writing must be factual and objective. Avoid the use of emotive and ambiguous language.

Remember to sign and date a report.

HOW TO WRITE A REPORT
Before you begin, ask yourself the following questions:
- What are the purpose and the theme of this report?
- What objectives am I hoping to achieve?
  Remember, a report is effective when
- it is understood without too much effort
- the findings are acknowledged to be valid and are acted on.

PRELIMINARY WORK
Because reports have very different objectives, it is necessary to put in a great deal of work in preparing the material before beginning the process of writing it. This preliminary work will determine the quality of the result and will enable you to structure and organise your material more effectively.

1. Establish the purpose or objective of the report. Is it to describe or evaluate a situation or set of circumstances? Is the report explaining a procedure or situation?

2. Once you have established the purpose of the report, decide on a title; this will help you to concentrate more clearly on what exactly the report is all about. You may be asked to write a report on how secondary schoolgirls use their free time at weekends. You could use a title such as 'The use of free time at weekends by schoolgirls aged 14–17.' Establishing a title will help you to limit the topic and to concentrate more clearly on what exactly you must write.
3. Find out who will read the report. This will affect the style of your report. Writing a report for the school committee will demand a different style from one for the managing director of a company.
4. Establish whether the report has a time limit, and if so, what this is.
5. Look at the resources at your disposal. What budget have you been allocated? What equipment have you got? What materials will you need?
6. Study how to structure your report. Will your report be structured in sections with sub-headings? Will the report be a summary?

CHECK-LIST FOR REPORTS
1. Does the title indicate clearly the nature of the report?
2. Are the objectives of the report clearly stated?
3. Are all the terms used in the report clearly defined?
4. Is the report written in the correct tense? Generally reports are written in the past tense.
5. Is the language of the report clear? Are there obscure phrases, evidence of bias, emotive terms or intemperate language in the report?
6. Are all the claims made substantiated clearly by facts?
7. Are the conclusions based on evidence?
8. Are the recommendations feasible?
9. Is the report signed and dated?

Media accounts

Media accounts of some event or happening generally give a factual and objective description of what they are reporting. However, such accounts are often influenced by a number of things: the type of publication, the readership aimed at, or the writer's own viewpoint on the event.

Instructions

Instructions can be written on technical or on human subjects. Technical subjects involve giving detailed guidelines on certain procedures, such as changing a fuse, fixing the plug of a hairdryer, or changing the bag on a vacuum-cleaner. These types of instructions will use specialised vocabulary and perhaps a series of numbered stages or steps.

On the other hand, instructions can be written on human subjects such as 'How to increase your self-confidence', 'How to benefit from the points scheme', or 'How to cope with exam stress'. In these type of instructions the use of generalised vocabulary and illustrations will help a great deal. The style will be more relaxed and informal.

In writing instructions, as in all writing situations, take into account
- your subject matter
- your audience
- the best techniques that can be used to communicate that subject matter to that audience.

Examine the following set of instructions on 'taking your children out of the rat race', then study the commentary that follows it.

Taking your children out of the rat race

Quality bus corridors, rising house prices, corrupt politicians, lack of child care facilities, the cost of the latest football strip—has your blood pressure shot up yet? If not, you're in a minority. It seems that stress levels for most of us have increased at a similar pace to economic growth. Have you noticed how aggressive other drivers have become? Or how casual and dismissive shop assistants are? Perhaps it is all symptomatic of the negative aspects of prosperity. The outcome of our new-found status is a population that appears less caring and more interested in promoting self-interest. In the middle of all this material mayhem, it is important for parents not to lose sight of the core values. How many of the following do you do regularly?

- Talk to your children. Do you know what your children did at school today? If not, why not?
- Play with your children. There can surely be no more rewarding experience for a parent than getting lost in the child's world. Your child likes nothing more than spending time with parents—no toy or bag of sweets is more cherished.
- Tell your child about your own experiences. Younger children love to hear about what life was like when Mammy and Daddy were the same age. This is also a useful strategy if you suspect that your child is experiencing some difficulties. For example, if you suspect that your child is being bullied, talking about when you were young can be a useful way of getting your child to open up.
- Listen. It's not an easy skill. Go for a walk and let the child do the talking. Sit and simply shoot the breeze. Try to say nothing. Let your child lead the conversation.
- Be yourself. There is no such thing as a perfect parent or a perfect child. Being trendy or over-generous will not enhance the relationship with your child; being yourself will. That means getting into the habit of leaving work outside the front door and tuning into the home environment as you find it.
- Inform your child about what is happening in the world.
- Watch your child. Children like nothing better than having their parents watching their activities. Whether this involves cringing as your child rides a bicycle with no supports for the first time, or freezing on the sideline of a football pitch for an hour, your child will appreciate it.
- Be present. Stress makes us spend all our time reflecting on the past and planning for the future. It means we miss the most important time of all. Try to come into the present and enjoy the magic and beauty of your children as they are today.

- Say 'no' sometimes. There is a temptation to make up for lost time by material goods. This can lead to frustrations on both sides when it becomes impossible to supply all your child's desires.

COMMENT
This passage is written in information format. Note the informal, almost chatty style of introduction. The layout is clear and unambiguous; all points are signalled, and no excessive information is used.

WRITING INSTRUCTIONS
1. Work out exactly what you want to achieve. What is the purpose of the instructions? Are you trying to teach children how to cook, or to outline the stages of a game, or to instruct people how to operate a machine?
2. Instructions must be clear. Make your statements specific.
3. Make sure there is a logical sequence in the stages of your instructions. Each stage should follow logically from the preceding one.
4. Say one thing in each sentence, and make sure your different stages are manageable.
5. Put the most important item in each sentence at the beginning.
6. Use the imperative form of the verb.
7. Use short sentences and short paragraphs.
8. Avoid jargon.

SAMPLE INSTRUCTIONS
Study the layout of the following set of instructions.

Tableware care

Detergents
Many different automatic dishwashing detergents are available. Choosing the correct one is vitally important, because some detergents with a high alkaline concentration can cause permanent damage to your tableware. Whenever possible, choose a detergent that can provide a good hygienic result without damaging your tableware; and never use more than the recommended quantity.

Temperatures
A washing temperature of 60°C (140°F) is accepted as the most suitable for the effective removal of food particles while minimising the risk of damaging the glaze or decoration. Excessively high temperatures will reduce washing efficiency and may damage your tableware.

Scraping
Use a plastic or rubber scraper to remove food residues. Do not use metal utensils, which can cause marking. Ideally also spray with water before washing.

Racking
Make sure that racks and baskets are plastic or plastic-coated. Replace damaged baskets immediately, as exposed metal will cause marking. Avoid the use of metal scourers. Rack your tableware correctly to ensure that items do not vibrate against each other during the wash cycle. Avoid placing cups of differing heights in the same basket.

Cutlery
Always wash cutlery separately in specially designed cutlery baskets to prevent marking of the tableware.

Microwave ovens
Tableware with metallised decorations, for example gold, is not suitable for use in microwave ovens.

Thermal shock
Ceramic tableware is not designed to withstand thermal shock, so avoid moving your tableware from a freezer to a hot oven or hob, or from a hot oven to a cold surface. Do not place tableware on or near a naked flame.

Staining
If glaze staining is a problem, use a recognised destainer, or soak the tableware in a weak solution of bleach or washing soda crystals. Avoid using abrasives to remove staining.

Memos

A memo can be defined as a brief and informal letter. The main differences between a letter and a memo are:

- A memo is informal.
- The message is immediate.
- Memos are written in offices or other work-places.

In general, both letters and memos involve

- getting the reader's attention
- making a claim
- supporting the claim by justification or explanation
- calling for action; this may include what you want the reader to do, or what you will do, or both.

Memos generally explain or outline all details in a short, terse form. Avoid long sentences and pompous words. Use information that is relevant; avoid digressing. Maintain a polite and courteous tone.

MEMO
Use of folders
It appears that manila folders are being used for internal data and for communication with

the regional sales offices, when it would be more satisfactory to use paper clips or simply staples on these documents. In the interests of economy it is suggested that for all internal and external mail, wherever practicable, either of the above two methods should be adopted.

COMMENT
This memo is long-winded and redundant. The sentence structure is too long and confusing. Avoid also the use of such phrases as 'wherever practicable'.
An alternative version could be written as follows:

> The use of folders is costing our company extra money. As an alternative, please staple documents or use paper clips.

Letters

There are different kinds of letters. *Formal letters* include business letters, letters of complaint, job applications, sales letters, and letters to the newspaper. *Personal letters* include letters of condolence and letters to a friend or pen-pal.
When writing any kind of letter,

- know what you want to say
- set out your information logically and in paragraph form
- use the correct layout and the correct tone.

Examinations on the writing of letters and memos are testing

- the coherent organisation of information
- the use of appropriate expression
- accepted standards of layout.

FEATURES OF A LETTER
1. Use the correct layout, and make it pleasing to the eye.
2. The sender's address is usually written in the top right-hand corner. (A letter on behalf of an organisation or a company will be on a printed letter-heading that includes the name and address.)
3. Write out the date fully: for example, '23 January 2001'. All letters must be dated, as they constitute a written record of a transaction.
4. Reference numbers are usually written either above or below the recipient's address.
5. Begin the letter by addressing the person by name or alternatively 'Dear sir/madam'.
6. The first sentence contains the main point of your letter.
7. Conclude your letter with either 'Yours sincerely' or 'Yours truly'. Remember, 'Yours' begins with a capital letter; 'sincerely' has an *e*; 'truly' has no *e*.
8. Use the correct tone for the context. Use a formal, tactful and courteous style, especially if you are conveying unwelcome information.
9. Choose appropriate language. Avoid clichés, verbose or wordy statements, and jargon. The language should be clear and simple.

How to write a letter
1. Decide what you want to say.
2. Set out your information logically and organise it into paragraphs. In a letter, paragraphs are signposts for the reader, which enable him or her to follow your message more clearly.
3. Choose a suitable tone when writing letters. Remember to be factual and not emotional in letters.
4. Use correct spelling and punctuation.
5. Choose the correct vocabulary for the person who is being addressed.
6. Avoid verbose language and clichés. Choose fresh and concise language that is free from jargon.
7. Write the main point of your letter in the first sentence.

Sample letters
Read the following letters, then study the commentary carefully.

Letter of application for a summer job

> 14 Moygrave Park
> Cork
>
> 13 May 2000

Mr John Naughton, Personnel manager
Bel Computers Ltd
Cloneen Industrial Estate
Cork

Dear Mr Naughton,
    I wish to apply for the position of computer operator advertised in the "Cork Examiner" on Thursday last. I am a fifth-year pupil at Crescent Comprehensive College, Cork, where I have just completed a special course in computers. I also spent some time during my transition year working in a computer firm as part of my work experience.
    I feel that I would be capable and proficient in carrying out this job. I would be available to start work from 1 June until September.
    I enclose a copy of my CV, and I will supply you with two recent references should you require them. You can contact me by telephone at (021) 6372334.

Yours sincerely,

Neil Dolan

Comment
This letter sets out clearly the important details concerning this applicant. The writer

makes use of short sentences and short paragraphs, which contributes to making the points striking and clear.

Letter to a Newspaper

4 Carew Park
Blakestown
Killarney

6 January 2000

Letters to the Editor
Irish Times
11 D'Olier Street
Dublin 2

Dear sir,

In recent weeks your paper has carried negative articles about travelling people. As a traveller and a member of the Irish Association of Travelling Women, I would like to invite the writers of these articles to live for a week in a travellers' site so that they can experience for themselves what it means to live without running water, toilets, or refuse collection.

Your article implies that travellers cause dirt and litter, which they leave to the local authority to clean up. I would challenge that writer to keep a site clean with no bin collections, no running water, and no toilets, not to mention settled people dumping their own rubbish in skips on travellers' sites. Many of these sites are indeed a disgrace; but whose fault is it?

Mr Davis states that travellers refuse to work, even when there is a labour shortage. I would like them to tell me who will give travellers a job, when they are followed by security people even as they go innocently into shops.

Finally, traveller parents have been criticised for making their children beg, subjecting them to 'emotional and physical slavery'. Yes, there is a minority of traveller children who beg—usually because of severe hardship at home; but anyone passing along any city street knows that the majority of people begging nowadays are settled people, and are mostly adults.

It does not befit your paper to allow space for articles and letters such as those of Mr Graham and Ms Moore, which contribute to anti-traveller prejudice and make the work of travellers' organisations much harder.

Yours sincerely,

Margaret Rushe

Comment

This letter is a complaint against unjust claims and statements made about travelling people. The style is clear and to the point. The sentence structure is short, and the vocabulary used is precise.

Remember, when writing a letter of complaint you must
- concentrate clearly on the results you want, rather than on the incompetence of the people involved
- describe your problem clearly, without giving way to anger; control of emotion is essential to get the desired result
- keep a record of all contacts and transactions made
- make sure you are complaining to the right person
- keep letters of complaint short.

NOTICES AND BULLETINS

Notices place the emphasis on layout and attracting the attention of the reader through short, catchy phrases and words. Their main aim is to attract the attention of different people. For that reason, their position on a notice-board must be
- well positioned for all to see
- big and attractively laid out
- up to date.

Notices are effective only if they produce the results that were intended. For that reason, the language should be vigorous and direct. The presentation should be simple and bold and the message comprehensible to everyone. Keep messages brief and terse. The opening or heading should be an eye-catcher.

> **Learn German—free!**
> If you would like to start learning German, hand in your name to the Personnel Office before Friday 10 October.
> Classes will be held at 6 p.m. in Block D on Tuesdays and Fridays. Classes will last one hour and are free.
> **Remember—**
> - you have nothing to pay
> - you can drop out whenever you like if you don't enjoy learning German.
>
> Places are limited! Hand in your name to Mary Dawson *now.*

COMMENT

The information in this notice is reduced to a minimum. The vocabulary is simple, and sentence structure and paragraphing are short. The layout makes it eye-catching. Note how two devices from advertising are used:

- the headline, which aims at catching the attention
- the appeal to action at the conclusion.

Forms and questionnaires

In filling out forms:

1. Read the instructions carefully and follow them.

2. Leave no part of the form unanswered.
3. Supply all details fully, such as first name and surname, dates of attendance at courses.
4. Where sections do not apply to you, draw a line through them or write *Not applicable*.

A *questionnaire* is a document that is circulated in order to obtain information by means of a series of carefully designed questions. This information is then collated, and deductions are made about the issues involved.

Sample composition

The following composition is written in the language of information. It is taken from actual pupils' work and is graded according to the standards required at Higher level. Study it carefully, and pay particular attention to the commentary that follows it. The task was: 'Write an informative newspaper article about your home town or parish, concentrating especially on the qualities that make it unique or memorable.'

> Lying south of Limerick rests the parish of Donaghmore. With a present population of approximately 2,600 and an area of 8,500 acres, this parish has evolved over the centuries as one of the most distinctive and distinguished areas of County Limerick.
>
> Since its beginnings as a parish in the thirteenth century, the area has undergone considerable change, and its inhabitants have witnessed and participated in some of the important events in local history. From the arrival of St Patrick to this land in the fifth century to the War of Independence in 1921, this parish has contributed greatly to the rich heritage of the south of Ireland.
>
> What makes the chronology of this parish so monumental and atypical has been the consistent involvement in both cultural and sporting activities. Rich architectural features are a striking hallmark of this parish. These bear witness to some of the more impressive changes that have been a constant feature of this region. As you saunter along the road, or drive through the narrow laneways, you will see the ancient ruins of castles and churches nestling snugly alongside more modern structures.
>
> This particular parish has played a large part in our history. The Great Famine of 1845 brought about considerable change for the Irish people at that time. Community spirit was at a low ebb, with the brutal reality of emigration rampant everywhere. It is ironic that precisely at a time of profound neediness and suffering the parish managed to construct one of the richest churches in the region, magnificently decorated with some outstanding stained-glass windows and fronting a large and elegant roof—an undoubted architectural achievement!
>
> A singular feature of Famine times was the famous Mass paths, and of course my parish boasts several—those secret paths where many local people stole silently along in early morning time, in spite of the danger involved, and attended their Mass gathered around a rock in a large bare field. Such are the strong remnants of a deep Christian community, which still remain in evidence today.
>
> One of the clearest documented facts is that some people from my parish participated in the Boer War of 1899.

Clearly some of the most memorable achievements of the people from this region will be in the area of sports. One of the greatest moments in history is recorded on the first Sunday of September 1973, when Éamon Grimes of Rootiagh captained Limerick to win the All-Ireland senior hurling title, a feat that has to be repeated by any Limerick man. Undoubtedly this was one of the proudest and most extraordinary events in the lives of many parishioners. Some other strong links in the sporting scene include Dromore Celtic and Glenview FC, which figure predominantly in the Limerick soccer scene. Indeed my parish is home to one of County Limerick's oldest and most well-established GAA clubs, South Liberties, which has attained numerous trophies over the years.

One of the striking features of some of the buildings bears witness to the existence of that strong feature of Irish educational life, the hedge school. In a corner of a large field lie the ruins of one of the most famous hedge schools in the country, a place that testifies to the eager attempts of the Irish to overcome oppression and struggle to retain some vestige of their identity by keeping the Irish language alive.

No parish would be complete without a focal point for its young people. And my parish stands foremost in providing a large hall, which is well endowed with stage and dance-floor. Our local group may not be the outstanding rock metallers but they do supply our lively youth with some good entertainment every weekend.

One of the most striking achievements of my community has been the establishment of a strong community centre, situated in the heart of the parish. It is here that the various social and educational activities take place; and it is here that many young people find an outlet for their various talents, from tap-dancing to disco dancing, and from community work to teaching arts and crafts.

Spearheaded by some students and a keen drama teacher, Youthbrief, a popular drama group, have set the parish on the map. Not only have this drama group been at the centre of a national festival but they have managed to entertain the local community on many long winter nights with various performances of *Riders to the Sea* and *The Playboy of the Western World*. This universally popular entertainment has become one of the most organic and dynamic initiatives undertaken in recent years.

In addition, there are voluntary projects that are organised and run by some young people of my parish. These embrace different activities, from visiting the old people, helping with odd jobs and shopping to teaching literacy skills to the local travelling community.

The community centre provides a rich forum for organising and sustaining these varied activities. Every Saturday the organisers of this community, who work voluntarily, run a disco for young and old alike to finance the different projects. Classes are held every Tuesday and Wednesday morning for all mothers. Here they have an opportunity to develop and improve various skills, from cookery to guitar, to acquiring another language or brushing up an already rusty one. To facilitate their lives, an extension has been added on to the centre where creche facilities make it easy to relax and enjoy the morning in peace, and perhaps engage in gossip and chat about the local news.

There are a host of various activities and areas of interest in this exciting community. This is an area that is characterised by a striking sense of good will, an area that is unique in the support and consolidation offered by its members to the old and disadvantaged. Truly my community is both unique and noteworthy.

Comment
Grade: A2
In this piece the writer has structured the information clearly into separate paragraphs, all of which deal with a distinct aspect of the subject. Each of these paragraphs gives a graphic and detailed insight into some particular feature of this parish that makes it noteworthy.

Remember, good informative writing has to be both clear and concise. This composition has hints of a personal touch, which prevent the subject from becoming boring. The whole article is comprehensive: it gives a thorough insight into the more striking features of this community and covers the central aspects of its life. The writer uses a variety of sentence structure and vocabulary to communicate the points effectively. The subject is handled confidently; this is evident in the style, which is smooth-flowing and lucid.

Perhaps the writer could liven up the vocabulary and language used, and perhaps vary the sentence structure.

Exercises on writing in the language of information
1. You are the secretary of a city youth club. Write a report that you will submit to the Department of Education and Science with an application for a grant. Include details of all the activities of your club and the numbers who attend.
2. You are the manager of a small restaurant. Write a list of instructions for your employees on the procedures to be followed in the event of a fire.
3. You wish to object to an advertisement that you consider to be unsuitable for viewing on television. Write a letter to the Advertising Standards Body setting out clearly your objections.
4. As a journalist for a local newspaper, write a factual report on an all-Ireland rugby match.

The language of persuasion

The 'language of persuasion' is used by writers to try to influence the way in which a person may think or act. Its primary purpose is to influence how a reader thinks. This is the type of writing that forms the framework of political speeches, advertising writing, and marketing.

Persuasion can be achieved in different ways:
- by manipulation
- by appealing to the emotions
- by argument.

The language of argument and that of persuasion are quite similar; however, the techniques used in both are distinctive. Because the aim of the persuasive writer is to manipulate feeling and emotion, there is a heavy reliance on emotive vocabulary, on using feeling and emotion to elicit agreement or acquiescence. Persuasive writing can be found in letters, political speeches and addresses, film reviews, some newspaper reports, and advertising.

Features of persuasive writing

Because persuasive writing has as its aim convincing you about something, most of the techniques used are directed at the emotions or the senses rather than the intellect. The language of persuasion relies on emotive argument to communicate its message more forcefully to the reader.

All types of persuasive writing use the same tactics. It is worth examining the following features of persuasive writing, in particular in the area of advertising, to persuade or convince:
- slogans
- repetition
- statistics
- imperatives
- the rhyming of words
- rhetorical questions
- buzzwords
- tones.

Slogans

A slogan can be described as a point made without any support, often in the form of a short, punchy phrase. Advertisements usually contain slogans.

> If you ache when you wake ...
> When it pours, we reign.
> You can with a Nissan.
> Every Rolex takes twelve months to make; no wonder time is so valuable.
> When you're healthy on the inside, it shows on the outside.

The purpose of a slogan is to fix an image in your mind; and so the writer will use graphic images, and perhaps a play on words wherever possible.

Repetition

Repetition is a hallmark of persuasive writing, and in particular of advertising.

> Introducing PURE COLOUR nail lacquer with a treat at the House of Fraser.
> Pure impact. Pure luxury. Pure colour. Pure treat.

The following extract from an article on drugs is a clear example of how repetition can be used effectively in persuasive writing:

> We know that good education and good training policies work. We know that strict

regulation is much more effective in keeping drugs such as alcohol and tobacco away from children than the anarchic market in illegal drugs has ever been. We know, above all, that what we're doing now is, by any objective standards, a failure so disastrous that no change could ever make things worse.

The repetition of the phrase 'we know' gives a strong and emphatic punch to the ideas here.

Statistics

Statistics are also used by persuasive writers. The use of statistics may lend an air of authority to an otherwise dubious claim.

> A nationwide study by a team of doctors has demonstrated that in 97 per cent of headaches, X works to give relief.
> Up to 80 per cent better sleep on the Tempur mattress.
> Syndol gives relief in half an hour.
> Now 82 per cent of people in the country have opted for the Maxi central heating system.

Imperatives and commands

These are also a feature of persuasive writing. Imperatives demand immediate action:

> Buy now ...
> Use this coupon to send for our free brochure ...
> Send in this form and you will receive ...
> Order today ...
> Pay in the next ten days and you will receive ...
> All you have to do is ...

Rhyming

Very often persuasive writing uses words that rhyme, which can give a sense of movement to the piece of writing.

> A flawless look ... imperceptible, undetectable.
> Firm up your flab in five weeks.

Rhetorical questions

A rhetorical question is one to which an answer is not really expected: the question usually implies the answer and is used merely as a device of persuasion.

> Have you problems getting your wash white?
> Would you believe there are bikes that cost more than this car?
> What really kills weeds?
> What gas heating is more simple than ...?
> Why not enjoy life with a Sunrise Scoota?
> What other cereal will provide a better balance of the things your body needs?

Buzzwords

Buzzwords are very fashionable, often pseudo-technical terms that are usually meaningless: 'empowerment', 'cyberspace', 'out there', 'in terms of', 'the bottom line'. They are widely used in persuasive writing to impress the reader.

Tones

Tone is the relationship a writer establishes with the reader. It is an important ingredient of effective persuasive writing. A writer wishing to persuade can adopt any number of tones, including
- humorous
- ironic or satirical
- didactic or instructive
- oratorical.

Humorous tone

A writer can use humour to illustrate a point, as for example in the following paragraph about computers:

> Bugs are the usual excuse for computer breakdown, but a London company had a particular problem with rats that liked to eat the insulation around the cables. Rodent exterminators were brought in and laid tubs of poison underneath the floorboards. The rats just dragged the dishes out of the way to get at the insulation. The ratters then spread special spy-dust, which, instead of laying a trail to the rats' nest, got swept into the air-conditioning system and made the staff sneeze.

The humour here mocks the attempts of humans to deal with computer breakdown.

Ironic tone

Both irony and satire can by used for purposes of ridicule or mockery. Irony can also be used to hammer home a point effectively. In the following paragraph the writer makes clever use of irony to condemn the growth of 'warlords' in eastern European countries.

> Much of the former Yugoslavia is now ruled by warlords. Their vehicle of choice is a four-wheel-drive Cherokee Chief with a policeman's blue light to flash when speeding through a check-point. They pack a pistol but they don't wave it about. They leave vulgar intimidation to the bodyguards in the back, the ones with shades, designer jeans, and Zastava machine-pistols. They themselves dress in the leather jackets, floral ties and pressed corduroy trousers favoured by German television producers. They bear no resemblance whatever to Rambo. The ones I met at the check-points on the roads of Croatia and Serbia were short, stubby men who in a former life were small-time hoods, small-town cops, or both. Spend a day with them touring their world and you'd hardly know that most of them are serial killers.

Satirical tone

In satirical writing the folly of human nature is exposed to ridicule. Dickens possesses the remarkable gift of drawing an exquisitely satirical portrait in some of his characters. The following passage is an example of humorous satire that describes Pip eating his Christmas dinner as a child:

> Among this good company I should have felt myself, even if I hadn't robbed the pantry, in a false position. Not because I was squeezed in at an acute angle of the table-cloth, with the table in my chest and the Pumblechookian elbow in my eye, nor because I was not allowed to speak (I didn't want to speak), nor because I was regaled with the scaly tips of the drumsticks of the fowls and with those obscure corners of pork of which the pig, when living, had had the least reason to be vain. No; I should not have minded that if they would only have left me alone. But they wouldn't leave me alone. They seemed to think the opportunity lost if they failed to point the conversation at me, every now and then, and stick the point into me. I might have been an unfortunate little bull in a Spanish arena, I got so smartingly touched up by these moral goads.

(Charles Dickens, Great Expectations)

The following description is an example of how character portrayal can be used effectively to gain maximum satirical effect:

> The worst of it was that that bullying old Pumblechook, preyed upon by a devouring curiosity to be informed of all I had seen and heard, came gaping over in his chaise-cart at tea time, to have the details divulged to him. And the mere sight of the torment, with his fishy eyes and mouth open, his sandy hair inquisitively on end, and his waistcoat heaving with windy arithmetic, made me vicious in my reticence.

The description of Pumblechook's physical appearance is based on a series of small graphic details: 'gaping over in his chaise-cart at tea time', 'fishy eyes', 'mouth open', 'sandy hair inquisitively on end'. The combination of these striking and effective details with a distinct tone of satire makes this piece a splendid example of ironic satire.

Didactic tone

Didactic writing sets out to instruct or teach the reader about something. The writer uses the imperative 'must' or 'have to' and a dogmatic tone in this type of writing.

> I have learnt that many people who take astrology seriously were first attracted to the field by their reading of horoscopes in the newspapers. It is deplorable that so many newspapers now print this daily nonsense. At the start the regular reading is a sort of fun game, but it often ends up as a mighty serious business. The steady and ready availability of astrological 'predictions' can, over many years, have insidious influences on a person's judgment. Faith in astrology and other occult practice is harmful insofar as it encourages an unwholesome flight from the persistent problems of real life. Other solutions must be found by people who suffer from the frustrations of poverty, from grief at the death of a loved one, or from fear of economic or personal insecurity.

The purpose of this passage is to persuade the reader against falling victim to astrology. The tone is an explicit condemnation of reliance on astrological predictions. The writer uses a dogmatic tone to point out the fact that faith in such practices results in an unwholesome escape from the problems that are a part of daily life.

ORATORICAL WRITING
Oratorical writing is also used by the persuasive writer, though it is more suited to the spoken than to the written word. Some features of this type of writing are

- a magnificent flow of thought
- the use of rhetorical questions
- a fine command of expressions and language.

Examine the following speech of St John Rivers to Jane Eyre, all in an oratorical tone:

> I am the servant of an infallible master. I am not going out under human guidance, subject to the defective laws and erring control of my feeble fellow-worms: my king, my lawgiver, my captain, is the All-perfect. It seems strange to me that all round me do not burn to enlist under the same banner—to join in the same enterprise.
>
> Humility, Jane, is the groundwork of Christian virtues: you say right that you are not fit for the work. Who is fit for it? Or who that ever was truly called, believed himself worthy of the summons? I for instance am but dust and ashes. With St Paul I acknowledge myself the chiefest of sinners: but I do not suffer this sense of my personal vileness to daunt me. I know my Leader: that he is just as well as mighty; and while he has chosen a feeble instrument to perform a great task, he will, from the boundless stores of his providence, supply the inadequacy of the means to the end. Think like me, Jane—trust like me. It is the Rock of Ages I ask you to lean on: do not doubt but it will bear the weight of your human weakness.
>
> (Charlotte Brontë, *Jane Eyre*)

In this extract, St John Rivers is urging Jane to leave everything and become his wife out on the missions. The tone is emotive. Examine the use of repetition and rhetorical questions: these are effective rhetorical devices in moving an audience over to your side and are hallmarks of oratorical writing.

The following is an example of a political speech written in an oratorical tone:

> Ladies and gentlemen, I would like to talk to you for a moment about the present situation. Never before has this country faced such a crisis, and what is now needed is a great deal of courage and honesty. Should we fail to deal with the economic crisis at once, the situation could be disastrous. It is at moments such as this that the true character of a nation shines through. I believe that the right action taken now will resolve the problems that have faced us so menacingly. What we must all realise is that the way ahead is hard, and sacrifices must be made; but on no account and in no circumstances must our resolve be shaken. It is obvious that those who do not firmly believe as I do that this is so are mistaken. Were we to act as they suggest we would face a situation from which we might never recover, and this must not be allowed to happen. I sincerely hope that

you will join with me in saying 'Yes' to what I am proposing, because saying 'No' would mean not only that I was defeated but that I was wrong.

This is an example of a speech that relies for its effect on arousing the emotions of the audience. Note the reliance on emotive vocabulary in the sentence beginning 'Should you fail to deal ...' In oratorical writing there is a certain degree of exaggeration, which is also a hallmark of persuasive writing. Phrases such as 'never before has this country faced such a crisis' and 'were we to act as they suggest' rely for their effect on exaggeration and drama.

Writing in the language of persuasion
A good persuasive writer must be able to

- express their views clearly and logically
- foresee all possible angles of opposition and be able to tackle them effectively.

Before you begin any type of persuasive composition, be aware of the following points:

- Know your audience.
- Know your subject.
- Establish the correct tone with your audience.
- State your purpose clearly.
- Use persuasive techniques.

Know your audience
Have a good knowledge of who your reader or audience is. A striking talk on drug-dependence is hardly likely to stimulate a group of pensioners. Similarly, an excellent article describing the advantages of pension schemes will not attract the attention of a group of teenagers. Identify as clearly as possible who your readers are, what level of knowledge they have about the subject, and their motivations and interest in reading the composition. Know clearly what type of persuasion will affect your reader.

The following headlines are taken from different magazines and are written in a persuasive style. Identify the intended audience in each case.

> When pop stars have to talk love, they only talk to their fave mag, *TV Hits*
> They're the cutest twosome in pop—but what makes Marvin and Tamara tick?
> Why we adore Dior

These headlines are obviously taken from magazines that are aimed at young people. Naturally this type of approach could not be adopted in an educational publication or a medical journal.

Know your subject
It makes no sense to start writing about something you know nothing about, particularly when you are trying to persuade somebody to adopt your viewpoint.

Consider the following two paragraphs on how fashion in clothes is the deliberate creation of waste:

> Fashion today is nothing more than creating a lot of waste. People buy clothes they do not need and so waste them. This is the case particularly with women, because they are in a sense more slaves of fashion than men. So clothes designers produce new designs each year, and they in turn contribute to this development of waste.

There is very little in this argument that will make you adopt any serious viewpoint. On the other hand, look at the following passage on the same theme:

> Over the years, the great majority of men have successfully resisted all attempts to make them change their style of dress. The same cannot be said for women. Each year a few so-called top designers in Paris or London lay down the law, and women the whole world over rush to obey. The decrees of the designers are unpredictable and dictatorial. This year they decide, in their arbitrary fashion, that skirts will be short and waists will be high; zips are in and buttons are out. Next year the law is reversed, and, far from taking exception, no-one is even mildly surprised.
>
> If women are mercilessly exploited year after year, they have only themselves to blame. Because they shudder at the thought of being seen in clothes that are out of fashion, they are annually blackmailed by the designers and the big stores. Clothes that have been worn only a few times have to be discarded because of the dictates of fashion. When you come to think of it, only a woman is capable of standing in front of a wardrobe packed full of clothes and announcing sadly that she has nothing to wear. Changing fashions are nothing more than the deliberate creation of waste. Many women squander vast sums of money each year to replace clothes that have hardly been worn. Women who cannot afford to discard clothing in this way waste hours of their time altering the dresses they have. Hem-lines are taken up or let down; waist-lines are taken in or let out; neck-lines are lowered or raised; and so on.

The writer here gives examples to support the argument; and the examples chosen are graphic and relevant. Remember to research your subject before beginning on the process of writing.

Establish the correct tone with your audience
Once you have identified your audience, adapt your message and tone accordingly. You cannot use a lofty or philosophical tone with a group of schoolchildren; neither can you use a colloquial tone in a speech to the board of management of your school. Similarly, do not use formal language if you are writing on pop music for a teenage magazine.

It can help sometimes to introduce a note of humour or irony into your writing, in order to gain the attention of your reader more readily.

State your purpose clearly and confidently
Outline clearly in your opening paragraph what your intention is.

Use persuasive techniques

Some examples can be the use of effective images or anecdotes to support your viewpoint. These can also serve the function of arousing certain emotions about your topic in readers and of getting them on your side.

The following paragraphs are an excellent example of how humour and the anecdote work together to communicate a point effectively:

> As everyone knows, 'getting away from it all' involves a lot more than just physical distance. For me, though, it has to be shoes: one hint of even the shortest weekend break and I feel I should get into shoes so comfortable I could conceivably sleep in them. I have a particular antipathy to flat shoes, because the stupid things make me feel short, fat, and flat-footed.
>
> This antipathy to flatties took on a more sinister note on a recent trip to Galway, when, as usual, I took the first, quavering step to really relaxing by donning my old school trainers. They're made of canvas with three bright blue stripes, and they're flatter than a glass of Seven-Up left in the sun. They go down very well in trendy night clubs and at casual brunches in friends' back gardens when everyone usually has a good chat about how they don't make trainers like that any more. This is all very well, but after two days of short wanders to the beach and back to the pub I was practically bed-ridden, with legs bent like nutcrackers. It didn't take an Einstein or even a Dr Scholl to work out that this complete seizure in the leg department was the result of wearing flat shoes for the first time in—oh, dear—seven years. The tendons in my calves were used to being made tight by two inches of heel and were complaining loudly about being stretched to their natural length.

The writer of this passage uses a familiar and homely vocabulary that is accessible to the ordinary reader. The humorous tone makes it a lively piece of writing. The writer also varies the structure of the sentences.

Remember

Bear in mind the following guidelines when writing a persuasive composition or article.
1. Avoid making sweeping statements or vague and broad generalisations, such as:

   All pupils suffer from extreme examination pressure.
   All governments are corrupt.
   All teenagers take drugs.
   All women are victims.

2. Don't make unsupported statements. Support each point you make with sufficient evidence or effective illustrations.
3. Avoid using an aggressive or bitter tone, as it will only alienate your reader.
4. Don't distort the truth. While a certain amount of hyperbole or exaggeration is permissible in persuasive writing, it is never acceptable to distort or pervert the truth or to tell a lie in your writing.

Sample composition

The following passages are written in the language of persuasion. They are taken from actual pupils' work and are graded according to the standards required at Higher level. Study them carefully, and pay particular attention to the commentary that follows.

The task here was: 'Write a persuasive article for a teenage magazine on the subject of dieting and weight.'

Lighten up—you'll never get stuck in the aisle
You're walking down the aisle of a crowded bus, and straight ahead you see the last vacant seat. Approaching it in slow motion, you realise that there are steel bars on each side of the seat. Everyone is watching as you sit down. Squeezing against the bars of the seat are your bulges of fat, and they're multiplying by the second. Wide-eyed passengers point and stare as you struggle to get out of your seat and walk back down the aisle in sheer terror. Oh, the relief when the alarm wakes you up to the Divine Comedy's 'National Express'.

A few weeks ago our transition-year class in St Jude's was busily discussing ideas for our magazine, *Voice from the Well*. We all got distracted and started to talk about weight. Within minutes we were heatedly deploring the emaciated appearance of Monica in 'Friends'.

Women through the ages have wasted their time worrying about their weight and their appearance, and I think it's about time we confronted our fears. We might feel tempted to blame anorectic actors, gaunt girl-groups or the supercilious models of today for making size 6 a figure. We could say that women's magazines are the cause of such mass misery, bombarding us as they do with revolutionary diets that just don't work. But the simple truth is that women were concerned about their weight and appearance long before such things even existed.

According to a tour guide in Bath, a lift built to honour Queen Victoria in one of the finest hotels in the city made no difference to her life-style. She overheard a peasant saying something like 'Oh, my goodness, would you look at the Queen's flat ankles,' and she fled the city in a huff, never to return. I can't help but feel a little sympathy for the petulant queen, because, in the words of Julian Browne, obesity is a condition that proves that the Lord does not help those who help themselves.

Imagine having to ask your sister to help you crush your lower chest cavity with a corset every morning and you would wonder how any woman could ever have inflicted those elephant-tusks of discomfort on herself. Yet women once chanced breaking the odd rib to gain some control of their figure.

Today dieting seems to have replaced the corset. After all, it takes a lot of self-discipline to stick to a diet consisting of a rice cake for breakfast, a cup of tea for lunch, and no dinner at all. Lots of women would be quite happy to be a little less pear-shaped, but successful control freaks, like Courtney Cox and Calista Flockhart, go much further and, not surprisingly, have been accused of being anorectic.

Scientists have proved that a woman with Barbie Doll proportions could not survive; yet many women strive for what they see as perfection.

'All the other reindeer used to laugh and call him names …' If you ever really thought about that jolly Christmas song, you'd realise that it isn't so jolly after all. You might even say that Rudolph epitomises our cultural over-emphasis on physical appearance. Poor old Rudolph was stigmatised for having a red nose and was accepted only when it dawned on the other reindeer that he might come in handy because of it. Being fat is also highly stigmatised, and women tend to use their weighing scales to evaluate their physical attractiveness. The average female star was dismayed when the *Titanic* star Kate Winslet was described as 'too fat to be attractive'.

On groggy-eyed days, when you sit sluggishly at the back of the classroom and feel your hair, you suddenly realise that the strange shampoo you used that morning must have been conditioner. Then you feel as if you had poured petrol over yourself before coming to school. And just as you were forgetting about your facial volcanoes you're asked to analyse the Prince of Morocco's line in *The Merchant of Venice*—'Mislike me not for my complexion.' By the time you get home and collapse in front of the telly nauseated with self-pity you're simply in no form for irritating Special K advertisements.

If you compare yourself with others you may become vain and bitter, for, as the 'Desiderata' says, 'there will always be greater and lesser persons than yourself.' You might never be a Naomi Campbell or a Kate Moss, but the chances are too that you'll never realise your recurring nightmare and make headlines for getting stuck in the aisle of a bus. I suggest that we all lighten up and become more like Rudolph. Do something useful, like buying a nice cream bun. Perhaps some shops and bakeries might even think of putting up a little sign saying 'Thank you for not dieting.'

COMMENT
Grade A2
This is a witty and light-hearted piece of writing on the topic of weight and dieting. The opening anecdote is entertaining and catches the reader's attention immediately. The language and style are both vibrant and humorous. There are some light-hearted yet clever hints of satire and sarcasm. The examples that are used are familiar and topical. There is clear identification of the audience: the article is written for a teenage magazine, and the examples and illustrations used are interesting and relevant. There is an energy and vibrancy in the ideas presented; it is clear that the writer is enthusiastic about the topic. The writer here seems to be very much in control of her subject at every stage. The writing is immediate and accessible, as the writer constantly addresses the reader.

Perhaps some of the references could be developed in more detail and depth to gain that higher mark. Also, the narrative moves on a bit too abruptly at times.

For the next composition, the task was: 'Compose a persuasive composition that seeks to establish the need for greater awareness of sex stereotyping today.'

Mam is cooking the evening meal. She glances at the saucepans every now and then as she runs the cloth over the kitchen work-top. This completed, she picks up the sweeping-brush. All this time, Father sits in his armchair, gazing with glassy eyes at the television screen. He hasn't moved from his cosy sanctuary for hours. He and the armchair have become one, as if he had been melted into it in a liquid state, and now they are inseparable. As my mother runs the brush over the floor, she protests feebly about the noises coming from the television. A typical scene on a Saturday in my house!

Suddenly, in a feat of incredible athletic ability, my father springs from his chair and dives for the television. (The remote-control is broken and he hasn't got around to fixing it.) He reaches the mute button in less than one second, and before my eyes have become adjusted to the sight of him actually out of his chair he is seated comfortably again. 'I hate that advertisement,' he declares in disgust. 'I'm sick of this incessant campaign against men. We're just as capable as women, and I'm tired of being told otherwise.'

It could be one of a range of advertisements running at the moment that irritate my father: the advertisements that suggest that men can do housework only with this wonderful product and should do so to seek approval from women; an advertisement that features a women spelling out the slogan 'So simple even he can do it'; an advertisement that depicts utter chaos when Father is looking after the house, and only with the return of the female is order restored.

These advertisements are nothing less than harmful. Women have been so oppressed and victimised in the past that now it seems we have veered too much to the other extreme. Now, marketing strategies base their tactics on portraying an image of a highly effective, highly capable woman, not realising that this excessive portrayal of supposed outstanding female talent runs the risk of undermining the male counterpart. Sex stereotyping still exists, in however subtle a form, and it is imperative that this issue is recognised and addressed as such.

Sex stereotyping affects us all, whether we realise it or not. As may be deduced from my earlier anecdotal reference, my parents fit neatly into this category of male and female stereotypes, as depicted by the media. My mother does most of the cleaning and housework, while my father carries out the 'male' jobs, such as washing the car and fixing whatever is broken. Although, genetically speaking, my father would be as capable of vacuum-cleaning and cleaning sinks as my mother, it is not difficult to see how this situation has evolved.

From birth they have been assaulted with images that subtly engrave on their consciousness certain ideas about the different roles of males and females in society. Who can blame them for their actions when they have experienced such brainwashing? My parents are certainly not alone in this. Can you think of a single household in which there are no preconceived notions about male and female roles? I certainly cannot. While many people may recognise the inanity and prejudice underlying such advertisements, there are other, more subtle methods that consolidate this attitude. Take, for example, the famous Simpsons, a programme that is watched by multitudes both old and young every night of the week. This programme is a key example of sex stereotyping in its depiction of an intelligent and hard-working daughter and a lazy, troublesome and intellectually challenged son. The long-suffering mother is more intelligent than her husband and looks after all the housework and child care. This type of presentation is more insidious, as it adopts a simple and fairly unassuming story line and cleverly uses the medium of comedy to communicate its content.

It is my firm belief that sex stereotyping is one of the greatest sources of friction between male and female in our society. Every person, whether male or female, holds some preconceived ideas about the opposite sex, whether they realise it or not. These prejudices on both sides sometimes lead to conflict and an unspoken agreement that it is the duty of all women to join together in hostility against men. Men feel compelled to defend their position and 'band together' against women. American chat shows illustrate how prominent this male-female conflict has become in American society. It is hardly surprising that the divorce rate in America is the highest in the world; and this is enough to provide ample evidence for the link between sex stereotyping in society and the damage done to male-female relations.

In the world of sport the damage done by sex stereotyping is once again in evidence. Society puts such pressure on both men and women to conform that people may become afraid to seek the job they truly want. Male nurses and female mechanics need to be strong individuals to deal with the inevitable mockery and harassment they will receive as a result of their career choice.

Sex stereotyping is a problem that must be addressed fully. In an age such as ours it is disturbing to think that we cannot behave as we please, or choose whatever career we wish, because of the reproductive organs we were born with. Both males and females must face their different strengths and limitations squarely and sincerely and try to transcend all the pressures to behave in a particular way. Since the mass media seem to be one of the main methods through which this attitude towards male and female springs, the problem needs to be remedied within this context. Media programmes and presentations of these issues must broaden the scope of their research and work at depicting a wider vision of the different roles of both male and female.

COMMENT
Grade B1
This composition is an example of an organised piece of writing, which is clearly constructed into different paragraphs, all of which keep to the topic throughout. The writer's enthusiasm for the subject is evident from the lively and rather witty style. The writer also makes use of some current examples and illustrations from the media to support the statements made. However, as is typical of a lot of young people's writing, a lot of very generalised statements are made: for example, 'Women have become so oppressed and victimised in the past that now it seems we have veered too much to the other extreme.' Remember that facts must be supported at all times by clear examples or statistics.

Exercises on writing in the language of persuasion
1. Write a short persuasive article for a local newspaper on the value of having sport as a compulsory part of the curriculum. Aim your article at a general readership.
2. Compose a persuasive article for a popular magazine on the topic 'Is it now time for men's liberation?'
3. Compose a persuasive composition for a teenage magazine that seeks to establish the

need for a greater degree of selectivity in the viewing of television programmes.
4. Write out an advertisement for your favourite make-up, aiming it at members of your own class. In the advertisement include price, special offers, and the imperative use of language.
5. Write a persuasive letter to a local newspaper about ways in which the environment could be kept cleaner.

THE AESTHETIC USE OF LANGUAGE

This section deals with the way in which language can be used to create an aesthetic effect in writing. In this section there is an emphasis on how language can be used to create concepts of beauty and harmony through the use of words that add up to striking images of things. The emphasis here is on the use of language as an artistic or creative medium.

Writing in which language can be used aesthetically includes fiction, drama, films, and poetry.

Features of the aesthetic use of language
1. The use of imagery: the capacity of words to create pictures. Imagery can also be defined as word pictures; it is the way a writer uses words to conjure up a picture or image of something. Imagery is the basis of all writing but in particular in the writing of poetry, drama, certain types of fiction, and, in a different manner, in films.
2. A stress on how language can be used in an artistic way.
3. The different ways in which words can be used to create concepts of beauty and harmony.
   Read the following descriptive passage, then study the commentary that follows.

> Smoke was rising here and there among the creepers that festooned the dead or dying trees. As they watched, a flash of fire appeared at the root of one wisp, and then the smoke thickened. Small flames stirred at the bole of a tree and crawled away through leaves and brushwood, dividing and increasing. One patch touched a tree trunk and scrambled up like a bright squirrel. The smoke increased, sifted, rolled outwards. The squirrel leapt on the wings of the wind and clung to another standing tree eating downwards. Beneath the dark canopy of leaves and smoke the fire laid hold on the forest and began to gnaw. Acres of black and yellow smoke rolled steadily towards the sea. At the sight of the flames and the irresistible course of the fire, the boys broke into shrill, excited cheering. The flames, as though they were a kind of wild life, crept as a jaguar creeps on its belly towards a line of birch-like saplings that fledged an outcrop of the pine rock. They flapped at the first of the trees, and the branches grew a brief foliage of fire. The heart of flame leapt nimbly across the gap between the trees and then went swinging and flaring along the whole row of them. Beneath the capering boys a quarter of a mile square of forest was savage with smoke and flame. The separate noises of the fire merged into a drum-roll that seemed to shake the mountain.
>
> (William Golding, *Lord of the Flies*)

Comment

This passage is highly dramatic and vivid. The effect here is achieved through a series of energetic verbs and vocabulary: 'a flash of fire appeared', 'the smoke increased, sifted, rolled outwards'. The writer is intent on conveying movement and energy. Through the expert combination of certain techniques, such as the use of vivid imagery, splendid descriptions, and energetic language, he paints a highly effective image of the whole scene.

Now look at the following extract, which has many examples of the figurative use of language:

> As the sun set, its light slowly melted the landscape, till everything was made of fire and glass. Released from the glare of noon, the haycocks seemed to float on the aftergrass: their freshness penetrated the air. In the far distance, hills with woods up their flanks lay in light like hills in another world—it would be a pleasure of heaven to stand up there, where no foot ever seemed to have trodden, on the spaces between the woods soft as powder dusted over with gold. Against those hills, the burning red rambler roses in cottage gardens along the roadside looked earthy—they were too near the eye.
>
> The road was in Ireland. The light, the air from the distance, the air of evening rushed transversely through the open sides of the car. The rims of the hood flapped, the hood's metal frame rattled as the tourer, in great bounds of speed, held the road's darkening magnetic centre streak. The big shabby family car was empty but for its small driver—its emptiness seemed to levitate it—on its back seat a coat slithered about, and a dressing case bumped against the seat. The driver did not relax her excited touch on the wheel: now and then while she drove she turned one wrist over, to bring the watch worn on it into view, and she gave the mileage marked on the yellow signposts a flying, jealous, half-inadvertent look. She was driving parallel with the sunset: the sun slowly went down on her right hand.
>
> (Elizabeth Bowen, *Summer Night*)

Comment

This is a splendid example of how language can be used in a highly creative and aesthetic fashion. In the extract, the writer gives us some beautiful images of nature. Note, for example, her reference to colour: 'everything was made of fire and glass', 'the woods soft as powder dusted over with gold', the 'burning red rambler roses'. All the images used are rich and sensuous and serve the function of painting a powerfully clear picture of an Irish landscape in summer.

The following extract, from the verse play *Murder in the Cathedral*, is a striking example of how language can be used aesthetically:

> *Chorus:*
> Numb the hand and dry the eyelid,
> Still the horror, but more horror
> Than when tearing in the belly.
> Still the horror, but more horror
> Than when twisting in the fingers,

Than when splitting in the skull.
More than footfall in the passage,
More than shadow in the doorway,
More than fury in the hall.
The agents of hell disappear, the human, they shrink and dissolve
Into dust on the wind, forgotten, unmemorable; only is here
The white flat face of Death, God's silent servant,
And behind the face of Death the Judgment,
And behind the Judgment the Void,
more horrid than active shapes of Hell;
Emptiness, absence, separation from God;
The horror of the effortless journey, to the empty land
Which is no land, only emptiness, absence, the Void,
Where those who were men can no longer turn the mind
To distraction, delusion, escape into dream, pretence;
Where the soul is no longer deceived, for there are no objects, no tones,
No colours, no forms to distract, to divert the soul
From seeing itself, foully united for ever, nothing with nothing,
Not what we call death but what beyond death is not death
We fear, we fear. Who shall then plead for me,
Who intercede for me, in my most need?

(T. S. Eliot, *Murder in the Cathedral*)

COMMENT
This passage is written in a highly poetic style, which is also a striking feature of the language of aesthetics. The vocabulary is rich and poetic; images are lyrical and emphatic. The writer uses splendid and fluid rhythms, together with effective repetition, to conjure up some frightening images of Hell and loss.

Writing in the language of aesthetics

The ability to write in order to demonstrate the whole aesthetic quality of language involves a capacity to use images. Language that is aesthetic is rich in beautiful imagery and description. Learn the art of writing description well. Good descriptive writing concentrates on giving a clear, vivid picture. Good description concentrates on involving all the senses.

Method of writing descriptive composition
1. Select details of what you are describing with great care, and concentrate on registering a few small points.
2. Be selective in what you write about when describing. Do not include every feature, but concentrate on one or two.

3. Refer to location in some way. This can be the geographical context, the country or region, the landscape, or the time, season, or historical period.
4. Remember, effective imagery is created through the association of words. This can be achieved
   - by means of similes or metaphors or rhythm
   - by direct description.
5. Use images and language that appeal to the different senses. Visual images can include features of colour or shape and size. The use of images that appeal to the ear create a deep and lasting impression on your reader.

> The scullery was water, where the old pump stood. And it had everything else that was related to water: thick steam of Mondays edgy with starch; soapsuds boiling, bellying and popping, creaking and whispering, rainbowed with light and winking with a million windows. Bubble bubble toil and grumble, rinsing and slapping of sheets and shirts, and panting Mother rowing her red arms like oars in the steaming waves. Then the linen came up out of the pot like pastry or woven suds or sheets of moulded snow.

The effect of this description is to conjure up a vivid picture of the scullery and how the washing was done. The writer draws on all the senses: the sense of smell by the starch and the soapsuds, the sense of touch in the references to slapping the sheets and 'rowing her red arms like oars in the steaming waves.'

Describing people

The ability to draw effective description of character requires
- drawing an image of their inner character, motivations, moods, or situation
- painting a picture of the background, age, professional situation, or emotional state.

Sometimes a writer will use the actions of a character or their particular environment to depict internal dispositions.

> Towards the end of her day in London Mrs Drover went round to her shut-up house to look for several things she wanted to take away. Some belonged to herself, some belonged to her family, who were by now used to their country life. It was late August; it had been a steamy showery day: at the moment the trees down the pavement glittered in an escape of humid yellow afternoon sun. Against the next batch of clouds, already piling up ink-dark, broken chimneys and parapets stood out. In her once familiar street, as in any unused channel, an unfamiliar queerness had silted up; a cat wove itself in and out of railings, but no human eye watched Mrs Drover's return. Shifting some parcels under her arm, she slowly forced round her latchkey in an unwilling lock, then gave the door, which was warped, a push with her knee. Dead air came out to meet her as she went in.

The following passages show how language can be used in an aesthetic way. They are taken from actual pupils' work and are graded according to the standards required at Higher level. Study them carefully, and pay particular attention to the commentary that follows.

The first assignment was: 'Compose an imaginative series of reflections on the topic "autumn".'

September and October can be the very worst months of the year. Look at the weather: rain, wind, mist, and damp; wind blowing in relentlessly from the Atlantic, heralding the first onslaughts of winter. Fog and mist roll in, and sometimes for days on end the countryside is enveloped in a thick blanket of grey. It clings to river banks, shrouds mountain tops, nestles in valleys and between the folds of hills. It deadens sound, obscures sight, and creates an eerie ghostly atmosphere.

There is dampness everywhere. On walls! On windows! On floors! Housewives become irritated and drivers frustrated as the damp of their windscreens lessens visibility. There is mud and mire on city paths and country lanes, and as you walk you hear the squelch as the water and mud ooze up around your shoes. Old people tread warily as all around 'moist green leaves rest in rotting rust.' Everywhere shoes make a lovely crunching, crackling, rustling, popping sound as you walk on the carpet of leaves underfoot.

Then again you may awake some October morning and the world appears transformed. You swish back your curtains and lo! you look out into a dazzling world, your eye marvels at the dizzy blue sky overhead, and here and there scattered in the high dome of the heavens, clouds like puffballs and torn tufts of cotton-wool glide lazily in the vast expanse of blue. You open your front door and your eye is assaulted and bombarded with glowing, jewel-bright colours. What colour! Hedgerows, wood ditches, forests and fields are clothed in a glorious array of colour: vivid orange, fiery reds, bright yellows, garish mustards, dull browns, and sombre black.

Trees, shrubs, flowers are now beginning to wear a tattered, forlorn look. They are no longer clothed in the glossy, green, luxuriant foliage of high summer. Trees are taking a gaunt, skeletal look as they raise brittle, bare branches to the sky. Ominous-looking brown and black spots are appearing like some malignant disease on the ripe blooms of roses and flowers. Leaves look as if they are sickening for some fatal disease: they shrivel up, become crisper and crisper, and then in the first gales of autumn flutter gently to the ground, yielding up their fragile, tenuous hold on life, and lie decaying on the ground.

Meanwhile, frenzied and feverish preparations go on in both the animal and the human world. Take a walk in your local woods—but tread carefully. Move stealthily through the undergrowth and you may see a sudden flash and a brown bushy tail belonging to a busy squirrel who is hurriedly scuttling out of your way as he clutches a pawful of nuts. You may hear a rustling sound and lo! you may see a mole or badger digging out their winter home in preparation for hibernation. Look overhead and your eye will marvel at the sight of birds congregating on wires, twittering excitedly in anticipation of their annual winter holiday when they migrate to sunny southern climates.

In cosy country kitchens filled with a smell of turf, plump, bustling housewives are sweating as they bend over hot stoves making delicious jams, pickles, mouth-watering pies, and potent wines and ales, and reminding us only too well of those vivid words of Shakespeare, 'and greasy Joan doth keel the pot.' Out in the straw-strewn farmyard the red-faced farmer is busy, bringing in the last of the crops. In both town and country, young folk with long, doleful faces are making last-minute and begrudging preparations for returning to school.

Comment
Grade: B1
This article is written in an imaginative and highly descriptive style. There is a strong emphasis on describing colour, movement, and shape, which is a hallmark of good, effective description. Some of the images used are rich and sensuous.

Areas for development
The opening of this composition is a bit too obvious. Openings have to be dynamic and arresting for the reader. There is an atmosphere of 'purple prose' throughout, a conscious striving for effect, giving the whole piece an unnatural air.

Perhaps the writer could concentrate on developing the description in more detail. Concentrating on the lives of people would perhaps broaden the scope and develop the theme in greater detail. The conclusion needs to be developed in more detail and depth, as it is a bit too abrupt and flat and a little disappointing.

The next passage is from an aesthetic composition on the topic 'Memories'.

> **'Children of the sun'**
> The black nannies congregated on the corner of Gillian Road, shouting out greetings of 'Sanibonai' and 'Ngikhona' in their loud, cheerful voices. The coarse sound of their voices was softened by the beautiful musical lilt of their language. Their vibrant exclamations hovered on the still hot air, and their infectious laughter lingered over the neighbourhood.
>
> Faint echoes of the carefree chatter floated out over the vast, dry, empty land in front and were carried downwards over the gently sloping field of burnt dry tufts of grass, which crackled underfoot, and sand of almost the same yellowish-brown shade, until they reached the river. The gurgle of the deep brown water mimicked the buoyant giggles, and the hadida bird's call from above echoed across the vlei. Children's playful shouting and a dog's excited barking reverberated among the cloud-like rocks bordering the river. Two bluish-white trees, though quite bare, provided the only source of shade from the blazing sun. But the refreshing sound of flowing water made the sun's crude heat more bearable.
>
> The only refuge from a scorching midday sun was beneath the cool, clear blue waters of a swimming pool. Happy and carefree children screamed in delight while splashing around in the water, duck-diving and dodging the bees and wasps that hovered on the surface. Around the edge of the pool, steam rose from the slabs of slate, roasting any feet that ventured out of the pool.
>
> Towards early afternoon little brown bodies lay glistening in the sun, stretched out on towels, shivering with warmth and with the ticklish feeling as each tiny droplet evaporated.
>
> But peace and serenity did not last long. Sharp ears perked up as the familiar tinkling tune of the ice-cream man drifted through the air. And the legs that had been stretched out in the sun sprang to life in anticipation. Money in shrivelled hands and children in

swimming costumes with stringy wet hair ran barefoot down the driveway in glee. And it didn't matter that the ice-creams melted before they reached their mouths, or that the raspberry sauce dropped down onto bronzed feet and made their toes stick together. The children walked slowly back up the driveway, heads bent forward in an attempt to catch as much of the liquid as possible. They sat on the patio's stone steps licking the ice-creams, with dots of white on their noses and red sauce smeared around their mouths, happy and content.

Even when empty, the patio held all the voices and memories of the neighbourhood. It was a place where many stories had been told, jokes shared, and tears shed. Overlooking the swimming pool and surrounded by luscious green tropical plants, its cold stone floor and cool shade were both refreshing and relaxing. Out in front, the garden sloped down towards the road, bordered on one side by a tall white wall and on the other by the long driveway running adjacent to a boundary of trees, plants, and hedges.

Once darkness fell, the lush flowerbeds, trees and shrubs provided an ideal place for 'tip the lantern', and, starting from the bottom of the garden, the children tried to sneak their way up to the top beside the patio without being seen. Scrapes and bruises on bare legs and arms were ignored as little bodies wormed their way through soil and plants like camouflaged snakes.

The rustle of shrubs was covered up by the shrill of the crickets, whose sound was so constant that it was forgotten but would be missed if absent.

Gay chatter drifted across from the adults around the candle-lit patio table, where they still sat hours after the braai was over. Floating candles on the pool created a magical glow, and the warm night was softly scented with the mingled fragrances of sweet pea and honeysuckle.

Life revolved around nature and the outdoors. Trees, plants, bushes and shrubbery provided innumerable playgrounds. A forest of tall bamboo supplied rich, cool shade and a soft leafy floor for exhausted children and an ideal storage place for caterpillars in shoe boxes, waiting for them to spin cocoons.

Long scrape marks on the syringa barks all over the neighbourhood marked the struggles of scratched legs' attempts to overcome the initial challenge of the bare tree trunk, before climbing through green leaves and rough branches. The tall sky-rockets were much easier to climb, for the thick coniferous foliage started at ground level. But a challenge was always welcomed; and syringas, with their beautiful, sweet-smelling pink flowers, had better-shaped branches for tree-houses.

Grubby children solemnly collected wood, planks and ropes from old compost heaps and fields full of shoulder-height yellow grass. They emerged, laden with precious materials and covered in blackjacks. Planks of wood were wedged between branches and tied meticulously, and gradually the tree-houses were erected. These were the sites of many tree parties and secret nocturnal meetings when even the crickets were asleep.

The silent whispers in this magical land of the large trees at night was a stark contrast to the shouting of children at play on the road during the day. BMX bikes skidded in the earth, sending up clouds of dust behind them. The bikes, which were once brightly coloured and shiny, were now almost indistinguishable from one another, for each was coated in the same layer of dry brown dust.

A stranger could not tell which children belonged where, for wooded stiles, built by the gardeners, provided easy access for barefoot children from garden to garden. Sandy children with messy hair, skimpy clothing and dirty bottoms scrambled in all directions.

But every Monday afternoon they all headed in the same direction, muttering Bible verses under their breath that should have been learnt over the past week. Children from even further afield than Gillian Road came to Good News Club, and the competition for a perfect memory verse record and the ultimate prize was tough.

But behind all the competitiveness, the love shown and taught among friends and neighbours shone back through the glowing eyes of their happy children.

Comment
Grade: A1
This is a highly original piece of writing and approach to the topic. The images and language are highly vivid and poetic, all of which are strong features of the aesthetic use of language. The whole composition is clearly punctuated with its striking emphasis on colour, sounds, and smells. There are some splendid touches of poetry: for example the sibilance in the lines 'around the edge of the pool, steam rose from the slabs of slate, roasting any feet.' The imagery used is varied, rich, and sensuous: 'little brown bodies lay glistening in the sun, shivering with warmth.'

This passage is written to emphasise how language can be used in an aesthetic manner. For that reason the subject matter does not have to be developed or analysed in a deep or weighty manner; instead there is a heavy reliance on the aesthetic use of language, on harmony, the use of images, sound patterns, and poetic touches.

Exercises on writing in the language of aesthetics
1. Write a descriptive article for a holiday magazine on a city scene preparing for a new millennium.
2. Compose a sketch or dramatic scene for a play on any topic you are interested in. Concentrate on drawing out specific features of the characters you are presenting.
3. Write a poem or a short story, paying particular attention to the use of imagery or description, on any scene from country life or nature that has impressed you.
4. Write a series of diary entries on your experiences in settling in another country.

6
Samples of Paper I with Model Answers

STRUCTURE OF PAPER I

Study the following samples of paper I. They follow the same layout as the examination at Higher level. In each paper there are four different comprehension texts. Some of these texts may include a photograph or an advertisement. Each text is followed by a number of questions, which correspond to the type of questions that will be asked in the examination.

Suggested answers are provided for the comprehension questions on each text (see pages 128–50). The purpose of these answers is to suggest a method of approaching a particular question. None of these answers is definitive: a variety of approaches may be adopted.

To improve your technique in answering comprehension questions, try answering the questions yourself first of all, then compare your own answers with the suggested answers provided.

PAPER I
Time allowed: 2½ hours.
- This paper is divided into two sections: Section I COMPREHENDING and Section II COMPOSING.
- This paper contains *four* texts on a general theme.
- Both sections of this paper (COMPREHENDING and COMPOSING) must be attempted.
- Each section carries 100 marks.

Section I: Comprehending
(100 marks)
- Read each of the texts carefully a number of times.

- Two questions, A and B, follow each text.
- You must answer a Question A on one text and a Question B on a different text. You must answer only one Question A and only one Question B. These questions carry equal marks.
- N.B. You may NOT answer a Question A and a Question B on the same text.

Section II: *Composing*
(100 marks)
Write a composition on *any one* of the topics provided.
    The composition assignments are intended to reflect language study in the areas of information, argument, narration, and the aesthetic use of language.

FIRST SAMPLE PAPER: CULTURE AND TRENDS

This paper contains *four* texts on the general theme of culture and trends.

Section I: *Comprehending*
(100 marks)

Text 1

Vitamin pills increase the risk of lung cancer and heart disease among smokers, according to a report to be published by the World Health Organisation (WHO). The claim—which concerns tablets that contain beta-carotene, a form of vitamin A—will shock millions of smokers, who believe that popping the pills can prevent cancer and limit the damaging effects of their habit.
    The warning follows an international meeting in Lyon at which scientists agreed that non-smokers who take beta-carotene pills and related carotenoid supplements in the hope of preventing cancer are probably wasting their money.
    Dr Harri Vainio of the International Agency for Research on Cancer, a WHO body comprising twenty-three experts from ten countries, said: 'Our group came to the conclusion that, until further information becomes available on how beta-carotene and other carotenoids influence the processes leading to cancer, none of these substances should be promoted to the general population as a tumour-preventive treatment.'
    Beta-carotene, the best-known of the six hundred identified carotenoids, is a pigment that gives colour to many foods, including carrots, apricots and oranges. It is also present in dark-green leafy vegetables.

QUESTION A
1. Identify the writer's purpose in this passage. Does the writer succeed in achieving this purpose? Make reference to the passage to support your answer.
2. What type of readership is targeted in this piece of writing? Support your answer by reference to the passage itself.

QUESTION B
Write an original and witty article for a popular teenage magazine on the subject 'We are what we wear.'

Text 2

Hellfire and hyperdrive: the Gospel according to *Star Wars*

'I am trying to bring up my children with Jedi values'—so wrote an earnest Christian recently in a discussion on an internet site devoted to modern culture. The combination of Christianity and *Star Wars* may seem one of the more bizarre bits of merchandising in the hype around *The Phantom Menace*, but now a Methodist university chaplain in Liverpool has written an entire book on the subject. 'I'm not into buying light-sabres, running around pretending to be Princess Leia, or anything like that,' said the Rev. David Wilkinson, who worked for six years as an astrophysicist before his ordination. He claims to be only a moderate fan, though he has already seen *The Phantom Menace* twice in the line of duty. But, he says, this is the way that schoolchildren and students get their moral discussions nowadays. 'I went to a school the other day and spoke to a group of around a hundred people. Half of them had already seen it on pirate video, even before the official release.'

Though *The Phantom Menace* has been generally panned, Wilkinson sees it as in some respects the most theologically interesting of the films, because it centres on a character changing sides. 'How does the boy Anakin Skywalker turn into the evil Darth Vader? What is it that conspires within us to produce evil?' That the answers to this question are not necessarily Christian ones does not bother him, though conservative Christians around the world have complained that *Star Wars* spreads New Age heresies.

In the climactic scene of *Return of the Jedi*, where Darth Vader returns to his original team and chucks the evil Emperor into the glowing maw of the hyperdrive, Wilkinson sees an echo of the Christian theme of redemption through self-sacrifice. He sees the Force as a sign of hope: 'It's not a picture of God, but it's raising the question of God. There is a tension in the films between the scientific–materialistic world view and the transcendence: the good guys rely on the Force and the bad guys rely on the death star. They even use a robot army in *The Phantom Menace*, which is an illustration of a western technological society trying to stamp out any sense of the transcendent.'

On the other hand, to most people the Force is nothing like the idea of a Christian God. The interesting bits of Christianity, from the Book of Job onwards, are adaptations to the fact that the spaceship does not rise miraculously from the swamp, even when the good guys want it to, really badly. This does not worry Mr Wilkinson. It seems to him that *Star Wars*, though it is one of the greatest consumerist phenomena of the age, opens up a vision of a world beyond technological consumerism. It is designed to appeal to the kind of characters—'a small boy and a whiny teenager'—who would never have anything to do with normal church life.

It's all an imposing theory, and will make an interesting companion to an earlier book he published on *The Spirituality of the X Files*. Both phenomena, he says, show evidence of a tremendous need to believe in the reality of stuff outside our narrow imaginations, and to anchor myth with detailed reality. There is a key difference, he insists. Christianity's gospel stories weren't made up in the way that those about Skywalker and Darth Vader were. *Star Wars* fans, of course, might not agree.

QUESTION A
1. Explain briefly the arguments the writer uses to draw a parallel between Christian ideas and those underlying the presentation of *Star Wars*?
2. What techniques does the writer use to back up or substantiate the claims made in the above passage?

QUESTION B
Write a short review of a film you enjoyed watching.

Text 3

Eating at Mama's

For the first time since the decline of Dadaism we are witnessing a revival in the fine art of meaningless naming. This thought is prompted by the film *Trainspotting* and by the opening of a new play on Broadway called *Virgil Is Still the Frogboy*. The play is not about Virgil: no frogs feature therein. The title is apparently taken from a Long Island graffiti, to whose meaning the play offers no clues. This omission has not diminished the show's success.

As Luis Buñuel knew, obscurity is a characteristic of objects of desire. Accordingly, there is no train-spotting in *Trainspotting*, just a predictable, even sentimental movie that thinks it's hip. (Compared with the work of, say, William Burroughs, it's positively cutesy.) The film has many admirers, perhaps because they are unable to understand even its title, let alone the fashionably indecipherable slang of the dialogue. The fact remains that *Trainspotting* contains no mention of persons keeping obsessive notes on the arrival and departure of trains. The only railway engines are to be found on the wallpaper of the central character's bedroom. Whence, therefore, the choo-choo moniker? Some sort of pun on the word 'tracks' may be intended.

Nowadays, dreary old comprehensibility is still very much around. A new film about a boy-man called Jack is called *Jack*. A film about crazed basketball fans is called *The Fan*. The new version of Jane Austin's *Emma* is called *Emma*.

However, titular mystification continues to intensify. When Oasis sing 'You're my wonderwall', what do they mean? I intend to ride over you on my motorbike, round and round at very high speed? Surely not.

And *Blade Runner*? Yes I know that hunters of android replicants are called 'blade runners'. But why? And yes, William Burroughs (again) used the phrase in a 1979 novel; and, to get really arcane, there's a 1974 medical thriller called *The Bladerunner* by the late

Dr Alan Nourse. But what does any of this have to do with Ridley Scott's film? Harrison Ford runs not, neither does he blade. Shouldn't a work of art give us the keys with which to unlock its meanings? Perhaps there aren't any; perhaps it's just that the phrase sounds cool, thanks to those echoes of Burroughs, 'Daddy Cool' himself.

In 1928 Luis Buñuel and Salvador Dali co-directed the surrealist classic *Un Chien Andalou*, a film about many things but not about Andalusian dogs. So it is with Tarantino's *Reservoir Dogs*. No reservoir, no dogs, no use of the words 'reservoir', 'dogs' or 'reservoir dogs' at any point in the film. No imagery derived from dogs or reservoirs, or dogs in reservoirs, or reservoirs of dogs. Nothing; or as Mr Pink and Co. would say '. . . nothing'.

The story goes that when the young Tarantino was working in a video shop his distaste for fancy European writer-directors such as Louis Malle manifested itself in an inability to pronounce the titles of their films. Malle's *Au Revoir, les Enfants* defeated him completely ('Oh reservoir les . . .'), until he began to refer to it contemptuously as—you guessed it—'those, oh reservoir dogs'. Subsequently he made this the title of his own film, no doubt as a further gesture of anti-European defiance. Alas, the obliqueness of the gibe meant that the Europeans simply did not comprehend. 'What we have here,' as the guy in *Cool Hand Luke* defiantly remarked, 'is a failure to communicate.'

But these days the thing about incomprehensibility is that people aren't supposed to understand. In accordance with the new *zeitgeist*,* therefore, the title of this piece has in part been selected—'sampled'—from Lou Reed's advice—'Don't eat at places called Mama's'—in the diary of his recent tour. To forestall any attempts at esotericism, I confess that as a title it means nothing at all; but then the very concept of meaning is now outdated.

Welcome to the new incomprehensibility: gibberish with attitude.

* *Zeitgeist*: spirit of the times.

QUESTION A
1. What is the main thrust of the writer's arguments in this passage?
2. Comment on
    i) the writer's use of reference in the above passage
    ii) the style of the passage.

QUESTION B
'Welcome to the new incomprehensibility: gibberish with attitude.' How apt a conclusion to the passage is this statement? Give reasons for your answer.

Text 4

QUESTION A

1. What type of life-style is suggested by this picture? Support your answer by reference to details in the photograph.
2. What kind of statement is this photograph making?

QUESTION B
Compose a short introductory paragraph that might accompany this photograph.

(For suggested answers on first sample paper see pages 128–32)

Section II: Composing
(100 marks)

Write a composition on *any one* of the following.

1. Write a narrative composition on your experience of making a film, or of an interview that you carried out with a film star.
2. Write a letter to your local newspaper on what you consider to be the advantages of health food shops.
3. Choose an exotic region that you would like to visit. Write a descriptive account of your trip and the particular cultural experiences that impressed you.
4. Write a persuasive speech for a debate entitled 'Discrimination is still rampant today.'
5. '*Star Wars*, though it is one of the greatest consumerist phenomena of the age, opens up a vision of a world beyond technological consumerism. It is designed to appeal to the kind of characters—"a small boy and a whiny teenager"—who would never have anything to do with normal church life.' Compose a series of arguments on what you consider should be the relationship between religion and ordinary life.
6. Imagine that you are working on the set of a film being made about your locality. Compose an imaginative account of your experiences of working with the film crew.
7. 'Vitamin pills increase the risk of lung cancer and heart disease among smokers, according to a report to be published by the World Health Organisation (WHO).' Write an informative article for a teenage magazine on the importance of healthy eating.
8. Write the speech you will deliver for a debate on the topic 'Young people today are slaves of fads and fashions.'

SECOND SAMPLE PAPER: VIOLENCE AND DESTRUCTION

This paper contains *four* different texts on the general theme of violence and destruction.

Section I: Comprehending
(100 marks)

Text 1

Animal cruelty and mass murder

Shortly before the killings at the US Capitol building in Washington, the chief suspect in the case shot sixteen cats with his father's revolver. This vitally important incident was barely mentioned in reports of 'the assault on the front door of democracy'. It should have received banner headlines.

In England a few years ago the 'Butcher of Hungerford', Michael Ryan, tested his vast array of weapons on cats and wildlife before blowing away his neighbours. At the age of fourteen he had set animals alight just to watch them burn. Yet the police never considered him a threat to society—not until Michael declared open season on humans.

Recently two schoolchildren in Arkansas made world headlines when they shot their teacher and several pupils. As it happened, the children had been taught from an early age to hunt and kill animals—and to enjoy doing it. Video footage showed them pumping bullets into deer at point-blank range, with smirking adults standing over them.

After the murders a local policeman was quoted as saying 'We just don't understand how something like this could happen in our small, peaceful, deer-hunting community.'

In Britain, neighbours had seen two children who abducted and killed a younger child cutting the heads off live pigeons. Gangsters Bonny and Clyde tortured livestock on a farm before embarking on their killing spree. In one of Ireland's most gruesome murder cases, the killer admitted in court that exposure to cruelty in a meat plant where he worked had brutalised him. After watching pigs die without being stunned, which his co-workers found amusing, he 'hadn't the slightest remorse' about using a butcher's knife on his victims.

The people involved in these and similar crimes had different motives, backgrounds and psychological profiles. But they all had one thing in common: ill-treatment of animals had made them insensitive to human suffering.

For example, one study found that sport hunters in the US were seven times more likely to beat their wives than non-shooters. This disturbing tendency was attributed to an 'excessive need among hunters to control and dominate their environment'.

In Ireland firearms abound. Our gun culture is getting out of hand. Parts of the countryside have become a virtual battlefield, with bird and animal corpses littering the woods and fields. We should tackle this issue before 'harmless' taking of life spawns a major tragedy. One effective measure would be to have all weapons electronically tagged. Police could then monitor their use and whereabouts. Sadistic or over-zealous gunmen could be given the same treatment, depending on how the situation developed.

It is, after all, a matter of life and death.

QUESTION A
1. Do you consider this passage to be an example of effective writing? Give reasons for your answer.
2. Distinguish the facts from the opinions in this passage.

QUESTION B
Write two paragraphs, using a descriptive style, on a street scene at night.

Text 2

A light flapped over the scene, as if reflected from phosphorescent wings crossing the sky, and a rumble filled the air. It was the first move of the approaching storm.

The second peal was noisy, with comparatively little visible lightening . . .

Then there came a third flash. Manoeuvres of a most extraordinary kind were going on in the vast firmamental hollows overhead. The lightning now was the colour of silver, and gleamed in the heavens like a mailed army. Rumbles became rattles. Gabriel from his elevated position could see over the landscape at least half-a-dozen miles in front. Every hedge, bush, and tree was distinct as in a line engraving. In a paddock in the same direction was a herd of heifers, and the forms of these were visible at this moment in the act of galloping about in the wildest and maddest confusion, flinging their heels and tails high into the air, their heads to earth. A poplar in the immediate foreground was like an ink stroke on burnished tin. Then the picture vanished, leaving the darkness so intense that Gabriel worked entirely by feeling with his hands.

He had stuck his ricking-rod, or poniard, as it was indifferently called—a long iron lance, polished by handling—into the stack, used to support the sheaves instead of the support called a groom used on houses. A blue light appeared in the zenith, and in some indescribable manner flickered down near the top of the rod. It was the fourth of the larger flashes. A moment later and there was a smack—smart, clear, and short . . .

Heaven opened then, indeed. The flash was almost too novel for its inexpressibly dangerous nature to be at once realised . . . It sprang from east, west, north, south, and was a perfect dance of death. The forms of skeletons appeared in the air, shaped with blue fire for bones—dancing, leaping, striding, racing around, and mingling altogether in unparalleled confusion. With these were intertwined undulating snakes of green, and behind these was a broad mass of lesser light . . .

Oak had hardly time to gather up these impressions into a thought . . . when the tall tree on the hill before mentioned seemed on fire to a white heat . . . It was a stupefying blast, harsh and pitiless, and it fell upon their ears in a dead, flat blow, without that reverberation which lends the tones of a drum to more distant thunder. By the lustre reflected from every part of the earth and from the wide domical scoop above it, he saw that the tree was sliced down the whole length of its tall, straight stem, a huge riband of bark being apparently flung off. The other portion remained erect, and revealed the bared surface as a strip of white down the front. The lightning had struck the tree. A sulphurous smell filled the air; then all was silent, and black as a cave in Hinnom.

(Thomas Hardy, *Far from the Madding Crowd*)

QUESTION A
1. Show how the writer succeeds in building up atmosphere in this extract.
2. Comment on how the writer makes use of small details to draw a realistic picture of the storm in this extract.

QUESTION B
Write a conclusion of about 150 words to this extract. In particular, concentrate on the effects of the storm.

Text 3

What is it possible to say about the loss of lives resulting from the Northern troubles? This. That so far it has all been in vain, quite purposeless. No cause was advanced in any way which would have not been better served by peaceful means. Who can say what this island would have been like if the depraved culture of violence had not once again taken root? Aside from the 3,600 lives lost, how much else has been lost? What opportunities to learn, to be civilised, to create art and order, were squandered in the cretinous squalor of war?

If we had listed the dead of 1916–22, described who they were and how they died; if we had studied the barbarous injustice of their fate, if we had dwelt on the sufferings of their families, if we had made the immorality of political violence a keystone of our political culture, we would have not tolerated the violation of law and life of the last thirty years.

Catalogue
There might be an excuse for being ignorant of the events of 1916–22. There is no excuse now for ignorance over the events of 1966–99. The definitive catalogue of those who died in our troubles, how, where and when they died, who their families were and how else their families might have suffered, has been produced by David McKittrick and published by Mainstream Publishing. It is the saddest, most sobering, most heartbreaking book I have ever read. Not a page on it is without an almost unbearable tragedy; each tragedy is real, each one was lived by actual people, each one spread vast repercussions through family, friends and the broader community to which they belonged.

Numbers numb. Very soon after one starts counting deaths they lose meaning. Three hundred, four hundred, five hundred; people become ciphers, their identity, their purpose in life, the people they loved and the people who loved them in return vanish behind the metronome ticking of digits passing through our minds. That is how we have been able to bear the unbearable during these troubles. We let the shutters of statistics conceal the mountain range of human suffering behind them.

In the greatest single piece of historical scholarship in either journalism or historical studies that has ever been conducted in this country, David McKittrick has liberated the dead from the limbo of statistics. The unliving live again. He has followed up each death, back to the first killings in 1966, and up to the most recent, that of Charles Bennett this last summer: the numbered corpses, and their poor bereaved families, come back to life on the page. And in their merely literary resurrection they serve as a terrible indictment of the culture of political violence that finds so many apologists throughout Irish life.

Utter futility
A page of David's masterpiece should convince any civilised person that a resort to violence to solve the communal problems of Ireland is no more than a celebration of idiot-barbarism. And it is not enough to say this is the case today. The resort to violence in the name of the Republic has been marked by two enduring features. The first is the enormous suffering it has caused; the second is its utter futility. The war for a united Irish republic has been going on intermittently now for nearly eighty-five years. It is no closer to achievement today than it was when the violent accounts were opened in Dublin in 1916 and two unarmed police officers—Constables Lahiffe and O'Brien—were murdered in the centre of Dublin.

How are these murders commemorated today? They are not. Children are not taught about these poor men butchered while doing their duty. They are not taught about Countess Markievicz capering around the body of the policeman she had just shot in St Stephen's Green joyfully shrieking, 'I shot him, I shot him.' There is a statue to her not far from where she gunned down this blameless man; he has vanished from history, as have the hundreds of others who died that Eastertide.

Those who are ignorant of the realities of the Easter Rising and of the violence of 1919–22 could be forgiven their ignorance. The issue is not individual atrocities. The issue is violence itself. That is the atrocity. It is the atrocity which we have had to live with for the greater part of this century, an atrocity which in each generation has re-emerged. But until the publication of *Lost Lives*, it has always been possible to hide the true evil of violence. Not any more. There can be no more searing indictment, not merely of the individual deeds of violence but of the political culture which justifies it, than this book.

Monstrosity
I defy anyone to browse through the pages of *Lost Lives* without being stunned by the sheer monstrosity of all that we have done, or allowed to be done, over the last thirty years. Evil, unspeakable evil, rose in our midst and we as a people were too weak, too indecisive, too pusillanimous to deal with it. And here now is a record of the consequences; in its encyclopaedic detail, in its towering integrity and in its moral compassion it could be the most influential study of Irish history that has ever been presented.

I know of no work which can alter behaviour as this one can, should, must. The argument it presents against the use of violence, for all that it is implicit, is compelling and complete.

Nothing more needs to be said. Buy *Lost Lives*. Nobody on this island can have an excuse for not knowing about the evils of violence. Nobody who can work through the 1,600 pages of murder it covers will ever find an excuse or a pretext for political violence again.

QUESTION A
1. Consider this passage as an example of effective persuasive writing.
2. In what type of publication would you read this type of article?

QUESTION B
Write a speech for your class, of about 200 words, outlining the reasons why you think they should read this book.

Text 4

Photograph A

Photograph B

Photograph C

Photograph D

Photograph E

QUESTION A
1. Study photographs A–E and describe briefly what comment is being made in each case.
2. Pick one photograph and identify three different techniques that are used to communicate its particular message.

QUESTION B
Write a headline that could accompany each photograph.

(For suggested answers on second sample paper see pagwes 133–7)

Section II: Composing
(100 marks)

Write a composition on *any one* of the following.

1. 'There might be an excuse for being ignorant of the events of 1916–22. There is no excuse now for ignorance over the events of 1966–99.' Write out a speech for a debate in which you would either challenge or support this statement.
2. Write a narrative composition on your experience of seeing a street fight.
3. 'In Ireland firearms abound. Our gun culture is getting out of hand. Parts of the countryside have become a virtual battlefield, with bird and animal corpses littering the woods and fields.' Write a letter to the newspaper on your own views of the hunting and shooting of wild animals.
4. 'The lightning now was the colour of silver, and gleamed in the heavens like a mailed army.' Use this statement as the starting point for a short story. Concentrate on using vivid and descriptive language.
5. Compose a series of arguments on the subject 'Violence has become a hallmark of our society.'
6. Write the dialogue for a screenplay on the subject 'Peaceful solutions'.
7. In an article intended for a serious magazine, write a persuasive account of your own experience of the horrors of war.

Third sample paper: Communication

This paper contains *four* texts on the general theme of communication.

Section I: Comprehending
(100 marks)

Text 1

A: Pope redefines the nature of Paradise

Just days after a leading Jesuit magazine redefined concepts of Hell, the Pope turned his attention yesterday to Paradise, declaring that it was not a place above the clouds where angels played harps, but a 'state of being' after death.

The Heaven in which we will find ourselves is neither an abstraction nor a physical place among the clouds, he told seventy pilgrims in St Peter's Square.

Looking invigorated and tanned after his summer break in the Italian Alps, the Pope, who has suffered from a series of debilitating illnesses, said he wanted to make it clear that Paradise was 'a living and personal relationship with the Holy Trinity'. Just as Hell was separation from God, so Paradise was 'close communion and full intimacy with God. Heaven is a blessed community of those who remained faithful to Jesus Christ in their lifetime and are now at one with his glory.'

At the end of last week, *Civiltà Cattolica*, the magazine of the Society of Jesus, said Hell was not a place where the souls of the damned were tortured eternally by fire and demons, as represented by Dante and others, but a state of being in which those who had consistently rejected God and 'consciously chosen not to do good' were condemned to permanent banishment from God's presence.

Earlier this year the Pope, rejecting artistic images from Michaelangelo to Blake, told pilgrims they should not see God as an old man with a white beard but rather as a supreme being with both masculine and feminine aspects.

Although many writers, such as Milton, have propagated a literal idea of Paradise, others have taken a sceptical view, with Proust observing in *Remembrance of Things Past* that 'the true paradises are the paradises we have lost on earth.'

The Pope told his listeners that they could gain some 'intimation' of what Paradise would be like by following the 'sacramental life, of which the Eucharist is the centre', and by devoting themselves to 'fraternal love for their fellow beings'.

B: Paradise redefined

Heaven must be one hell of a place.

Paradise is no longer the place it used to be. Like one of those seaside resorts most frequently compared to it, its delights are looking tackier with time. So the Pope, the principal salesman of this time-share retreat, has suggested that the prospectus be sent for a reprint. Apparently the traditional selling points—the angels and ambrosia and eternal sunshine—now seem a little outmoded. Heaven, the Pope told pilgrims yesterday, is not a physical place above the clouds but a state of being after death, and Paradise a living personal relationship with the Holy Trinity.

Of course the Pope is quite sensible in making such suggestions. The human condition is thrown quite out of kilter by the prospect of perpetual bliss. Man's earthly delights are held in delicate balance by desires that admit of only passing satisfaction if they are not to destroy themselves. Unlimited pleasure, much like retirement to the Costa, can seem rather less than perfect when offered in perpetuity. And surely, deep down, Disraeli knew that even a glutton would soon sicken of ortolans eaten to the sound of soft music.

Anyway, eternity must keep pace with the times. Our less sophisticated forebears may have been beguiled by the prospect of a simple blow-out banquet; but life on earth in their day must have been pretty tough to endure. How easy it must have been to imagine Elysian satisfactions when an ingrowing toenail could make existence a living hell.

It was only when Plato came up with his ideas about archetypes, of ideal worlds that were so much more real than his own, that Paradise had to start measuring up to increased expectations. From then on, unthinkable bliss had to adapt itself to the ideals of different religions, each trimming and tweaking it according to their various systems of value. The Pope now adds his own interpretation to this visionary pageant. But he finds himself facing the same problem that has perplexed all those who have grappled with portrayals of perfect happiness. Like the great spiritual poets Dante and Milton before him, the pontiff is finding out how notoriously hard it is to make Heaven sound even half as good as Hell. Certainly, to the average Christian teenager, his papal ideal of chilling out with the Paraclete will not sound like too much fun. Perhaps everyone should be left to conjure up his own personal vision of the expected afterlife, for in the end all anyone can really guess is that Heaven is bound to be one hell of a place.

QUESTION A
1. Study the two articles above and identify the purpose of each. Comment on which you consider to be more effective in achieving that purpose. Give your reasons why.
2. In what type of publication would you expect to find each article? In your answer take into account the type of language and arguments that are used.

QUESTION B
Write a short review, of about 150 words, for a popular magazine on what you consider should be the main priority of a journalist.

Text 2

Brutal but moving

A few poignant moments—a whisper, a glance, a touch—are the only glimpses of true humanity in this film, in which the outlook for the future is portrayed as very bleak indeed. Set on the streets of Belfast, the story of the 'Boxer' unfolds in a chaotic world where violence is a part of everyday life and where to fall in love may be not just dangerous but deadly.

Danny Flynn, played magnificently by Daniel Day-Lewis, is a former IRA man trying to build a life on the outside after spending fourteen years in prison. His long years inside have convinced him that it's time to do things differently; but in a world where order is imposed by the authority of the IRA, that means breaking social mores.

As is his custom, Daniel Day-Lewis immersed himself completely in the role, and once again his strict method approach has paid dividends. His emotional portrayal of Danny is complex, subtle and utterly convincing. His training with Barry McGuigan turned him into a muscular fighting machine, and the scenes in the ring are every bit as compelling as those in *Raging Bull* and that other great, underrated boxing film *The Big Man*.

QUESTION A
1. Identify the main purpose of the writer in this article.
2. Comment on two different techniques used by the writer to achieve this purpose. Make reference to the passage to support your answer.

QUESTION B
Write two paragraphs for a serious journal on the topic 'Family life is in conflict with television.' In the first paragraph outline the problems you see in this area. In the second paragraph propose some solution to these problems.

Text 3

A virtual nation

The pioneers of telecommunications have always looked further than others, seeking new ways to bring people together over seemingly impossible distances. Now, with the birth of Turly, worldwide portable telecommunications has been achieved. In the space of seven short years since the company was spun off from its founder, Motorola, Iridium has turned a vision into a reality.

Like many great inventions, Iridium has grown out of a simple challenge. On holiday in the Caribbean in 1985, Karen Bertinger found she could not call the United States on her mobile phone. 'Why can't you make my phone work out here?' she asked her husband, Bary Bertinger, an executive with Motorola. She convinced him that there was a real need for a system that would provide wireless communication between any two points on the planet; and that's where the Iridium story really begins.

But to quote Thomas Edison, arguably the greatest of telecommunications pioneers, 'Genius is one per cent inspiration, ninety-nine per cent perspiration.' In this respect, Iridium is no different from any other major technological leap forward: from the original idea flowed thirteen years of tireless hard work as the talents of more than 10,000 people were harnessed with the single goal of making the vision a reality.

Now satellites are in place, circling the globe in their orbits 780 kilometres above Earth. Agreements have been signed with more than 300 telecommunications providers.

The palm-sized Iridium handsets are in production and will be available soon to the first customers, bringing them the power to make and take calls anywhere in the world, using one telephone, with one number, and receiving only one bill. What was once a visionary project is now a technological and commercial triumph.

QUESTION A
1. Describe clearly how the writer illustrates the opening statement: 'The pioneers of telecommunications have always looked further than others, seeking new ways to bring people together over seemingly impossible distances.'
2. Do you think the writer develops the argument effectively here? Support your points by detailed reference to the text.

QUESTION B
Write an original and interesting opening paragraph on the topic 'Isn't it time to limit the use of private cars?'

Text 4
QUESTION A
1. Write a description of the photograph that accompanies the advertisement on page 114. What do you consider to be the relation between the photograph and the advertisement?
2. Identify three different techniques used by the writer. In your answer take into account the layout of the advertisement together with the writer's use of words.

QUESTION B
Write a speech for your class on what you consider to be the benefits of having a mobile phone.

(For answers on third sample paper see pages 137–41)

Section II: Composing
(100 marks)

Write a composition on *any one* of the following.
1. Write a prose composition, using the language of argument, on the topic 'The media's role is to uncover and expose the truth.'
2. Imagine you are a journalist who has been asked to report on a famine or war in a country in southern Africa. Compose an imaginative article on that topic.
3. 'To quote Thomas Edison, arguably the greatest of telecommunications pioneers, "genius is one per cent inspiration, ninety-nine per cent perspiration."' In the light of this statement, write an informative article for a serious journal on your views of recent technological developments.
4. 'The Pope turned his attention yesterday to Paradise, declaring that it was not a place above the clouds where angels played harps but a "state of being" after death.' Write a narrative account of your vision of Paradise.
5. Compose a persuasive speech either for or against the argument that the media must respect people's privacy.
6. 'Looking invigorated and tanned after his summer break in the Italian Alps, the Pope, who has suffered from a series of debilitating illnesses, said he wanted to make it clear that Paradise was a "living and personal relationship with the Holy Trinity".' Imagine you are asked to represent the young people of Ireland at an International Conference in Rome. Compose an autobiographical sketch on your impressions of attending the conference and your experience of having a private audience with the Pope.
7. Write a persuasive letter for a serious journal on your ideas about the topic 'Freedom of information is a necessary right in a democracy.'

FOURTH SAMPLE PAPER: LIFE-STYLES

This paper contains *four* texts on the general theme of life-styles.

Section I: Comprehending
(100 marks)

Text 1

Reach for the stars

Seriously rich women are different from you and me: they have time to think ahead. Do you know what you are going to wear on New Year's Eve? Neither do I. But there they were this week, lining the front rows at the final Paris *haute couture* showings, picking their frocks for the party to end all parties.

Ivana Trump thought she might go for Thierry Mugler; Muna al-Ayub seemed certain to choose Dior; Catherine Deneuve was considering Yves Saint-Laurent; while Joan Collins was enraptured by Valentino. The Bridge of Wildenstein hadn't made up her mind. Nan Kempner, the American socialite, chuckled throatily. 'When you get to my age

darling, every day seems like New Year. So I shall be at home in bed, in New York, wearing nothing at all.'

The New Year's soirées were a fabulous brief for the couturiers. Even Paco Rabanne, who seems convinced that Paris will be wiped out during the eclipse on the eleventh of August (he thinks that the Mir space station will crash to Earth) had spared a thought for the socialising that will doubtless continue elsewhere. Rabanne, who retired from the couture circus after his show on Sunday, produced his own made-to-measure version of Mir. There was no sense of millennium minimalism: this was a season for vamps and voluptuaries, and for the visionary designers to create their ultimate fantasies. It was a season of sybaritic fashion moments, and a time to wallow.

Exotic skins (crocodile, python) and furs (fox, rabbit, mink, marmot) fashioned skirts and dresses, trimmed the inside of coats and caressed the cleavage. Fabulous plumage (guineafowl, ostrich, bearded vulture) soared from heads, was woven into knits and trailed from hems of taffeta opera-coats.

Brocade glistened with jewels, crystals winked from silk tulle and knickers sparkled with gold studs. There were miracles of invention, such as velvet appliquéd with mink, rabbit painted to look like panther and tweed interlaced with feathers. Not everything was what it seemed. John Galliano's Brer Fox and rabbit toppers were real; his boar's head hat was papier mâché.

Flight was a key inspiration, whether expressed in billowing parachute gowns, paratrooper gear, woman-as-bird or woman-as-satellite. Fashion was reaching for the stars—enough to make the imagination soar.

QUESTION A
1. Who are the intended target audience of this article? Support your answer by reference to the passage.
2. In what type of publication would you read this type of review? Give reasons for your answer.

QUESTION B
Write an imaginative and witty opening paragraph for a teenage fashion magazine on the topic of hairstyles.

Text 2

Does anywhere on earth sound more exotic? Or does the name Bali evoke an image long since past of a Mecca for artists in the nineteen-thirties and hippies in the nineteen-sixties? Does it offer adventure, romance, peace and quiet, spiritual rejuvenation? Well, yes. Bali has volcanoes, jungle, elephants, wild monkeys, amazing birds, vistas of rice paddies, azure seas, gleaming sands, colourful culture and captivating music and dancing. It also has bungee-jumping, go-karting, paragliding, white-water rafting, paint-balling, and an internet café—this last lot are present because Bali is to Australians what Torremolinos is to British and Irish people.

The views of the jungle and rice paddies opposite are luscious. At night the sound of the stream at the bottom of the gorge and the clatter of insects provide an auditory environment just as compelling.

Plenty of tours will take you on a boat to a desert island or bird park. In any of these places you will come across the monkeys. As well as being charming, they are adept pickpockets, but can usually be bribed with food to return whatever they have purloined. Who is to say whether or not the nearby vendors who sell you the titbits of food are in league with the monkeys?

QUESTION A
1. Do you consider this to be an effective piece of persuasive writing? Give reasons for your answer.
2. Identify the facts in this passage.

QUESTION B
Write out an advertisement that would accompany this article. Include a slogan and an arresting caption, and concentrate on using some persuasive techniques in the language you use.

Text 3

The wind blew the smell of rain down the valley ahead of the rain itself, the smell of wet earth and aromatic plants. The old woman pulled in her washing and fetched the cane chairs off the terrace. The old man, Anton Hahn, put on boots and a waterproof and went into the garden to check that all the catchments were clear. The peon came over from the barn with an empty bottle and the woman filled it with apple *chicha*. He was drunk already. Two red oxen stood yoked to a cart, bracing themselves for the storm.

The old man walked round his vegetable garden and his flower garden bright with annuals. Having seen that they would get the full benefit of the rain, he came inside the house. Apart from its metal roof nothing distinguished it from the houses of a southern German village, the half-timbering infilled with white plaster, the grey shutters, the wicket fence, scrubbed floors, painted panelling, the chandelier of antler tines and lithographs of the Rhineland.

Anton Hahn took off his tweed cap and hung it on an antler. He took off his boots and canvas gaiters and put on rope-soled slippers. His head was flat on top and his face creased and red. A little girl with a pigtail came into the kitchen.

'Do your wish your pipe, *Onkel*?'

'*Bitte*.' And she brought a big meerschaum and filled it with tobacco from a blue-and-white jar.

The old man poured himself a tankard of *chicha*. As the rain slammed on the roof, he talked about the Colonia Nueva Alemania. His uncles settled here in 1905 and he had followed after the Great War.

'What could I do? The Fatherland was in a bad condition. Before the war, no family could have enough sons. One was a soldier. One was a carpenter, and two stayed on the farm. But after 1918 Germany was full of refugees from the Bolsheviks. Even the villages were full.'

His brother lived on the family farm on the borders of Bavaria and Württemberg. They wrote letters once a month but had not met since 1923.

'The war was the biggest mistake in history,' Anton Hahn said. He was obsessed by the war. 'Two peoples of the Superior Race ruining each other. Together England and Germany could have ruled the world. Now even Patagonia is returning to the *indígenas*. This is a pity.'

He went on lamenting the decline of the West and, at one point, dropped the name Ludwig.

'Mad Ludwig?'

'The King? Mad? You call the King mad? In my house? No!'

I had to think fast.

'Some people call him mad,' I said, 'but, of course, he was a great genius.'

Anton Hahn was hard to pacify. He stood up and lifted his tankard.

'You will join me,' he said.

I stood.

'To the King! To the last genius of Europe! With him died the greatness of my race!'

The old man offered me dinner, but I refused, having eaten with the soprano two hours before.

'You will not leave my house until you have eaten with us. After that you may go where you will.'

So I ate his ham and pickles and sun-coloured eggs and drank his apple *chicha*, which went to my head. Then I asked him about Wilson and Evans.

'They were gentlemen,' he said. 'They were friends of my family and my uncles buried them. My cousin knows the story.'

The old woman was tall and thin and her yellowing skin fell from her face in folds. Her hair was white and cut in a fringe across her eyebrows.

'Yes, I remember Wilson and Evans. I had four years at the time.'

It was a hot, windless day in early summer. The Frontier Police, eighty of them, had been hunting the outlaws up and down the Cordillera. The Police were criminals themselves, mostly Paraguayos; you had to be white or Christian to join. Everyone in Río Pico liked the North Americans. Her mother, Doña Guillermina, dressed Wilson's hand, right here in the kitchen. They could easily have gone over into Chile. How could they know the Indian would betray them?

'I remember them bringing in the bodies,' she said. The *Fronterizas* brought them down on an ox-cart. They were here, outside the gate. They had swelled up in the heat and the smell was terrible. My mother sent me to my room so I shouldn't see. Then the officer cut their heads off and came up the steps, here, carrying them by the hair. And he asked my mother for preserving alcohol. You see, this *Agencia* in New York was paying five thousand dollars a head. They wanted to send the heads up there and get the money. This made my father very angry. He shouted them to give over the heads and the bodies and he buried them.'

The storm was passing. Columns of grey water fell on the far side of the valley. Along the length of the apple orchard was a line of blue lupins. Wherever there were Germans there were blue lupins.

By the corral a rough wood cross stuck out of a small mound. The arching stems of a pampas rose sprang up as if fertilised by the bodies. I watched a grey harrier soaring and diving, and the sweep of grass and the thunderheads turning crimson.

The old man had come out and was standing behind me.

'No one would want to drop an atom bomb on Patagonia,' he said.

(Bruce Chatwin, *In Patagonia*)

QUESTION A
1. Good narrative writing depends for its effect on recording small details vividly. In the extract above, identify how the writer has drawn some vivid description by means of small details.
2. From your reading of this extract, comment on the type of person you think the narrator is. Give reasons for your answer.

QUESTION B
1. Sum up in your own words the anecdote given above, and say how much it contributes to the power of the passage.
2. Point out some features of narrative writing from the passage.

Text 4
QUESTION A
1. Identify the target audience of the advertisement on page 121.
2. Do you consider this to be an effective advertisement? Give three reasons for your answer.

QUESTION B
Write a paragraph of about 100 words on your reaction to this advertisement.

(For answers on fourth sample paper see pages 141–5.)

Section II: Composing
(100 marks)
Write a composition on *any one* of the following.
1. 'By the corral a rough wood cross stuck out of a small mound. The arching stems of a pampas rose sprung up as if fertilised by the bodies. I watched a grey harrier soaring and diving, and the sweep of grass and the thunderheads turning crimson.' Compose a descriptive account of some particular scene in nature that impressed you. Concentrate on using some original images and small details in your descriptions.
2. 'But there they were this week, lining the front rows at the final Paris *haute couture* showings, picking their frocks for the party to end all parties.' Write a review for a magazine on a fashion show you attended.
3. 'Or does the name Bali evoke an image long since past of a Mecca for artists in the nineteen-thirties and hippies in the nineteen-sixties?' Compose an article, using a persuasive style, on what you consider to be the advantages of taking holidays abroad.
4. 'Apart from its metal roof nothing distinguished it from the houses of a southern German village, the half-timbering infilled with white plaster, the grey shutters, the wicket fence, scrubbed floors, painted panelling, the chandelier of antler tines and lithographs of the Rhineland.' Write a narrative account of your experiences abroad. Include some details of your impressions of the people, food and culture.
5. 'Travelling broadens horizons.' Taking this topic as the subject for a debate, write out the arguments you would use in your speech.
6. Compose a series of diary entries by a person who is engaged in working on a Third World project. Include details of the people, their life-style, food and culture.
7. Write a letter to a local newspaper on your opinion of modern culture.

Fifth sample paper: Home and identity

This paper contains *four* texts on the general theme of home and identity.

Section I: Comprehending
(100 marks)

Text 1

The westernisation of the world

A traditional scene

In Singapore, Peking opera still lives, in the back streets. On Boat Quay, where great barges moor to unload rice from Thailand, raw rubber from Malaysia, or timber from Sumatra, I watched a troupe of travelling actors throw up a canvas-and-wood booth stage, paint on their white faces and lozenge eyes, and don their resplendent vermilion, ultramarine and gold robes. Then, to raptured audiences of bent old women and little children with perfect circle faces, they enacted tales of feudal princes and magic birds and tragic love affairs, sweeping their sleeves and singing in strange metallic voices.

The performance had been paid for by a local cultural society as part of a religious festival. A purple cloth temple had been erected on the quayside, painted papier mâché sculptures were burning down like giant joss-sticks, and middle-aged men were sharing out gifts to be distributed among members' families: red buckets, roast ducks, candies, and moon-cakes. The son of the organiser, a fashionable young man in Italian shirt and gold-rimmed glasses, was looking on with amused benevolence. I asked him why only old people and children were watching the show. 'Young people don't like these operas,' he said. 'They are too old-fashioned. We would prefer to see a high-quality western variety show—something like that.'

He spoke for a whole generation. Go to almost any village in the Third World and you will find youths who scorn traditional dress and sport denims and T-shirts. Go into any bank, and the tellers will be dressed as would their European counterparts; at night the manager will climb into his car and go home to watch television in a home that would not stick out on a European or North American estate. Every capital city in the world is getting to look like every other, and not just in consumer fashions: the mimicry extends to architecture, industrial technology, health care, education and housing.

Perverting development
The Third World's obsession with the western way of life has perverted development and is rapidly destroying both good and bad in traditional cultures, flinging the baby out with the bath water. It is the most totally pervasive example of what historians call cultural diffusion in the history of mankind. Its origins lie in the colonial experience, in which a variety of European conquerors suffered from the same colonial arrogance. Never a doubt entered their minds that native cultures could be in any way—materially, morally, or spiritually—superior to their own, and they firmly believed that the benighted inhabitants of the darker continents needed enlightening. And so there grew up, alongside political and economic imperialism, that more insidious form of control: cultural imperialism. It conquered not just their bodies but the souls of its victims, turning them into willing accomplices.

Reference-group behaviour
The most insidious form of cultural imperialism works by what sociologists call reference-group behaviour, found when someone copies the habits and life-style of a social group they wish to belong to, or to be classed with, and abandons those of their own group. This desire to prove equality surely helps to explain why Kwame Nkrumah of Ghana built the huge stadium and triumphal arch of Black Star Square in its capital, Accra. Why the tiny village of President Houphouet-Boigny in Côte d'Ivoire has been graced with a four-lane motorway, starting and ending nowhere, a five-star hotel and an ultra-modern conference centre. The aim was not to show the old imperialists but to impress other Third World leaders in the only way everyone would recognise: the western way. Fashions and dress codes have also fallen victim to this compulsion to westernise. In post-war Turkey a ruthless policy was pursued which saw the replacement of the Arabic script with the roman alphabet, while the wearing of the traditional hat, the fez, became a criminal offence. Launching this campaign the president declared: 'The people of the Turkish Republic must prove that they are civilised and advanced persons in their outward respect also. A civilised international dress is worthy and appropriate for our nation and we will wear it. Boots or shoes on our feet, trousers on our legs, shirt and tie, jacket and waistcoat—and of course, to complete these, a cover with a brim on our heads. I want to make this clear. The head covering is called a hat.'

QUESTION A
1. Describe briefly the writer's views on the impact the 'obsession with the western way of life' has made upon the people of the Third World.
2. Do you consider this passage to be an example of effective writing? Give reasons for your answer.

QUESTION B
Write a descriptive passage of between 150 and 200 words for a holiday brochure, describing what you consider to be the ideal holiday. In preparing your writing, pay careful attention to the way the author of the above passage uses detail in the opening two paragraphs.

Text 2

Pioneers: A view of home

I'm just a little picky about what I take pride in. There are actually people who take pride in their race. This is stupid. Not that anyone should be ashamed of his or her race, it's just that when you think about it you had nothing to do with it. Not your race, not your age, not your nationality. Not even your name.

Family feud

Recently I was watching a repeat of a television show called 'Family Feud', in which two families compete in guessing the answers to the most silly questions. The 'right answer' was the one that had been given earlier by a fabled 'one hundred people'. (We asked a hundred people to name a friendly neighbourhood bird, and the families had to guess what this one hundred had said—'buzzard'.) Whichever family reached 350 points first was the winner. A black family consisting of father, mother, two daughters and a son-in-law were playing a white family of father, mother and three sons in uniforms. As luck would have it the black family won. The show's presenter went over and shook the hands of the white family and thanked them for coming. Then one of the sons piped up with: 'Well we can still fly.' I guess they were Air Force; but mostly that was a racist remark: you blacks may know what one hundred people think, but hey—we whites can fly. Totally unnecessary. And tacky. I don't object to the boys being proud of flying—if I could fly I'd be proud of myself when I board a flight! No. It was the context in which the remark was made. As if 'Well, after all, we're still white' could make up for the fact that they lost.

We are not so important after all

It's so clear, now that we have photographs from the moon, and man-made satellites even farther away, that Earth resembles nothing so much as a single cell in the human body. What a concept—that the planet on which we live is no more than a specimen on a slide. We, who think humans are nature's invention, may well turn out to be no more than the life we see swimming in an ordinary drop of water. What is really important then? What does that do to our notions of race, fatherland, and home?

Where is home?

They say home is where when you go . . . they have to take you in. I rather prefer the idea that home, when you could go anywhere, is where you would prefer to be. The true joy of being a black American is that we really have no home. Europeans bought us; but the Africans sold. We might not have come to America of our own volition, but that is true of so many of the people who have come here from the overcrowded, disease-ridden cities of Europe. And what of those who had to flee religious persecution, or the unspeakable Catholic Inquisition, or starvation in Italy, or the black rotten potatoes lying in the fields of Ireland? No-one came to the New World in a cruise ship; they all came because they had to. They were poor, hungry, criminal, persecuted individuals who would rather chance dropping off the end of the earth than stay inert, knowing that both their body and spirit were slowly having the life squeezed from them. A pioneer has only two things: a deep desire to survive and an equally strong will to live. Home is not the place where our possessions and accomplishments are deposited and displayed; it is this earth that we have explored, the heavens we view with awe, these humans who, despite the flaws, we try to love and those who try to love us. It is the willingness to pioneer the one trek we all can make, no matter what our station or location in life: the existential reality that wherever there is life, we are at home.

QUESTION A
1. Characterise, in your own words, the attitudes of the writer of this passage to questions of identity and belonging.
2. Consider this passage as an example of predominantly persuasive writing.

QUESTION B
Write a short letter (100–150 words) to the television company which produces the show 'Family Feud', commenting on the behaviour of the families as described in this passage.

Text 3

In this passage taken from a recent publication (1990), the English novelist, John Braine, establishes a link between the appearance and atmosphere of places and the people who live in them.

Writing about home
People are places, and places are people. This isn't to dazzle you with its originality; it's simply another working rule. Whenever you write about places you also write about people. It isn't always that you mention the people when you write about the place. Sometimes it's necessary, sometimes it isn't. On the whole the best way is to concentrate on making the reader see the place.

The most revealing place of all is the home. Imagine yourself suddenly in the home of a complete stranger. Within five minutes you'll have an accurate general picture of what sort of person he is. There are obvious guides, like the kind of books or, for that matter, the absence of books, and the pictures and ornaments, and the quality of the furniture. There are different kinds of tidiness, from the house-proud to the clinically obsessive; different kinds of untidiness, from profusion to squalor. There is, over and above all, the atmosphere of a home. Some people have the gift of creating comfort, some have not. But be careful about this. If you describe a home properly, if you see it accurately, there's no need to say anything about the atmosphere. Or, to be more precise, your reader instantly makes the inference of falling between a shot of a man swaying on a windowsill ten storeys up and the same man sitting on the ground.

This isn't to say that we are exclusively the creatures of our economic environment. We aren't, for instance, made what we are by our homes (using the word in its narrowest sense). We make our homes. We were there first, so to speak. We even make impersonal places, like offices and factories, bear the imprint of our personalities: pin-ups on the walls behind the workbench, trendy executive toys, gold pens, silver mounted portraits on the executive's desk (or, equally revealing, nothing at all).

QUESTION A
1. Describe accurately and concisely the author's illustration of his opening statement: 'People are places, and places are people.'
2. Do you think he states his argument well? Support your points by detailed reference to the text.

QUESTION B
Imagine yourself in the home of some well-known figure from the world of entertainment or political life. Write a short account (150–200 words) for a popular magazine of what you imagine this home to look like, and give some indication of what you have chosen to include as significant detail.

Text 4
QUESTION A
1. What life-style is suggested to you by the collection of images on page 127?
2. How is this life-style suggested?
3. In what type of publication would you expect to find images such as this? Refer to the images in support of your point of view.
4. Compose an introductory paragraph of about 200 words that might accompany this image in the publication you have chosen in response to question 3.

QUESTION B
Imagine you are employing a graphic designer to compile such a photo gallery of your own life. Write a brief letter to him or her in which you outline the kind of images or objects you would include, giving the reasons for their inclusion.

Section II: Composing
(100 marks)
Write a composition on *any one* of the following.
1. 'Home, when you could go anywhere, is where you would prefer to be.' 'Home is not the place where our possessions and accomplishments are deposited and displayed.' In an article intended for a serious journal, present a case for or against one of these views of home.
2. 'There are actually people who take pride in their race. This is stupid.' Write an article in which you challenge or support these views.
3. 'Tales of feudal princes and magic birds and wars and tragic love affairs.' Compose a fable or fairy-tale suggested by one or more of the details in this quotation. You may, if you wish, give your composition a modern setting.
4. 'If you describe a home properly, if you see it accurately, there's no need to say anything about its atmosphere.' Write an informative newspaper article about your home town, parish, or locality, concentrating especially on the qualities that make it unique or memorable.
5. 'Fashions and dress-codes.' Compose a persuasive article or a speech for a debate that discusses the issue 'We are what we wear.'

6. 'The most revealing place of all is the home. Compose a series of thoughtful diary entries of a person returning to their native country after an absence of some years.
7. 'Days in my life.' Imagine you are working in the household of the person in the images under Text 4. Compose an autobiographical sketch or dramatic scene in which you characterise your experience in the house, and comment on your relationship with the householder.

(For answers on fifth sample paper see pages 145–50.)

Model answers to comprehension questions

First sample paper

Culture and trends: Text 1
ANSWERS TO QUESTION A
1. The purpose of this passage is to warn the reader about the dangers of taking certain vitamin pills. The writer succeeds in conveying this point clearly. The passage begins by pointing out the fact that certain types of vitamin pills may increase the risk of lung cancer and heart disease among smokers. To substantiate or back up this statement the writer makes reference to a number of different sources, in particular a report by the World Health Organisation. The article develops its points by showing the conclusions that have been drawn from an international meeting in Lyon. References are also made to some words of Dr Harri Vainio, which are used to support the main statement of the article: that beta-carotene should not be promoted to the general population as a tumour-preventive treatment.
2. This article is aimed at the ordinary reader who is concerned about their health. In particular it addresses itself to those people who might be inclined to take vitamins as a food supplement. The article opens with a straightforward assertion: 'Vitamin pills increase the risk of lung cancer and heart disease among smokers.' It then develops its points by using several short, terse statements about the dangers of certain types of pills. This approach is ideal for the ordinary reader who simply wants clear information on the topic.

ANSWER TO QUESTION B

> **We are what we wear**
> 'You!' the choreographer pinched my arm to guide me. 'You'd be better off dancing in the back row. And for God's sake, why don't you smile?'
>
> I glanced round the stage. *Joseph and His Amazing Technicolour Dreamcoat* is set not long after biblical times, so we would all probably have been stoned for wearing these pastel pink and blue-and-white halter-neck tops and short skirts. In the other corner the producer was vainly trying to teach the fellas how to dance in their gold slave-skirts. Perhaps the previous six hours of standing inconspicuously in the background trying to remember the words to 'Ba, ba, ba, ba, ba, ba, ba' had caused something in my head to snap. But as I looked at the pompous producer gesticulating wildly I saw a curly-haired Adolph Hitler in black leggings. I turned my attention back to the choreographer and bared my teeth.
>
> 'That's better.'
>
> 'Good humour is one of the best articles one can wear in society.' William Makepeace Thackeray, a contemporary of Dickens and author of *Vanity Fair*, knew the importance of a smile. A smile is not only a sign of humour or pleasure, because the face we present to the outer world is rarely our real face. We rarely show what we really feel in our facial expressions or in our actions. In the words of Billy Joel, 'We all have a face that we hide

away forever, and we take them out and show ourselves when everyone has gone.'

So we smile our way through the day, though in fact we may feel angry and annoyed beneath the smile. We smile at customers, or the boss, or the fact that we have just lost our job. Very few smiles have any real significance; they are simply a part of the suit of armour we don in order to face the world, like the masks we wear on a stage.

Society expects us to conform to a certain standard or idea in what we wear. Jung believed that the psychological struggle throughout life is to become more and more yourself, to continually discover and sculpt your own sense of uniqueness. However, my grandad laughs when I suggest he wear jeans. Him? Wear jeans? It is as if I had suggested he wear a frilly pink leotard to his next Legion of Mary meeting.

Both the clothes we wear and the hairstyles we fashion give scope for expression, though only within the glass confines of our particular culture, age, sex and social status. This kind of predictability led Bill Vaughan to observe that 'before you know it, the little girl in the frilly feminine dress is a woman in blue jeans.'

The old adage of first impressions being lasting only exacerbated my self-consciousness on my first week in first year. The existence of certain norms leaves the way open to all types of stereotyping. So within seconds of setting our eyes on new people, we make general and rigid judgments about them, right down to the very soles of their shoes.

We all know that being a teenager is often like being the reluctant star of a slapstick comedy, so I wasn't too surprised when the usually austere face of my home economics teacher contorted into a devilish grin. As she tore a hole in the top of the L&N shopping bag for my head, she was a fifteen-stone child delighting in having found a 'look what happens when you forget your apron' example.

The closest I can get to an analogy of rattling back to my table to cook those scones amid the stifling laughter is the way an early Christian would have worn a punishment sack. While the comfort of wearing horsehair was a noble and self-sacrificing deed, I on the contrary felt both victimised and absurd. Just as wearing a clown suit rids you of inhibitions about acting the clown, so too does sporting a plastic bag give you the freedom to act as scatter-brained as someone who . . . well . . . wears a plastic bag.

Take for example the distressing case of King Louis XIV of France. The narcissism of men as portrayed on those shampoo ads that we see today is a faint echo of the male pursuit of beauty under his reign. In the country where the Eiffel Tower was initially considered an eyesore, the Sun King introduced the wig, and the rouged men of his day would compete for the longest, curliest locks. As if that wasn't feminine enough, Louis also encouraged the late sixteenth-century innovation of high heels, which he wore to increase his own modest height.

'It will make or break him, so he's got to buy the best, 'cause he's a dedicated follower of fashion.' The Kinks could just as well be talking about Julius Caesar. Caesar kept for his own exclusive use the very thread of history: silk. Because it was sleek and synonymous with splendour and lustre, the Chinese guarded the secret of silk for more than two thousand years, and decreed death by torture to those who disclosed it. It makes you wonder whether Cleopatra was interested in Julius the man, or simply his silken image.

We are all guilty of judging by appearance. No-one would give Superman a reporting job because he just does not fit the image. But we must try to remember that what we wear is just a fraction of who we really are. After all, the only difference between Superman and Clark Kent lies in a pair of glasses and a different outfit. It takes a lot longer than a few seconds to catch a glimpse of the other side of a person's mask. Stevie Wonder never wanted pity for his blindness because he has the precious gift of never judging a book by the cover. 'The people I feel sorry for,' he said, 'are those with sight but who still cannot see.'

Culture and trends: Text 2
ANSWERS TO QUESTION A

1. The writer begins by referring to a Methodist university chaplain in Liverpool who has written a book on the subject of linking the film *Star Wars* with Christianity. This man—Rev. David Wilkinson—states that the film *Star Wars* is one of the most interesting films theologically, because it centres on a character changing sides. He goes on to pose the question: what is it in us that produces evil? He draws a parallel between the situation in the film where the evil Emperor is thrown into the glowing maw of the hyperdrive and the theme of redemption through self-sacrifice. He goes on to claim that the Force is a sign of hope. While it is not a picture of God, it is raising the question of God. The tension in the film is based on a scientific–materialistic world view and the idea of transcendence. In the film, we are told, the good guys rely on the Force and the bad guys rely on the death star. Rev. Wilkinson maintains that *Star Wars* is one of the greatest consumerist phenomena of the age, as it opens up a vision of a world beyond technological consumerism.

2. The writer uses the following techniques in order to develop the arguments in the passage. The passage opens with reference to words expressed by 'an earnest Christian' on how they are trying to bring up their children with Jedi values. The writer moves on to outline how there exists a direct correlation between some of the values of Christianity and those underlying the film *Star Wars*. He uses some words expressed by Rev. David Wilkinson in order to substantiate this claim.

The article develops by illustrating the clear correlation between certain Christian ideas, such as the theme of redemption and self-sacrifice, and those that are shown in the film.

ANSWER TO QUESTION B

> One of the films which I have truly enjoyed watching is *Life is Beautiful*. The film consists of two parts, which are closely related. In the first part, Guido (played by Roberto Benigni) falls in love with a school teacher in the town of Arezzo. The second part of the film takes place five years later and deals with the Nazi occupation. Guido, his wife and son are taken to a concentration camp because Guido is part-Jewish. Here, Guido uses all his wit and ingenuity to keep his son alive. For me the striking effect of this film is its ability to show the triumph of the human imagination over adversity. Guido pretends to his son that the death camp is a resort and that all the inhabitants are engaged in a game, and the best players will win an enormous prize.

Some people have objected to the fact that this film trivialises the Holocaust. However, I disagree with this view. For me, the film portrays death and suffering in a highly realistic manner. The effect of this serves the purpose of identifying more clearly the enormous horror of the Holocaust. This becomes very obvious for me when Guido himself is compelled to face the ultimate horror in the picture of the piled-up bodies.

I enjoyed this film very much, as it gives a very realistic and human portrayal of characters who suffered from the horrific effects of war and genocide.

Culture and trends: Text 3
ANSWERS TO QUESTION A
1. The writer begins his argument by stating that we are witnessing a revival in the art of giving names which are totally meaningless to things. To support this statement he uses several examples from films, for example *Trainspotting*, *Blade Runner* and *Reservoir Dogs*. The stories of these films have nothing whatever to do with their titles.

To illustrate his argument more clearly, the writer uses a humorous and almost ironic anecdote. In this anecdote we learn how Tarantino supposedly got the title *Reservoir Dogs* for his film because of his inability to pronounce the title of the film *Au Revoir, les Enfants*.

The writer concludes his argument by claiming that nowadays things are not meant to be understood; the more incomprehensible they are the better. The concept of meaning has become outdated.

2. i)   The writer's references mainly deal with cinematic allusions. He supports his main argument about the revival of the 'fine art of meaningless naming' by referring to a play, *Virgil Is Still the Frogboy*, and the films *Trainspotting* and *Blade Runner*. He also refers to several film directors, among them Luis Buñuel and Louis Malle, and to William Burroughs. He mentions the actor Harrison Ford in order to comment humorously that in the film *Blade Runner* he neither runs nor blades, and to emphasise the fact that the title has nothing whatever to do with the film's content.

Then, to demonstrate the fact that dreary comprehensibility does still exist, the writer makes reference to the films *Emma* and *The Fan*.

ii)   A number of very effective features of style are used in this passage to support the writer's main points. The tone of the entire passage is ironic and humorous. The writer uses colloquial expressions that would be familiar to the American reader, such as 'positively cutesy', 'hip' and 'Daddy Cool'; all examples of the writer's use of colloquial language and his mocking use of buzzwords.

The writer makes effective use of illustrations to support his argument: for example, the reference to the title of the film *Trainspotting* illustrates his main point that incomprehensibility is popular nowadays. In addition, there are copious references to various film directors and their films. The use of the colourful anecdote also illustrates very effectively how the young Tarantino got the name for his film *Reservoir Dogs*.

The sentence structure is varied; most of the sentences are terse, snappy statements that are in keeping with the colloquial or informal tone that is used. The writer also uses a series of short paragraphs that are clearly linked.

ANSWER TO QUESTION B
The conclusion of this passage is very suitable for the preceding argument and the tone used in it. The whole thrust of this article, conveyed by a series of striking examples, is how we are now confronted with a culture of incomprehensibility. The examples the writer uses throughout are taken from popular films and the work of modern artists. The writer also shows how directors give their films names that have nothing to do with their content. The examples he gives include films such as *Reservoir Dogs* and *Trainspotting*.

The conclusion is very effective. It sums up succinctly the writer's central arguments in a neat, effective and compact manner.

Culture and trends: Text 4
ANSWERS TO QUESTION A
1. The life-style suggested to me by this photograph is one of poverty and need. The clothes of the two boys are old and torn. The bigger boy has no shoes, and the ground is rough and seems to be filled with rubble. In addition, the cart is roughly made: it seems to be made of a cardboard box and wiring, and the wheels are broken. The metal bar propelling this old car is also rough-and-ready. The boys, however, seem to be happy. We can tell this from the smile on the face of the older boy and the fact that they are united in the picture.
2. The statement that seems to be made in this photograph is of a sense of initiative on the part of the boys. Even in conditions of poverty these two boys can find something to smile about: the older boy is happy as he pushes the younger boy along in this home-made cart. There is a strong sense of unity between the two, shown in the small detail of both boys holding the one pole and driving forward.

ANSWER TO QUESTION B

> Even in the midst of extreme hardship and poverty, Kiko and Yami can still find something to smile about. Born and bred in the Kikuyo tribe, in the North Kenyan mountains, both boys were left destitute at an early age. Their father abandoned their mother and ran to the mountains, and later on their mother died from disease and starvation. These two boys survived and now live with their uncle, spending their time entertaining each other and the kids from the nearby village by giving each other joy-rides in the local BMW.

Second sample paper (pages 102–110)
Violence and destruction: Text 1
ANSWERS TO QUESTION A
1. This passage is a dramatic example of persuasive writing. The writer's contention is that cruelty to animals is closely allied to cruelty and violence against people. The passage opens with a series of short anecdotes that illustrate the main point: how certain people who inflict cruelty on animals become dominated by a thirst for

violence, which is then used on humans. Each point made by the writer is clearly laid out in a series of neat, terse paragraphs, which make it easy to follow the writer's train of thought.

The writer uses language that is accessible and effective. Phrases such as 'pumping bullets', 'gruesome murder cases' and 'the countryside has become a virtual battlefield' serve the function of hammering home more forcefully the writer's message about the profound impact of violence on human consciousness.

The writer concludes by using an authoritarian tone in order to motivate the reader to do something about the problem: 'We should tackle this issue', 'It is, after all, a matter of life and death.' This tone is a hallmark of effective persuasive writing.

2. The following are examples of facts used in the article. (i) The chief suspect in the killings at the Capitol in Washington shot sixteen cats with his father's revolver. (ii) Michael Ryan, also called the 'Butcher of Hungerford', tested his weapons on cats and wildlife before shooting his neighbours. At the age of fourteen he had set animals alight. (iii) In Arkansas two schoolchildren, who had been taught by adults to hunt and kill animals, shot their teacher and several pupils. (iv) Neighbours in Britain had seen two children who abducted and killed a younger child cut off the heads of live pigeons. (v) Bonny and Clyde tortured livestock before they embarked on a killing spree. (vi) In Ireland a murderer claimed that exposure to cruelty in a meat plant had brutalised him. (vii) Research shows that sport hunters are seven times more likely to beat their wives than non-hunters.

The following are examples of opinions expressed in the article. (i) The killings at the Capitol in Washington should have received banner headlines. (ii) The violence in sport hunters is attributed to an excessive need among hunters to control and dominate their environment. (iii) Our gun culture is getting out of hand. Parts of the country have become a virtual battlefield. (iv) We should tackle this issue before the killing of animals spawns a major tragedy. (v) One effective measure would be to have all weapons electronically tagged so that police could monitor their use. Sadistic or over-zealous gunmen could be given the same treatment.

ANSWER TO QUESTION B

A street scene at night

It is almost three hours since the black veil of darkness covered the city. Now and then a sliver of moonlight penetrates through the smog and illuminates the streets below. The screeching of tyres—scarcely audible above the booming noise of nightclubs—fills the air as two stolen cars race each other down the main street, driven by teenage joyriders. A lone drunk stumbles along the footpath, using parked cars for handrails.

Across the street in a dark and gloomy alleyway two wretched tramps huddle in a doorway begging for money. One of them covers the scars of a lifetime of pain and suffering beneath a coarse, wrinkled face and dull beard. Drops of rain slowly trickle down an old rusty drainpipe. At the side of the disco a young man deals drugs to his clients before they enter the club. Other people pass by in fancy clothes eager for a night of enjoyment.

Violence and destruction: Text 2

ANSWERS TO QUESTION A

1. The writer builds up atmosphere in the passage by drawing a vivid description of nature as the storm begins to break. The atmosphere is a distinct one of threat and violence. The world of nature begins to take on almost a life of its own as the storm gathers momentum.

The passage opens with a reference to the light 'flapping' and the rumbles from the thunder filling the sky. As the lightning begins to flash, we witness how the whole atmosphere becomes transformed; every hedge, bush and tree becomes distinct in the landscape. The animals begin to react in wild confusion. This atmosphere of violence and tension intensifies as the passage develops. Just as the storm unleashes itself onto the world of nature, we become exposed to the profound destruction in its wake. The tall tree on the top of the hill is struck by lightning. As Gabriel struggles with the haystacks, his ricking-rod is also struck by a flash of lightning.

2. The writer concentrates on a series of sharp and vivid details to paint a striking and realistic image of the development of this storm. He uses a number of similes to describe the destruction in the world of nature. As the storm begins to break we are told how 'A light flapped . . . as if reflected from phosphorescent wings . . .'. Then the lightning is compared to the colour of silver, and we are told how it gleams 'like a mailed army'. With the outbreak of the storm, Hardy describes how every hedge, bush and tree 'was distinct as in a line engraving'. Through the use of a vivid simile the writer shows us the image of a poplar tree, which is 'like an ink stroke on burnished tin'. When the lightning strikes the landscape and trees, we are told how 'all was silent, and black as a cave in Hinnom'. Through the use of such vivid and precise similes the writer succeeds in painting an authentic picture of the whole landscape.

Hardy also makes use of personification to depict how nature assumes a lifelike quality. As the storm batters its way across the landscape, the lightning flashes are like 'forms of skeletons' appearing in the air, 'dancing, leaping, striding, racing around, and mingling altogether in unparalleled confusion'. These images are given added intensity through the writer's emphasis on colour: 'undulating snakes of green', 'black as a cave', 'the colour of silver'.

The writer makes use of a number of small but effective details, as well as personification, similes and active verbs, to paint a truly realistic and authentic picture of the whole scene.

ANSWER TO QUESTION B

> All night the storm raged on. At last the heavens opened and began to rain down huge undulating sheets of water. At six o'clock the dawn began to break in a sombre ash colour. The air began to stir and the temperature changed. Some of the trees began to rock to the base of their trunks, and the twigs clashed in strife as the wind gathered in intensity. For miles around one could see nothing but havoc: trees lay sprawled on the ground uprooted from their bases and lying in twisted and gnarled positions. Gates and fences were

smashed and broken. The barrier around the paddock was battered and completely destroyed. The storm had wreaked its full havoc. All that remained was the general devastation, which fronted the whole landscape. Morning came on, heavy, dull and leaden in intensity.

Violence and destruction: Text 3
ANSWERS TO QUESTION A
1. This is a very good example of writing as propaganda. The writer opens the article with a number of rhetorical questions: 'What is it possible to say about the loss of lives?', 'Who can say what this island would have been like?', 'How much else has been lost?'. Rhetorical questions are a hallmark of such writing and are a powerful device for gaining the attention of the reader.

The writer makes use of emotive vocabulary in order to present his controversial views; images such as, 'the most sobering, most heartbreaking book . . . not a page of it is without an almost unbearable tragedy'. This type of language is very effective, as it serves the function of involving the reader on an emotional level.

Another feature of persuasive writing is the use of repetition. This device illustrates a writer's points or arguments in an emphatic way. The following examples of emphatic repetition illustrate the writer's arguments very well: 'each tragedy is real, each one was lived by actual people, each one spread vast repercussions through family, friends . . .'.

Another feature of persuasive writing is the use of metaphor and images. The writer of this article makes abundant use of images and particularly metaphors to express an idea more forcefully; for example such images as 'we let the shutters of statistics conceal the mountain range of human suffering behind them', 'liberated the dead from the limbo of statistics'.

One effective device in persuasive writing is the technique of reinforcing a positive or affirmative statement by means of a negative. The writer of this article succeeds in doing this in a highly effective and striking way in statements such as 'The issue is not individual atrocities. The issue is violence itself.' and 'Not a page on it is without an almost unbearable tragedy; each tragedy is real, each one was lived by actual people'.

The most striking feature of this passage is the one-sided view it presents of complex and controversial events, which are reduced here to a simple emotional level, the purpose of which is to undermine the legitimacy of any alternative point of view.

The writer concludes the article by making use of the imperative: 'Nothing more needs to be said. Buy *Lost Lives*. Nobody on this island can have an excuse . . .'.

2. This article would probably appear in a newspaper aimed at a readership already inclined to agree with such opinions. The views put forward are expressed in such a provocative manner that there is little likelihood that they would convince an objective reader at the level of rational argument. The article uses highly selective facts and dubious analogies, such as equating the Northern violence with the War of Independence, all aimed at rousing the reader to an emotional involvement that will make them more ready to accept the writer's extreme views.

Answer to question B

I would like to inform you about a book called *Lost Lives*. My purpose in addressing you today is to put forward a number of reasons why you should buy this book. *Lost Lives* addresses itself directly to our own history. It deals with all the deaths arising from political conflict this century, from 1916 up to the events of the last thirty years. There can be no excuse for not knowing about the history of these events. This book describes the enormous suffering experienced by a huge number of families because of these deaths. Many negative as well as positive acts characterised the struggle for national independence, and the negative ones must be confronted honestly. Some people use these facts to put forward a one-sided view that gives the impression that the recent campaign of violence was not only wrong but happened for no reason. They try to ignore the years of sectarian discrimination and repression that led large numbers of people—wrongly, in my opinion—to resort to violence. We must study the causes as well as the effects of political violence if we are serious about making certain that it never happens again.

Violence and destruction: Text 4
Answers to question A

1. Photograph A shows someone who is engaged in a parachute jump. He is being helped by two other people who are sitting in a plane. The main comment that is made in this photograph seems to be that this man is trusting absolutely in his two friends. It shows his dependence on other people, and yet what can be achieved by people working together in harmony. In addition, the photograph seems to be suggesting the enormity of the world of nature and how small we humans seem to be within it.

Photograph B shows the football champion Jack Charlton playing with a schoolgirl and attempting to paint her face. It is a situation of fun, as can be seen from the stance of the girl, who is turning away and laughing. The expression of the other girl in the picture is also one of amusement. In some ways this photograph could represent the need for heroes and a type of hero worship.

Photograph C shows two elderly women studying an old cannon. The comment that seems to be made by this picture is how fascinating antique things can be. The fact that they are looking at a cannon, which has a pile of cannonballs beneath it, could also make a statement about the grim reality of war.

Photograph D shows a family at the seaside with their young son. He has made friends with a dog and is obviously fascinated by it. The photograph shows the power and meaning of friendship and communication.

Photograph E shows a man standing on a rough, rocky surface with his face hidden. In the distance stand two donkeys. The man appears to have climbed, as he is leaning on the stick and wears what appear to be walking-boots. The significance of this photograph could be that the man is reflecting deeply on something, perhaps in a spirit of prayer or of repentance.

2. Photograph A: This is a very effective image in depicting how humans engage in the art of flying. Two men seated in an aeroplane are holding a rope that is attached to another man, who is in mid-air. This serves the function of emphasising the unity of

the action and how they can achieve so much when working together in unison. In addition, a contrast is drawn between the man and the enormity of the landscape behind him. The face of the man who is in mid-air shows a sense of satisfaction at a feat that has been accomplished.

ANSWER TO QUESTION B
Photograph A : 'A leap of faith'
Photograph B : 'Picasso Jack'
Photograph C : 'The way we were'
Photograph D : 'Man's best friend, or kid's worst enemy?'
Photograph E : 'The pilgrim'

Third sample paper (pages 110–15)
Communication: Text 1
ANSWERS TO QUESTION A
1. The primary purpose of the first article is to give a detached and objective account of certain words expressed by the Pope on the subject of Heaven. The writer uses an informative style in order to achieve this purpose. For example the writer tells us how the Pope turned his attention to Paradise after the publication of a magazine that redefined concepts of Hell. The writer refers repeatedly to the actual words used by the Pope on the subject of Paradise. These statements are objective and clear: Paradise is 'a state of being' after death, a 'living and personal relationship with the Holy Trinity', 'close communion and full intimacy with God'.

The writer develops the points made by using a number of short paragraphs, each of which contains a different point made by the Pope on the subject of Heaven and Hell.

The second article is on the same subject, but the purpose of the writer here is distinctly different. This writer uses a subjective approach in commenting on the Pope's words. Much of the article is based on using certain kinds of tone, in particular sarcasm and irony. There are many ironic references throughout the passage, which serve the function of mocking or undermining the validity of the Pope's address. The writer's use of phrases such as 'even a glutton would soon sicken of ortolans eaten to the sound of soft music', the delights of paradise 'looking tackier with time', 'the Pope, the principal salesman of this time-share retreat' are all sarcastic.

The opening of the passage is both dramatic and sensational: 'Paradise is no longer the place it used to be.' The function of this approach is to shock the reader. The language is colloquial and casual; phrases such as 'chilling out with the Paraclete', 'a simple blow-out banquet', 'unlimited pleasure much like retirement to the Costa', are designed to entertain rather than inform the reader.

The first article has the function of informing the reader about the actual address of the Pope in a much more factual manner. The writer here is more objective and detached. The second article serves the function of shocking and startling the reader. The whole approach is informal and even sensational.

2. The first article would most likely be found in a serious newspaper or journal. The

writer appeals to reason and logic in developing the points in the article. Each point is supported by a clear example, which is obviously well researched and rational. There is direct reference to the actual words spoken by the Pope, and both evidence and facts are used throughout the article to illustrate each point made.

On the other hand the second article would most likely appear in a tabloid newspaper. The language and approach are clearly designed to shock. There are few facts mentioned and no reference to any ideas mentioned by the Pope.

ANSWER TO QUESTION B

In my opinion the main responsibility of a journalist is to serve the prevailing ethos of society. People have a right to the truth; they need to be informed correctly about the truth surrounding public events in order that they can play their part in society. However, commercial success and profitability are often in conflict with truth and with the needs of society.

A journalist has the responsibility to ferret out the truth and to publish it. An effective journalist, in my opinion, should have the aim of informing and educating the public, not merely reflecting surface symptoms. The journalist is an advocate of truth and the primary consideration should be both the truth and the welfare of the reader.

Communication: Text 2

ANSWERS TO QUESTION A

1. The primary purpose of the writer here is to give a review of the film *The Boxer*. The writer sets out the main details of the plot and the chief features of the central character.
2. The writer opens the review on an emotive tone: 'a few poignant moments—a whisper, a glance, a touch . . .'. This approach serves the function of attracting the reader's attention. The writer then moves on to give the main outline of the plot. He uses facts and names to give us certain information. We know, for example, that the story is set in Belfast and that the main character is Danny Flynn, a former IRA man. The writer also uses certain images, such as how the film unfolds in a chaotic world and how falling in love is both dangerous and deadly. This type of imagery shows clearly the nature and style of this film. The writer concludes by commenting on how the central actor performs in this film. The evaluation is subjective; for example the writer comments how Daniel Day-Lewis' portrayal of the central actor is 'complex, subtle and utterly convincing'.

The whole review is structured into a series of short, terse paragraphs. This particular structure makes it easy to follow the writer's development of ideas and the flow of thought. As a result of this approach, the review flows swiftly along. Note how the writer uses a minimum of words. Look at the second sentence, for example: 'Set on the streets of Belfast, the story of the "Boxer" unfolds in a chaotic world where violence is a part of everyday life and where to fall in love may be not just dangerous but deadly.'

ANSWER TO QUESTION B

The main question which must be asked is 'Will family life be able to resist the massive competition of television in our civilised society today?' The content of many television programmes presents a great number of unsolved problems and anxieties for a child. Often questions and themes continue to worry children subconsciously, and this can cause the appearance of mental or bodily disorders that are inexplicable to parents. In addition, sustained television viewing can reduce a child's creative imagination and impulses, and can cause a deficiency in their literacy and cultural development. Some of the consequences of excessive television viewing are laziness, indifference, lack of concentration and increased aggressiveness.

I feel that parents must play a part in preventing television from dominating and dictating life in their homes. Parents can stimulate children's creative capacities by playing with them from an early age. In this way children develop their talents, learn how to give and take, how to narrate imaginary stories and so stimulate their imagination. This in turn will enable them to communicate better on every level.

It can be helpful for the whole family to watch a particular programme together. This can create an opportunity to react and perhaps discuss the subject matter of that programme. Also, family life needs to be safeguarded by ensuring that television does not dominate the household at meal times. Meal times are a great opportunity to consider the others in the house and give ourselves to them and find out how their day was. Television is only an instrument that we must dominate and that must not be allowed to dominate us.

Communication: Text 3
ANSWERS TO QUESTION A

1. The writer develops this statement by claiming that with the birth of Turly, worldwide portable telecommunications has been achieved. Then the writer moves on to show how this company, founded by Motorola, has changed a vision into reality through Iridium.

To illustrate this point, the writer uses a short anecdote about Karen Bertinger, who was on holiday in the Caribbean in 1985 and was unable to phone the United States on her mobile phone. She convinced the company's chief executive of the need for a system that would provide wireless communication between any two points on the planet.

The writer goes on to declare that the work of bringing this into operation was based on a great deal of effort. Many people's talents were harnessed in order to bring this idea about.

The writer declares that there are now satellites circling 500 miles above the Earth.

The Iridium handsets are palm-sized and are now in production. The writer shows how these handsets are now in operation and will give people the power to make and take calls anywhere in the world. They will use only one telephone and one number and will receive only one bill. The writer concludes that what was once a visionary project is now a commercial success.

2. The writer uses effective argument to develop the points made in this passage. The article opens with a deductive argument: that is, the writer makes a general statement about how pioneers of telecommunications have always looked further than others in

order to expand their possibilities. The article goes on to illustrate this point by citing a particular example: that the birth of Turly has managed to bring about worldwide telecommunications.

This argument is given effective clarity by means of the short but vivid anecdote about Karen Bertinger, who managed to convince the company of the need for a wireless system of communication between any two points on the globe.

To illustrate the point that this project necessitated a lot of hard work, the writer refers to Thomas Edison's remark that 'genius is one per cent inspiration, ninety-nine per cent perspiration'. The writer develops this point in more detail by means of statistics. 'From the original idea flowed thirteen years of tireless hard work as the talents of more than 10,000 people were harnessed.' There is also a reference to the presence of satellites 500 miles above the Earth, and how agreements have been signed with more than 300 telecommunications companies.

The writer concludes by describing the nature of Iridium handsets: how they are palm-sized, can make calls anywhere, and involve only one number and one bill.

ANSWER TO QUESTION B

> Particularly in the past five years, the economic boom has brought prosperity for many people. There are disadvantages to all this growth and acceleration, however. With the development of Dublin as the centralised economic and social nucleus of the country, there has been a huge increase in the number of cars in the city. In the past seven years alone, car ownership in the greater Dublin area has increased by forty-two per cent. This has given rise to a situation where Dublin's most commonly used words are now 'gridlock', 'chock-a–block', and 'bumper-to-bumper'. The unprecedented growth in the number of cars on the road is a rapidly worsening problem that Ireland, and in particular Dublin, now faces.

Communication: Text 4
ANSWERS TO QUESTION A
1. The photograph shows us a picture of a man who is standing with one leg on the ground while the other is stretching in the air. At the same time the man is reading a book. This stance suggests that he is completely set for action. Everything in his life is under control.

The relationship between the advertisement and the photograph is intended to show that with a mobile phone you are ready to take on anything. In other words, a mobile phone enables you to take control of your life.

2. The writer uses an effective caption underneath the photograph—'Total control'—to advertise the mobile phone called 'Ready to Go'.

The advertisement also uses a direct address to the reader: 'Whatever way you look at it, a Ready to Go mobile phone gives you more than freedom, it gives you control over the way you live your life.' The advantages of this type of phone are spelt out in short punchy statements, all of which are negative but serve the function of hammering home the writer's message: 'No bills; no rental, no connection fee, no hassle!'

Answer to question B

I would like to outline some of the benefits of using a mobile phone. For me, there are numerous benefits, and indeed I feel that a mobile phone is now almost an indispensable means of communication.

One of the chief advantages of having a mobile phone can be seen in the case of accidents and other emergencies. A mobile phone can enable you to make almost immediate contact with a doctor or ambulance. Likewise, a mobile phone can be a life-saver if you happen to be attacked or trapped in an awkward situation. In the event of a robbery, contact can be made with the local Garda station, and the culprit may be apprehended more quickly.

In the world of work, the mobile phone fulfils a number of functions. Mobile phones can be the means of securing an effective business deal. They can help in making contact with someone if you happen to be late for a meeting, or if you have to cancel an appointment. Doctors on call must now consider the mobile phone one of their most indispensable instruments.

On a more day-to-day level, the mobile phone enables you to communicate with home if you know you are going to be late and let your family know where you are and how you can be contacted. As we can see, there are considerably more advantages than disadvantages in using a mobile phone.

Fourth sample paper (pages 115–21)
Life-styles: Text 1
Answers to question A

1. The audience for this type of article is probably women who have a moderate income. The writer begins by attracting the attention of the ordinary reader with the phrase 'Seriously rich women are different from you and me.' Before moving on to capture the exciting and exotic features of this fashion show, the writer asks the question 'Do you know what you are going to wear on New Year's Eve?' The sharp reply in the next sentence—'Neither do I'—demonstrates clearly that the writer identifies with the ordinary reader, who will not be planning so far ahead. Many of the references are to television and film stars, to 'socialites' and to trendy dress designers.

2. This type of review would probably be published in the features section of a daily newspaper, or in a popular magazine. The style is informal and lively. Many of the references to celebrities such as Joan Collins and Ivana Trump, and fashion designers such as Paco Rabanne, Dior and Yves Saint-Laurent would be familiar to many readers. The language used is simple and accessible to a wide readership, for example: 'there they were . . . lining the front rows . . . picking their frocks for the party to end all parties'.

The writer also makes use of a series of short and clear paragraphs to develop the points made. The images used are graphic: 'Nan Kempner, the American socialite, chuckled throatily', 'the couture circus', 'a season of sybaritic fashion moments, and a time to wallow'. In addition there are lots of examples of the style of clothes displayed at this show. The writer draws on fashion trends to illustrate the styles that dominated:

the exotic skins and furs, the brocade glistening with jewels, the crystals winking from silk tulle, the velvet appliquéd with mink, and the fabulous plumage soaring from heads, woven from knits and trailing from the hems of taffeta opera-coats. These all serve to show how the exotic and novel are a hallmark of the present time.

The writer also uses humour to conclude the article. 'Flight was a key inspiration, whether expressed in billowing parachute gowns, paratrooper gear, woman-as-bird, or woman-as-satellite. Fashion was reaching for the stars—enough to make the imagination soar.'

ANSWER TO QUESTION B

Hairstyles
Hairstyles have become the new medium of expression. Hair is clearly not 'hip' these days if it is not bleached, crimped, permed, thickened or fried to within an inch of its life.

One of the most distinguishable species of teenager today is the 'metaller' or, affectionately, the 'headbanger'. These rock-music-loving Neanderthals can be clearly distinguished from the rest of the teenage type by their flowing manes of unkempt hair. This windswept style is all-important to the headbangers. It allows them, literally, to let their hair down at social gatherings such as rock concerts. On the other hand, the skinhead brings a new meaning to the old reliable short back and sides. They prefer the hygienic and practical method of simply shaving all the hair from the head. However practical and hygienic it may be, it must be admitted this looks pretty scary as it glints in the darkness under the multicoloured disco lights.

Certainly hairstyles have become a rather complex issue. Formerly flags and signs distinguished different ethnic groups; nowadays it is hairstyles which distinguish the various groups of people that comprise society today.

Life-styles: Text 2
ANSWERS TO QUESTION A
1. This is a very effective example of persuasive writing. The article opens with several rhetorical questions, a hallmark of persuasive writing: 'Does anywhere on earth sound more exotic? Or does the name Bali evoke an image long since past of a mecca for artists . . . . Does it offer adventure, romance, peace and quiet . . .?'

The article develops by answering the question using a colloquial tone: 'Well, yes.' The writer gives a list of attractions offered by this exciting place, among them 'volcanoes, jungles, elephants, wild monkeys, amazing birds'. The writer gives a list of the activities that can be engaged in, such as go-karting, paragliding, white-water rafting, paint-balling and an internet café. To illustrate Bali's popularity the writer makes use of a simile: 'Bali is to Australians what Torremolinos is to British and Irish people.'

The writer makes use of richly sensuous images, for example, 'The views of the jungle and rice paddies opposite are luscious. At night the sound of the stream at the bottom of the gorge and the clatter of insects provide an auditory environment just as compelling.' The function of such imagery is to attract the reader on an emotive level.

The article concludes by drawing a humorous illustration about the monkeys and the food vendors. This technique adds a sense of colour and interest to the writing.

2. (i) Bali was a Mecca for artists in the thirties and sixties. (ii) There are volcanoes, jungle, elephants, wild monkeys, birds, rice paddies, seas, music and dancing in Bali. (iii) In Bali there is bungee-jumping, go-karting, paragliding, white-water rafting, paint-balling, and an internet café. (iv) Tours will take you by boat to a desert island or a bird park where there are monkeys.

ANSWER TO QUESTION B

Want that perfect paradise?
You have it now in BEAUTIFUL BALI.
Escape to the blissful beaches of Bali where you can have the time of your life
- wallowing on the golden sandy beaches
- soaking up the glorious sunshine
- lying by cool mountain streams

Bali has an amazing mixture of adventure sports, magnificent views of the jungle, exotic boat tours, and delicious and exciting food.
All you have to do is *Book Now* for that perfect holiday.
No better value than Bali –
Book your holiday today!

Life-styles: Text 3
ANSWERS TO QUESTION A

1. The writer opens this section by appealing to the different senses: we can almost smell the rain as it blows down the valley, with 'the smell of wet earth and aromatic plants'. We gain an insight into the habits of this community as they prepare for the oncoming storm. We can visualise the old woman gathering up her washing and the old man putting on his boots and waterproofs before he goes out to the garden. The writer also registers colours vividly with a series of striking adjectives: 'two red oxen', 'the half-timbering infilled with white plaster, the grey shutters', 'the painted panelling', the 'tobacco from a blue-and-white jar'. As he leaves the house at the conclusion he notes that there is a line of blue lupins, a favourite of German people. There is an emphasis on delineating small details in a vivid and economical way, for example Anton Hahn takes off a tweed cap and hangs it up on an antler. Features of the characters are shown very vividly: 'a little girl with a pigtail', 'his head was flat on top and his face creased and red', the old woman's 'yellowing skin fell from her face in folds', her hair was 'white and cut in a fringe across her eyebrows'.

From the use of small detail we gain an insight into the type of characters represented. We learn that Anton likes his tobacco and chicha. We also learn from his conversation that he is bitter about the war, and that he is loyal to the former king, Ludwig. In a headstrong gesture he compels the writer to drink to the health of Ludwig, and he forces him to stay to dinner in spite of his protestations. It is also clear that these people were humane from their reaction to the death of the two Englishmen.

Anton's father had insisted on giving them a proper burial, and before leaving, the writer notes this in the small detail of the rough wooden cross that lay beside the corral.
2. The narrator is observant. This can be seen from his expert and skilful registering of small details in both character and the environment. The old woman is described as 'tall and thin', her skin is 'yellowing' and 'falling from her face in folds'. Anton wears a tweed cap which has its own place: it hangs on an antler. The writer also carefully notes certain customs and habits such as Anton putting on his rope-soled slippers before he settles down with his pipe and tankard of chicha. As the narrator leaves the house he notes the beauty of nature: the arching stems of a pampas rose, the grey harrier soaring and diving. He also observes the small cross over the graves of the two Englishmen who were killed.

The narrator is also quick and resourceful. He makes the mistake of calling the former king 'Mad Ludwig' but is quick to qualify this by claiming 'he was a great genius'.

The narrator is sensitive. He registers the details of the anecdote about the two people who were victims of the frontier police with a great deal of insight and sensitivity. He is also courteous. At the insistence of Anton, he eats what is put before him even though he maintains that he just had a meal with the soprano. He also joins Anton in a toast to King Ludwig out of respect for Anton's view.

ANSWERS TO QUESTION B

1. Wilson and Evans were friends of the Hahns. They were betrayed to the frontier police who claimed their heads in order to get money. However, the father became angry and insisted on burying them. The anecdote contributes to the power of the passage by showing more clearly the type of people the Hahns were. Though they were Germans and had apparently suffered because of the war, they retained a great deal of humanity and sensitivity, as is evidenced by their reaction to the murder of the two men.
2. The story begins with the narrator coming down into the valley as the rain is starting. It recounts how he meets Anton Hahn and his wife and how he is invited to dinner. He then develops the narrative by giving us an insight into the character of Anton. Through the conversation we learn that Anton is bitter about the Great War: he believes that the war was the biggest mistake in history. We also see Anton's loyalty to the former German king, Ludwig. The reference to the Englishmen shows us another side to Anton's family: the humanity and generous spirit of his father, who insisted on giving the two men a proper burial. The passage concludes with the writer noting the passing of the storm, and the blue lupins, which are a favourite of German settlers. Hahn's philosophical comment that no-one would want to drop an atom bomb on Patagonia concludes this passage. The narrative has a distinct shape; a definite beginning, middle and conclusion.

There is also a realistic insight into the characters present in this narrative—a hallmark of good narrative writing. The dialogue is immediate and shows clearly the more striking features of these characters, and in particular Anton, who is more dominant and headstrong. The style and manner of the narrative shows us different features of the narrator: his capacity for observation, his love of nature, his sensitivity and ability to record small events in a vivid manner.

Another feature of effective narrative is the ability to draw realistic description. Here, by focusing on a series of details—on colour, movement and shape—we can almost visualise the whole scene before us. Images such as 'So I ate his ham and pickles and sun-coloured eggs and drank his apple chicha, which went to my head' and 'The Fronterizas brought them down on an ox-cart . . . . They had swelled up in the heat, and the smell was terrible' bring the whole situation alive.

Life-styles: Text 4
ANSWERS TO QUESTION A
1. The intended audience for this advertisement is the ordinary reader. The advertisement addresses itself to the reader who is in a position to help an underprivileged person in another country more effectively.
2. The advertisement is very effective, in the following ways: (i) The photograph of a young boy is highly effective in attracting the attention and sympathy of the reader. The boy's eyes and facial expression suggest someone who is desperately in need and who would greatly appreciate some small help. (ii) The heading at the top of the photograph is arresting and vivid. The underlying idea is one of helplessness in the young boy and his need for effective help, with a clever play on the term 'guardian angel'. (iii) The use of a coupon is a good way for people to find out how to help. In addition, the logo of the organisation Actionaid is clearly positioned and makes it obvious that help is being sought.

ANSWER TO QUESTION B

> My reaction to this photograph is an immediate impression that the boy is in urgent need of help. His eyes and the position of his hand convey a strong impression of a cry for help. The whole image is one of vulnerability and helplessness. This image is reinforced by the words at the top of the photograph: 'An angel in search of a guardian'.

Fifth sample paper (pages 122–7)
Home and identity: Text 1
ANSWERS TO QUESTION A
1. The writer of this article makes several powerful points about the consequences of the Third World's obsession with the western way of life. He believes it has stunted development and destroyed both the good and the bad in traditional cultures. He contends that this obsession is a striking example of 'cultural diffusion', the roots of which lie in colonialism. He maintains that colonialism, blinded by its own sense of superiority, imposes its culture while ignoring that of the country it has conquered. The

writer concludes that cultural imperialism has become a hallmark of such societies, and that it controls both the body and the soul of its victims.

The writer identifies the most insidious form of this type of dominance as 'reference-group behaviour', with the imitation of the habits and life-style of another culture and the simultaneous abandonment of one's own. He illustrates this by referring to Ghana and Turkey. In both instances the western life-style was adopted to impress other Third World leaders, and to show them that this was superior to their own culture.

2. The passage is a clear example of effective argument, for the following reasons.

The writer begins the article with a vivid and colourful anecdote to illustrate his argument that adherence to traditional culture in Third World countries is maintained mostly by older people, while younger people prefer to see a performance from the western world.

The topic sentence in each paragraph stands out clearly and is supported by graphic examples. The writer defines the term 'reference-group behaviour' and then cites examples to support this definition. This method of supporting his points with evidence makes the argument coherent and effective.

The passage concludes very effectively. The writer uses direct reference to an imposition made by the Turkish authorities, which made it compulsory to wear western dress. The language and tone of the quotation communicate the point with added effectiveness.

ANSWER TO QUESTION B

We are living in a material world, but you are not a material thing. Even if you were that bony bathing goddess lying on a Mediterranean beach, you know you wouldn't be happy. Sometimes the brochures with the blue skies and the even bluer seas serve only to give you the blues. It's a change of mind that you really want, not a change of scenery. But how do you get what you want, what you really want?

Sri Nisargadatta Maharaj, a guru in India, tells you what you already know: 'You are living in a dream world—seek the truth!'

Enlightenment awaits when you conquer the body and mind. This all-inclusive holiday to India offers you not just a superficial tan, but enables the sun to shine from your very soul as you wallow in a form of eternal bliss. You've heard the message, but the empirical knowledge is the only one of value. Seek!

This magazine also offers you tape-recorded conversations with Sri Nisargadatta Maharaj in the best-selling book *I am That* for the special price of €10.99.

Home and identity: Text 2
ANSWERS TO QUESTION A
1. The writer speaks about the subject of identity and belonging in the following points: he draws attention to the moral obtuseness underlying racist behaviour, in the anecdote about the television programme 'Family Feud'. He goes on to question the

importance of our identity by commenting on the size of the planet Earth, which 'resembles nothing so much as a single cell in the human body'. Having stated that the planet on which we live may be little more 'than a specimen on a slide', the writer proceeds to ask the question: How does this affect our notions of home and race?

The writer goes on to contend that home is where you would prefer to be when you are in a position to go anywhere in the world. He concludes by stating that home is the place we belong and where we find our identity. Home is the earth we explore, the people we live with and try to love in spite of their faults, the ability to pioneer the road we have undertaken no matter what situation we are in, the realisation that 'wherever there is life, we are at home'.

2. The passage is an effective example of persuasive writing. The tone of the passage is subjective. The writer uses personal references together with the subjective 'I' to show his objection to people who espouse racist views. The use of the personal pronoun 'we' is a subtle persuasive device which presupposes the reader's acquiescence in what the writer is contending. For example, phrases such as 'Home is not the place where our possessions and accomplishments are deposited and displayed: it is this earth that we have explored, the heavens we view with awe . . .' take for granted that the reader is agreeing with the arguments or points being made.

The writer uses a colloquial tone in order to address the reader more directly. The passage is structured clearly into a series of sub-sections, which make it easy to follow the writer's train of thought. The use of the anecdote about the television programme is a vivid method of illustrating his point about the destructive impact of racism. The writer also uses several rhetorical questions; another effective device to persuade the reader.

The conclusion of this passage is very effective. The writer first of all presents a negative statement, then reinforces this with a series of affirmations in order to hammer home his point more effectively: 'Home is not the place where our possessions and accomplishments are deposited and displayed: it is this earth . . . it is the willingness to pioneer . . .'. This is a very effective technique for use in persuasive writing.

ANSWER TO QUESTION B

Mallow Road
Cork
13 July 2002

Dear Sir,

I would like to draw your attention to the recent edition of 'Family Feud' that was broadcast at 8 p.m. on Tuesday 9 July.

I consider the incident involving the two families to be in very poor taste. It was shocking to see that there are people who can behave with such blindness and arrogance towards another group of people. Programmes and references like this serve to do nothing other than undermine the dignity and integrity of the person. In this particular case the people who came out badly were the white family. A programme of this type only highlights the innate ignorance and insensitivity of some people with regard to the real truth about the human person.

Perhaps, in the event of being unable to show such issues in a balanced and mature manner, you would refrain from dealing with them in any future programmes.

Yours sincerely
Mary McMahon

Home and identity: Text 3
ANSWERS TO QUESTION A
1. The writer illustrates his argument that 'People are places and places are people' by maintaining that whenever you write about people you also write about a place. He maintains that the best way to describe a place is to make the reader see it.

He goes on to make the statement that the most revealing place of all is the home. He uses the idea of imagining yourself in the home of a complete stranger. He declares that within five minutes you will know what type of person lives there. This will be revealed clearly through the way objects are positioned: the books (or absence of books), furniture and ornaments. The different kinds of tidiness or untidiness will tell you a lot about the person. The writer claims that if you can describe a home correctly you will not need to talk about the type of atmosphere in it, because the description will have done this for you. To illustrate the power of accurate description he uses a graphic image, showing how your reader will be able to make an inference between the image of a man swaying on a windowsill ten storeys up and the same man sitting on the ground.

The writer concludes by stating that we are not 'exclusively the creatures of our economic environment'. It is people who make a home and not the opposite. He cites some familiar examples to support this statement. We make impersonal places, such as offices and factories, bear the imprint of our personality by putting pictures on the wall or by displaying gold pens or 'executive toys'.

2. Yes, I believe that the writer argues his position clearly. He begins with a short, terse sentence that introduces his main argument: 'People are places, and places are people.' A variety of sentence structures is used to develop the argument that we can determine the atmosphere of a place from its description.

Each paragraph is clearly laid out and easy to follow. The writer sets out the topic or main sentence at the beginning of each paragraph. The first paragraph develops the argument by addressing the reader directly in a colloquial tone, 'This isn't meant to dazzle you with its originality: it's simply another working rule.' In the following paragraphs the topic sentences are developed and expanded by means of effective and apt analogies. The second paragraph opens with the statement that 'The most revealing place of all is the home.' To develop this statement the writer uses the argument about being in the home of a complete stranger and how we can make a judgment on what type of person he or she is. The examples used are simple and accessible: the novel description of different types of tidiness and untidiness, the positioning of material things. The concluding paragraph also makes use of familiar and relevant examples, such as the type of accessories one can accumulate in a place of work, whether pictures on the wall, gold pens or 'trendy executive toys'.

ANSWER TO QUESTION B

Hello, and welcome to this special edition of *Empire*. Today we are going to take a peep into the private life and home of none other than Jack Nicholson. The world-famous actor now lives in Los Angeles, where his new three-storey villa is some sight!

Let's start with the outside. The front gates form part of an enormous electric fence, with two security cameras and a tough-looking bodyguard. The long drive up to the house is interesting, filled with exotic plants and luxurious smells. The garden looks like something from ancient Rome, with its two Jacuzzis and its enormous pool surrounded by magnificent marble statues.

Inside this large and lavish house we gain another insight into the type of man Jack Nicholson is through the existence of a small but significant detail: a striking oak cabinet in the front hall. Here we are confronted with not one but two Academy Awards and numerous Golden Globes for Nicholson's many starring roles.

The hall and dining room are filled with prestigious masterpieces, such as works by Van Gogh and Picasso.

The large drawing room contains an amazing view over the lake, and in the centre of the parquet floor lies a large leopard-skin rug. The seats are made of black Italian leather and make it enormously difficult to emerge from them once you sink into their luxurious folds. Certainly this home is worth a visit to see how the other half lives!

Home and identity: Text 4
ANSWERS TO QUESTION A
1. The life-style suggested to me by this collection of images is one of wealth. The image of the old mansion, together with the pictures of antiques and horses, suggest a country estate of grandeur and elegance.
2. This life-style is suggested by the various pictures, for example the horse, the binoculars which are obviously old and precious, and the two dogs that lie indolently on each side of the picture. The picture of the woman with pearls suggests a person of wealth.
3. The type of publication that would show such images is a 'country life' magazine such as *Town and Country* or *Horse and Hound*. Such publications are aimed at a very selective readership, including rich landowners, aristocratic families and other wealthy people.
4. Introductory Paragraph for the magazine *Horse and Hound*:
Set in the heart of Connemara, the ancient castle of Ballyglunin Park lies secluded on its own grounds of several thousand acres. The River Cloon flows through the grounds. Stretching out beyond the huge grounds at the back are the splendid stables, which shelter many of the finest thoroughbreds this area has ever seen. The castle itself is famous for its distinctively wide hallway, containing a splendid stained-glass window. This carries the date 1415, the year in which it was taken over by its previous owners, the Butlers. The present owners, the O'Brien family, are renowned for their great love of animals. Once a year Ballyglunin Park opens its doors to host the annual Antique Fair, an event that draws people from all over the country. This castle and its heritage are something we can all take pride in.

Answer to question B

9 Laurence Terrace
Huntstown
Co. Limerick
14 December 2003

Ms Marie Heraughty
Graphic Design Centre
Arch Row
Belfast

Dear Ms Heraughty,
I am planning to compile a photo gallery of things that are important to me and that I have accumulated throughout my life.

I have been given your name by a friend of mine who has praised your expertise in this area. I wish to include some pictures that would show an image of happiness and success. For that reason, perhaps you could include some large maps of the world to show that I have travelled a great deal. I would also like you to include pictures of my home and family, and in particular a picture of my youngest daughter.

Could you contact me at the above address, or by phone (061) 2276893, to let me know whether this is possible?

Yours sincerely,
Joan Dunne

Paper II

Paper II, the literature paper, is divided into three sections: fiction, drama, and poetry. Each of these sections is dealt with separately below.

Examination Technique in Paper II

7

Prescribed texts for examination in 2003

Students are required to study:
1. *One text* on its own from the following texts:
BRONTË, Emily	*Wuthering Heights*
ISHIGURO, Kazuo	*The Remains of the Day*
MILLER, Arthur	*Death of a Salesman*
McGAHERN, John	*Amongst Women*
SHAKESPEARE, William	*Macbeth*
2. *Three other texts* from the list below, in a comparative manner, according to the comparative modes prescribed for this course.
   Any texts from the list below, other than the one already chosen for study on its own, may be selected for the comparative study.
   A film may be studied as one of the three texts in a comparative study.
   The comparative modes for examination in 2003 at Higher level are:
   (i) Theme or issue
   (ii) Cultural context
   (iii) General vision and viewpoint

Texts prescribed for comparative study for examination in 2003
(texts marked with an asterisk are discussed in this book)
ACHEBE, Chinua	*Things Fall Apart*
ANGELOU, Maya	*I Know Why the Caged Bird Sings*
ATWOOD, Margaret	*Cat's Eye*

AUSTEN, Jane	*Pride and Prejudice*
BALLARD, J. G.	*Empire of the Sun*
BARKER, Pat	*Regeneration*
BELL, Sam Hanna	*December Bride*
BRONTË, Emily	*Wuthering Heights**
DEANE, Seamus	*Reading in the Dark*
DICKENS, Charles	*Great Expectations*
FRIEL, Brian	*Dancing at Lughnasa*
HARDY, Thomas	*Far from the Madding Crowd*
ISHIGURO, Kazuo	*The Remains of the Day**
JOHNSTON, Jennifer	*How Many Miles to Babylon?*
JOYCE, James	*A Portrait of the Artist as a Young Man*
KAZAN, Elia (Dir.)	*On the Waterfront* (film)*
LEONARD, Hugh	*Home before Night*
LESSING, Doris	*The Grass Is Singing*
LONCRAINE, Richard (Dir.)	*Richard III* (film)*
LUHRMANN, Baz (Dir.)	*Strictly Ballroom* (film)*
MALOUF, David	*Fly Away Peter*
MILLER, Arthur	*Death of a Salesman**
McCABE, Eugene	*Death and Nightingales*
McGAHERN, John	*Amongst Women**
MacLAVERTY, Bernard	*Lamb*
OZ, Amos	*Panther in the Basement*
O'BRIEN, Kate Cruise	*The Homesick Garden*
O'CASEY, Seán	*The Plough and the Stars*
O'CONNOR, Frank	*My Oedipus Complex and Other Stories*
REED, Carol (Dir.)	*The Third Man* (film)*
SHAKESPEARE, William	*Othello**
	*Macbeth**
	Twelfth Night
SHERIDAN, Jim (Dir.)	*My Left Foot* (film)*
SOPHOCLES	*Antigone*
SYNGE, J. M.	*The Playboy of the Western World*
TORNATORE, Giusseppe (Dir.)	*Cinema Paradiso* (film)*

3. *Shakespearean drama*
   At Higher level a play by Shakespeare must be one of the texts chosen. This can be studied on its own or as an element in a comparative study.

4. *Poetry*
   A selection from the poetry of the following eight poets is prescribed for the Higher level examination in 2003:
   DONNE

HOPKINS
YEATS
FROST
BISHOP
PLATH
HEANEY
MAHON

Students will be expected to have studied at least six of the prescribed poems by each poet.

Prescribed texts for examination in 2004

Students are required to study:
1. *One text* on its own from the following texts:
BRONTË, Emily	*Wuthering Heights*
ELIOT, George	*Silas Marner*
IBSEN, Henrik	*A Doll's House*
McGAHERN, John	*Amongst Women*
SHAKESPEARE, William	*Macbeth*

2. *Three other texts* from the list below, in a comparative manner, according to the comparative modes prescribed for this course.

   Any texts from the list below, other than the one already chosen for study on its own, may be selected for the comparative study.

   A film may be studied as one of the three texts in a comparative study.

   The comparative modes for examination in 2004 at Higher level are:
   (i) Literary genre
   (ii) Theme or issue
   (iii) Cultural context

Texts prescribed for comparative study for examination in 2004
(texts marked with an asterisk are discussed in this book)

ACHEBE, Chinua	*Things Fall Apart*
ANGELOU, Maya	*I Know Why the Caged Bird Sings*
AUSTEN, Jane	*Pride and Prejudice*
BALLARD, J. G.	*Empire of the Sun*
BARKER, Pat	*Regeneration*
BIELENBERG, Christabel	*The Past is Myself*
BINCHY, Maeve	*Circle of Friends*
BRONTË, Emily	*Wuthering Heights**
CHATWIN, Bruce	*In Patagonia*
ELIOT, George	*Silas Marner**
FRIEL, Brian	*Dancing at Lughnasa*
GORDIMER, Nadine	*The House Gun*
HUSTON, John (Dir.)	*The Dead* (film)*

IBSEN, Henrik	*A Doll's House**
ISHIGURO, Kazuo	*The Remains of the Day**
IVORY, James (Dir.)	*A Room with a View* (film)*
JOYCE, James	*A Portrait of the Artist as a Young Man*
KAZAN, Elia (Dir.)	*On the Waterfront* (film)*
KEENAN, Brian	*An Evil Cradling*
LEONARD, Hugh	*Home before Night*
LONCRAINE, Richard (Dir.)	*Richard III* (film)*
LUHRMANN, Baz (Dir.)	*Strictly Ballroom* (film)*
MACKEN, Walter	*The Silent People*
MacLAVERTY, Bernard	*Lamb*
MADDEN, Deirdre	*One by One in the Darkness*
McGAHERN, John	*Amongst Women**
MEHTA, Gita	*A River Sutra*
MILLER, Arthur	*A View from the Bridge*
MOORE, Brian	*Lies of Silence*
O'CASEY, Seán	*The Plough and the Stars*
OZ, Amos	*Panther in the Basement*
SHAKESPEARE, William	*King Lear**
	*Macbeth**
	Twelfth Night
SOPHOCLES	*Oedipus the King*
SPARK, Muriel	*The Prime of Miss Jean Brodie*
STEINBECK, John	*Of Mice and Men*
SYNGE, J.M.	*The Playboy of the Western World*
TORNATORE, Giuseppe (Dir.)	*Cinema Paradiso* (film)*

3. *Shakespearean drama*

   At Higher level a play by Shakespeare must be one of the texts chosen. This can be studied on its own or as an element in a comparative study.

4. *Poetry*

   A selection from the poetry of the following eight poets is prescribed for the Higher level examination in 2004:
   WORDSWORTH
   DICKINSON
   HOPKINS
   FROST
   KAVANAGH
   PLATH
   HEANEY
   MAHON

Students will be expected to have studied at least six of the prescribed poems by each poet.

Examination technique in Paper II

1. The total number of marks required for Paper II is 200, or 50 per cent.
2. The time allowed for Paper II is 3 hours and twenty minutes.
3. You must answer from four different sections:
    - one question on a single text (total marks: 60)
    - one question on comparative study of texts (total marks: 70)
    - one question on prescribed poetry (total marks: 50)
    - questions on an unseen poem (total marks: 20).
4. Divide your time in the following way:
   The single text: 60 minutes
   The comparative study of texts: 70 minutes
   The prescribed poetry: 50 minutes
   The unseen poetry: 15 minutes
5. Give yourself 5 minutes to read back over the paper and to check your answers against the questions asked. *Do not exceed this time.* Remember, good time-keeping in an examination is essential in order to gain the necessary marks. *You will not receive extra marks by writing beyond the time.*
6. Attempt all sections of the paper.
7. Remember, you must answer a question on Shakespeare drama either as a single text or as part of a comparative study.

Answering literature questions

1. Do the question that you find easiest first. This will cause you to peak; it will boost your confidence and help you with the other sections.
2. Do not rush at answering questions. Spend time working out the implications of the question. Make sure you understand clearly what is being asked in the question. To do this, analyse or decode every aspect of the question.
3. Know the difference between such terms as 'justify', 'analyse', 'discuss', 'compare', 'contrast', 'evaluate', 'assess', 'comment', 'paraphrase'.
4. Remember, you don't have to agree with the question that is asked. Show clearly what stance you are taking on the question. Use evidence from your text or texts to support your stance on the question.
5. Rephrase the question in your own words. It can help to formulate it as a direct question: for example, '*Far from the Madding Crowd* explores the effects of flattery, obsession, and love' can be rephrased as 'How are the issues of flattery, obsession and love evident in *Far from the Madding Crowd*?'
6. Draw a circle around the main points of the question, and begin to organise a rough draft.
7. Brainstorm the topic. Use trigger questions: How? Why? Where? When?
8. Begin by *answering* the question asked. Your opening paragraph should simply make a *firm* and *clear* statement on the question that is asked.
9. Use the present tense in your answer. Use modern English as much as you can.
10. Give yourself time to look back over the answers. Check your answer for irrelevant

statements, incoherent argument, and repetition of ideas.
11. Before you construct a paragraph in your answer, consider:
    - What is the topic sentence or main idea of this paragraph?
    - What relationship has this paragraph to the question?
    - Are the ideas in the paragraph given support through evidence or quotation?
    - Does the concluding paragraph tie up all the ideas and refer back to the question?

Remember in each paragraph to refer to what is being asked in the question. And remember that each paragraph in your answer has to advance your argument to another stage. Each paragraph is a logical stage in a coherent and developing argument. If the paragraph has not got a bearing or relationship to the question, then discard it.

Features of a good answer on literature

1. A unity of impression. All paragraphs relate to one another and to the topic in general. The concluding paragraph must synthesise or tie up all the preceding ideas and arguments.
2. Answers that focus on what is asked, that don't beat around the bush, digress, or introduce material that is irrelevant.
3. A style that is familiar and clear to your reader. Remember that you are communicating with, not impressing, your reader. Avoid
    - awkward syntax
    - long-winded sentences
    - repetition
    - the self-conscious 'I think', 'I hope to prove that', 'I feel I have shown that ...' These are redundant and weaken your argument. A good literature essay does not need such statements: it should speak for itself.
4. A clear understanding of the question asked. The opening paragraph must focus your position on the question and show the direction your answer will take.
5. An individual or personal response. Don't rehash notes or critiques: make the answer your own. Support what you say by reference to or quotation from the text.
6. A maturity of response. Answers in the literature section must show that you have evaluated all sides and are presenting an objective, balanced and coherent answer.
7. A structured and organised argument, with supporting evidence that leads logically to a conclusion. Good essays make progress: they advance an argument, explore an issue, and arrive at a conclusion.

Incorporating quotations in answers

Every question on the literature paper requires reference to or quotation from the text. Quotations must be positioned in such a way that they play a central role in advancing your argument. The length of quotations must be appropriate to the point being made: give as many words from the text as are strictly relevant to your point—no more and no less. You must explain the relevance of a quotation, how this quotation relates to the point or points being made.

Use a colon to introduce a quotation. 'Doris Lessing makes use of many symbols in her book *The Grass Is Singing* in order to communicate her themes more forcefully. The store operates as a symbol of South African society on one level: "For thousands of people up and down southern Africa the store is the background to their childhood. So many things centre round it." On the other hand the store symbolises the "greyness and misery of Mary Turner's childhood".'

The Study of a Single Text 8

The questions on this section will take for granted that you have acquired a thorough knowledge of the novels or plays you have studied. This means you must
- know the main features or characteristics of the central characters well
- study the plot and how it develops in the text
- know how language and imagery are used to serve the writer's purpose
- study the principal quotations that describe the motivation of the characters, and the attitude of the writer to the characters and to the issues that are treated in the text.

How to answer a question on the study of a single text

1. Rephrase the question. Sometimes it can help to formulate the task as a direct question.
2. Take a definite stance on the question. Decide clearly whether you agree, partly agree or disagree with the question. You are free to take whatever stance you like, as long as you support it clearly with evidence and reference to the text.
3. Your opening paragraph should state clearly, in one or two sentences, your position on the question and the direction your essay will take.
4. Begin to organise your ideas before you start to write the essay. Jot down several points—six or seven—in note form. These will deal with different aspects of the question and will be constructed in paragraphs. The graph illustrates these points more clearly.

How to answer the question on the study of a single text

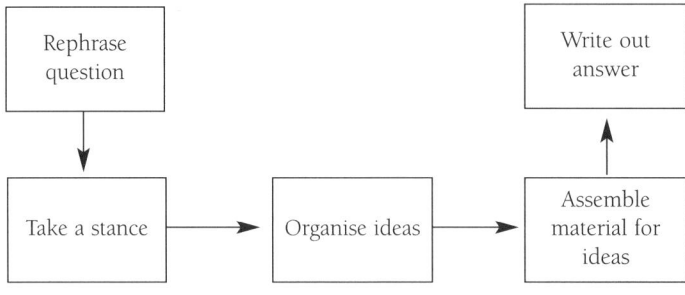

Sample draft answers

Here are three sample draft answers to questions on *Amongst Women*, *Wuthering Heights* and *The Remains of the Day* that illustrate these points. In each case the sample opening paragraph is written out fully; the points for the other paragraphs are written in note form. Examine closely the technique used in answering the questions in this section.

Amongst Women
(2003 and 2004 exams)
Discuss the position and role of the woman in the novel *Amongst Women*.

Stage 1
Rephrase the question. Examine what part does the woman play in the novel *Amongst Women*.

Sample opening paragraph
There are many different types of female character shown in the novel *Amongst Women*, written by John McGahern and set against an Irish background in the years following the War of Independence in 1921. In spite of the fact that these women have very different types of personality, their role is seen as essentially subservient to that of the male at this particular time in Irish history.

Paragraph 2
Discuss the personality of Rose Brady; that she is an independent girl who had worked in Glasgow and comes home to nurse her sick father. Show how she defies her family and succeeds in marrying Moran.

Paragraph 3
Develop some points that draw out the different characters of the Moran girls: Sheila, Mona and Maggie. Show how they are dependent on Moran's moods and sensitive to his erratic behaviour.

Paragraph 4
Discuss the changes that take place in the house with the arrival of Rose; how she sets a 'tone that would not be easily wrested from her'. Show the girls' joyful reaction to her personality when she arrives in the house. Show the changes in the lives of the girls with the arrival of Rose; how Maggie manages to go to England and become independent.

Paragraph 5
Develop the relationship between Rose and the Moran family, and in particular show how she withstands the erratic and violent behaviour of Moran. Show her strength of character in standing up silently for her rights, and how she reacts to his verbal violence by announcing that she will leave the house if he thinks she is not wanted.

Show how, through her moral strength, she manages to help the girls attain their independence and find good jobs.

Paragraph 6
Show the progress of the girls and how they are very anxious to please Moran by bringing their boyfriends to the house for approval. Draw a contrast between the position and reaction of Luke and Michael to Moran, and that of the girls. Develop the point about their unstinting devotion to Moran through all the years in spite of his tempestuous character.

Concluding paragraph
Draw together all the points made. Make reference again to the background of this novel—Ireland in the early twentieth century. Show how the role of the woman was slowly changing from working in the home all day to becoming professionally independent. Sum up the main points on the role of the Moran girls, and outline how Rose has contributed to helping them, through the particular way she behaved as Moran's wife.

Wuthering Heights
(2003 and 2004 exams)
'Emily Brontë makes use of an original and distinctive method of narration in her novel *Wuthering Heights*.' Assess the truth of this statement in the light of your reading of *Wuthering Heights*. Support your answer by reference to or quotation from the novel.

Stage 1
Rephrase the question. The narrative technique in the novel *Wuthering Heights* is both unique and original. Discuss.

Sample opening paragraph
This statement is true. Brontë makes use of two very ordinary narrators to tell this extraordinary story: Lockwood, a young man from London, and Nelly Dean, a housekeeper.

Paragraph 2
Discuss the reason for this extraordinary narrative technique—how it is used as a means of bringing otherwise incredible and supernatural events within the reader's grasp.

Paragraph 3
Discuss the narrative of Lockwood in the first four chapters. Develop his character by drawing a contrast with that of Heathcliff, and the whole environment of the Heights. Comment on the effect of this. Show how the author is able to introduce the theme of the supernatural (the figure of the ghostly Catherine outside the window) through the medium of Lockwood, and so make it credible and acceptable to the reader.

PARAGRAPH 4
Develop the point on how this story is given an anchor in the normal everyday world by commenting on Lockwood's first reaction to the inhabitants of the Heights. Take particular note of his first reaction to young Cathy.

PARAGRAPH 5
Discuss the character of Nelly Dean. Show how she continually shifts loyalties between Edgar Linton and Heathcliff, and comment on how she contributes to bringing about a good deal of the tragedy that happens in the lives of the people in the story.

PARAGRAPH 6
Comment on Nelly's part in facilitating Heathcliff's revenge plans by foolishly allowing young Cathy to be trapped in the Heights, and later on to marry young Linton.

CONCLUDING PARAGRAPH
Tie up all the points made and restate the particular type of story and genre of this novel. Draw a contrast between the two narrators and their contributions in developing the plot. Show how the novelist skillfully succeeds in revealing an unfamiliar world of heightened passions and violence, and yet makes it credible through her extraordinary narrative technique.

The Remains of the Day
(2003 exam only)
'Stevens is a character who has lost out a lot in life and who gains the sympathy of the reader in the novel.' Would you agree with this statement? Support your answer by reference to or quotation from the text.

STAGE 1
Rephrase the question. Stevens is someone who has missed out in life and who we feel sorry for.

SAMPLE OPENING PARAGRAPH
This statement is not completely true. While the title of the novel *The Remains of the Day* refers to Stevens's life at the conclusion, it is not necessarily true that Stevens has missed out completely in life. There is no doubt, however, that in many ways the sympathy of the reader lies with Stevens throughout a great deal of this story.

PARAGRAPH 2
Outline Stevens's great vision of the role of butler, and his notions of dignity. Show how these ideas are embodied in the figure of his father, through the constant references to his father's sustained loyalty to his employer.

PARAGRAPH 3
Develop the point on how Stevens modelled himself on this vision of his father as an

unquestionably loyal and dignified butler, and how he, Stevens, gave single-minded service and commitment to Lord Darlington.

Paragraph 4
Discuss the strained relationship between Stevens and Miss Kenton, and outline how Stevens attracts sympathy here because of his emotional sterility and blindness to the fact that he has cut himself off from a life of affection and love.

Paragraph 5
Concentrate on Stevens's motivations in his work. Show how commitment to his professional work as a butler has always superseded all other considerations. Write about his behaviour on the night of his father's death, when he continued to serve Lord Darlington because there was an important meeting of international delegates. Show how in this section (Day 2, Salisbury) Stevens recalls this night with a strong sense of triumph.

Paragraph 6
Analyse Stevens's motivations—how at each stage he truly felt he was serving society and his fellow human beings through carrying out a good service to Lord Darlington. Mention how he reacted to the news that Miss Kenton was leaving to get married; how he sustained his commitment that night to doing the best job he could do and how he firmly believed he behaved with true dignity.

Paragraph 7
Point out the contrast with Stevens at the conclusion of his career, when Lord Darlington is dead and has been exposed as a misguided man who was clearly supporting the Nazis. Show how Stevens remains faithful to the memory of Lord Darlington and believes that he was a good man who wanted justice in the world.

Paragraph 8
Discuss Stevens's meeting at the end of the novel with Miss Kenton (Mrs Benn). Show how he feels inside when she mentions that she could have had a better life had she married Stevens. Show how the reader's sympathy is drawn towards Stevens at this stage. Mention the conversation that Stevens has on the pier with the obscure butler at the end. Show how Stevens articulates for the first time how he feels his life has been a waste, and yet how he adopts a positive attitude towards this.

Concluding paragraph
Sum up by tracing the various factors that motivated Stevens throughout his career, and show how many significant events contributed to making him feel triumphant about his commitment as a butler. Contrast this with the events which occurred: the exposure of Lord Darlington, Stevens's lack of emotional fulfilment and the sense that he had wasted his life. Show how he reconciles his losses and balances them out, and how at the conclusion he counts the gains more than the losses and decides to adopt a positive attitude; to stop looking back at the past and lamenting it.

Sample complete answers

The following are complete sample answers that can be used in the study of a single text. They include an answer on one of Shakespeare's plays, *Macbeth*, and on the novel *Silas Marner*. Study the way in which the answers are constructed, and in particular the commentary at the conclusion.

Macbeth
(2003 and 2004 exam)
Would you agree with the statement that the witches in the play *Macbeth* are evil, malevolent creatures who originate deeds of blood and have a power over the soul? Discuss this statement with quotations from or reference to the play.

Sample answer
The witches are indeed creatures of evil who have access to secret knowledge; from the beginning of the play they know Macbeth's name. 'Hail to thee, Thane of Glamis.' However, the power of the witches is limited. They can incite, tempt and induce characters to do evil, but they can never cause a character to commit sin or carry out evil deeds except indirectly. We see the limited quality of their powers early on in their own reference to the sailor:

> Though his bark cannot be lost,
> Yet it shall be tempest-tost.
> (I, iii, line 24–5)

The witches are agents of evil who seek to reverse the normal order of things and by so doing to obscure reality. From the outset they make their role clear: to create hurly burly from what is stable. As agents of the Devil they disturb the normal order of things and thereby distort reality. The essence of their intention can be summed up in the lines

> Fair is foul, and foul is fair:
> Hover through the fog and filthy air.
> (I, i, line 11–12)

The witches are clearly intended to represent the metaphysical world of evil spirits roaming around Scotland. Their meetings take place in conditions suggestive of cosmic disorder. Their function on a symbolic level is to mirror the spirit of evil roaming around Scotland. They belong to the equivocal world of seeming. Their every action is a perversion of the natural order. They hover in the fog and filthy air. They appear amid thunder and lightning. They are neither wholly male nor female; they look like women yet have beards:

> you should be women,
> And yet your beards forbid me to interpret
> That you are so.
> (I, iii, line 45–47)

It is Banquo who recognises this satanic quality inherent in their natures when he asks the question:

> What! Can the devil speak true?
> (I, iii, line 108)

Banquo also recognises their manner of working:

> oftentimes, to win us to our harm,
> The instruments of darkness tell us truths,
> Win us with honest trifles, to betray's
> In deepest consequence.
> (I, iii, line 123–5)

Evil works through deception in the play. Shakespeare works into the texture of his drama the theme of appearance versus reality in order to clarify the whole theme of evil. The witches as instruments of evil operate in terms of false appearance. Their verse style is an indication of their function; their incantatory utterances communicate only equivocal and uncertain meanings. In other words, the witches are 'imperfect speakers'.

Macbeth is in some way unconsciously bound up with the evil world of the witches from the very beginning of the play. His first words, 'so foul and fair a day I have not seen' are an unconscious echo of the witches' words in act I, scene i. From his first encounter with them, Macbeth falls victim to their fatal temptations. After this first meeting with them (act I, scene iii), Macbeth begins to move in a world of darkness, which is the domain of evil. It is no surprise therefore to hear him say shortly afterwards, 'Stars, hide your fires!' Macbeth is simultaneously attracted and repelled by the prophecies. He is 'rapt' in a world apart from his fellows. His soliloquy

> Two truths are told,
> As happy prologues to the swelling act
> Of the imperial theme.
> (I, iii, line 127–9)

shows us how he is beginning to become involved in the dark world of half truths. This interior battle within Macbeth between good and evil is dramatised as a seesaw rhythm in his musings and in particular his soliloquies:

> This supernatural soliciting
> Cannot be ill, cannot be good;
> (I, iii, line 130)

It is obvious that Macbeth has begun to equivocate within himself in this juggling with the sense of good and evil. The witches tempt Macbeth with the possibility of kingship. However, he himself is his own destroyer. He is the one who falls victim to their fatal temptations and carries out murder after murder in his quest for 'sovereign sway and masterdom' (act I, scene v, line 69). So the witches indeed give rise to deeds of blood and violence through their subtle temptations, but they do not have power over the soul. Macbeth and his wife, Lady Macbeth, each end up as their own destroyer. They both go to their own damnation freely.

After carrying out the murder of Duncan, Macbeth is dominated by a sense of guilt. An agony of restlessness dominates him. His mind is full of scorpions, he cannot sleep, and he keeps alone, moody and savage. Everything within him condemns itself for being there. There is a fever in his blood, which urges him on to ceaseless action in his search for oblivion. Ambition, love of power and an instinct for self-preservation are too potent in him to permit him to give up. Motivated by a new will to live and a renewed desire for the crown, he challenges 'Fate' to come 'into the list'. He is 'bent to know, by the worst means the worst'. A frightful result ensues. He speaks no longer of conscience, remorse or pity, but instead becomes active and purposeful in his dedication to evil. By the time he has reached the witches in act IV, scene i, his relationship with them has changed. He is determined that

> Things bad begun make strong themselves by ill:
> (III, ii, line 55)

His decision at this stage is free, fully conscious and deliberately calculated. He wishes to know the future even though there is universal chaos. After this last encounter with the witches, the whole flood of evil in his nature is unleashed.

The final stage of their operation against him is shown in Hecate's words:

> raise such artificial sprites
> As by the strength of their illusion
> Shall draw him on to his confusion:
> (III, v, line 27–29)

The apparitions that the witches show to Macbeth are mocking illusions. They offer a false confirmation of his own desires while at the same time symbolising through tragedy and violence the final birth of a new order. In this way they turn out to be dramatically ironic. It is Macbeth's tragedy, however, that he accepts the version of the world offered to him by the witches. Yet at no stage do they compel acceptance of what they offer to him. The crime to which they incite him is committed by himself, and the responsibility for succumbing to the temptation is Macbeth's alone. He is his own betrayer. Macbeth's security depends on assumptions such as Birnham Wood moving to Dunsinane, and the fact that no man born of a woman will harm him. His life depends on appearances like these. His realisation about the falsity of this world of appearance and half-truths comes too late; only at the end of the tragedy does he realise that the witches have been

> juggling fiends . . .
> That palter with us in a double sense;
> (V, vii, line 48–49)

The witches tempt and entice. As evil agents they are catalysts with limited powers, but bring to the surface the latent evil that lies buried in the subconscious mind. Macbeth is his own destroyer, and at every stage in the play freely chooses his own course of action and freely commits himself to the whole world of evil and violence.

COMMENT
This is a question about the witches and whether or not they are creatures of absolute evil who control the soul of a character. The answer shows how the evil inherent in the witches is not absolute but simply sparks evil in others.
1. The first section of this answer explains the nature of the witches in the play and shows how they operate in deceiving characters.
2. The answer then develops by showing us the particular manner of the witches' evil operation in the play—their misleading language and statements.
3. The peculiar relationship between Macbeth and the witches is then outlined and Macbeth's free reactions are clearly drawn.
4. The answer concludes by demonstrating how the evil that governs the play begins in the witches' initial incitements but is freely adopted by Macbeth himself and carried to a dreadful extreme.

Silas Marner
(2004 only)
'The novel *Silas Marner* is not just a fairytale but also explores problems that affect real life.' Discuss this statement supporting your answer by quotation from or reference to the novel.

Sample answer
George Eliot described the novel as a 'tale of old-fashioned village life which unfolded itself from the merest millet-seed of thought'. Set in the imaginary village of Raveloe before the onslaught of the Industrial Revolution, the novel celebrates the strong old-fashioned and integrated sense of neighbourliness that prevailed before industrialisation. The central elements of a fairytale—loss of gold, recovery and restoration of happiness—govern the plot; yet the setting, characters, plot, dialect and detailed insight into life at that time prevent the novel from being merely a fairytale.

On one level, the novel *Silas Marner* could indeed be read as a simple fairytale about good and evil, beauty and ugliness, the rich man's folly and the poor man's triumph. Silas, with his bag of linen on his back, setting out from Lantern Yard, could seem like a figure from a fairytale as he goes to seek salvation in a distant land. This land is Raveloe, nestled in a snug well-wooded hollow in the heart of merry England, resembling a hamlet in a fairytale. The stone cottage heightens the air of romance that surrounds this story, resembling as it does a humble woodcutter's home. Even the characters could be figures that have stepped from a fairytale. Eppie with her golden hair and blue eyes could be a fairy princess, Dolly a fairy godmother, and Dunstan the age-old villain. Godfrey is the wicked brother who suffers for his wickedness and wildness, while Nancy saves him at the end. The evil characters are punished, and the good inevitably are rewarded. Like all fairy stories, the novel is made up of inexplicable events, such as the enigmatic disappearance of the gold, Godfrey's hidden past and double life, Dunstan's disappearance, and the mysterious arrival of Eppie.

The characters also resemble those of a fairytale. Eppie the princess is offered her rightful place in the castle (Red House) at the end; Silas's capacity to cure with herbs and potents emphasises the elements of mystery and magic that permeate the whole novel.

The language itself has fairytale connotations. The writer tells of the 'sleeping child', the 'shrunken rivulet', the 'song of birds and loving sunshine', the guineas rising in the iron pot year after year', with the miser counting his gold.

Despite these fairytale elements, however, the world of the novel is firmly rooted in reality and deals with real issues. Raveloe is set in the 'rich central plain of Merry England, where it was never reached by the vibrations of the coach horn or of public opinion' (Chapter 1). The time is clearly stated: before the Industrial Revolution. Raveloe becomes a symbol of a place that enjoys perfect freedom from industrialisation. Places such as the Rainbow are also symbolic of a certain style of life: 'the Rainbow was a luxurious resort for rich and stout husbands, whose wives have superfluous stores of linen.' (Chapter 5).

Our first glimpse into the Squirarchy, set against the background of the Napoleonic Wars, is given through the Red House, where we see Squire Cass's undisciplined lifestyle. We are told that in a very short space of time he idly feeds his deerhound with enough bits of 'beef to make a poor man's holiday dinner' (Chapter 9). This frequent comment on social waste is another issue that is treated ironically by the author. Early on in the novel we are told that 'there were many chiefs who could farm badly at their ease' (Chapter 1).

The novelist's purpose is not merely to describe character and incident in a vivid manner but to sustain, throughout the text, a subtle moral comment on many of the important social issues of the time. Her focus is on how weak will or evil can spread throughout society. For her the greatest sin is voluntary isolation from the community. Both of her leading protagonists, Godfrey and Silas, are reintegrated into Raveloe society. Through solidarity with other people they regain their self-esteem and status.

Eliot frequently interrupts the narrative to moralise or to teach some lesson. She condemns Godfrey's reliance on chance: 'Chance, the god of all men who follow their own devices instead of obeying a law they believe in,' (Chapter 9). The writer's view of life is 'as you sow so shall you reap'. Dunstan's soul sows spite and hatred, and he meets his death from a broken neck in the stone-pits. Marner's soul is simple and truthful, and he is rewarded with the love of Eppie.

Eliot has managed to balance her art in the novel and achieve a perfect blending of fantasy and realism. The fairytale elements are incorporated into a realistic setting where problems that are important to humankind are explored and analysed. She succeeds in creating a novel that not only entertains but also conveys rich insights into many important social issues of the time.

COMMENT

This is a question on two aspects of the novel—the fairytale features and the issues which make it a realistic social document.

The answer begins with a quotation from the novelist herself about her purpose in writing the story. It also sets out the background of the story clearly. The answer then develops by showing different aspects of how this novel could be treated on the level of a fairytale.

At each stage this answer makes reference to and quotes from the text to support the points made.

The second part of the answer takes account of the other aspect of the question, showing how the novel deals with real social issues. The answer concludes by referring back to the question and tying up all the points that have been made.

Possible types of questions for the study of a single text

Macbeth
(2003 and 2004 exams)
1. Discuss the way in which the language and imagery used in the play contribute to creating a world of evil and violence. Make reference to or quotation from the play in your answer.
2. What relevance has this play for a modern audience? Support your answer by reference to the play.
3. 'Banquo is not an innocent soldier who scorns the prophecies of the witches; he is a man whose upright principles have been deeply compromised.' Would you agree with this assessment of Banquo's character? Support your answer by quotation from or reference to the text.

Wuthering Heights
(2003 and 2004 exams)
1. 'The most interesting aspect of *Wuthering Heights* is the pattern of human relationships, especially the relationship between Catherine and Heathcliff.' Discuss this statement with reference to the novel.
2. 'The novelist has succeeded in creating an exciting world of imagination and passion.' Discuss this statement making reference in your answer to the writer's use of language and imagery.
3. 'Even though Catherine dies half way through the novel her presence dominates the entire plot.' Would you agree with this statement? Support your answer by reference to the text.

Silas Marner
(2004 exam only)
1. The novel *Silas Marner* is a realistic social document. Would you agree with this statement? Support your answer by reference to the novel.
2. Discuss the power of love to redeem in this novel. Make reference to the main plot and the sub-plot in your answer.
3. What is the role of the villagers in the novel *Silas Marner*? Support your answer by reference to the novel.

Amongst Women
(2003 and 2004 exams)
1. 'The novel *Amongst Women* is a realistic insight into Ireland in the early twenties.'

Comment on this statement in the light of your reading of the novel.
2. The story *Amongst Women* is about one man's attempts to impose his will on others. Test the truth of this statement from your reading of the novel.
3. Comment on the relevance of this novel for a modern reader. Make reference to the text to support your answer.

The Remains of the Day
(2003 exam only)
1. 'The situation of the woman is seen in a negative light in this novel.' Would you agree with this statement about the novel *The Remains of the Day*? Support your answer by reference to the novel.
2. Would you agree with the view that Stevens is a victim of the society at that time? Support your answer by reference to the novel.
3. The novel shows Stevens's blindness to the reality of his own life and the life around him. Would you agree with this statement? Support your answer by reference to the novel.

Death of a Salesman
(2003 exam only)
1. 'The play *Death of a Salesman* sets two different worlds side by side—the dreams of the past and the agonies of the present.' Would you agree with this statement? Support your answer by reference to the play.
2. Comment on the relevance of this play for a modern audience. Make reference to the play in your answer.
3. 'Linda is a tragic heroine who deserves the sympathy of the audience more than Willy.' Would you agree with this assessment of the character of Linda? Support your answer by reference to the play.

A Doll's House
(2004 exam only)
1. 'The play *A Doll's House* is a tragic play, which offers no solutions at the conclusion.' Would you agree with this statement? Support your answer by reference to the play.
2. 'Helmer is a tragic victim of blindness who gains the sympathy of the reader at the conclusion.' Would you agree with this assessment of Helmer's character? Support your answer by reference to the play.
3. 'The play *A Doll's House* is a realistic social document, which offers a vivid insight into the position of the woman in the mid-nineteenth century.' Would you agree with this assessment of the play? Support your answer by reference to the play.

The Comparative Study of Texts

What is a comparative study?

A comparative study of texts (play, novel or film) means the ability to focus on similarities or differences between texts, under such headings as
- the treatment of different issues or themes
- the genre and techniques used by the writer
- the social or cultural background or context
- the general vision or outlook of the text.

Theme or issue
(2003 and 2004 exams)
This is the central message presented by the writer, for example the themes of evil and the supernatural world in *Macbeth*, or the theme of revenge and passion in *Wuthering Heights*. At Higher level you must examine how a theme is developed in the text and what the writer's approach to it is.

The genre of a text
(2004 exam only)
Is the text
   a tragic play?
   a romantic novel?
   an autobiography?
   a travel book?

Plot and sub-plot
A plot is the sequence of events that happen in a story. A sub-plot is a lesser story within it, which may reflect the central action of the text.

Soliloquy
A soliloquy is a speech made by a character when alone; it is often an insight into the soul of a character.

Narrative technique
This is the way the story is told in the text. A story can be told in the *first person* or *third person*. In first-person narration the story is told from the point of view of the writer or narrator ('I'). In third-person narration the writer has an overview of the whole story, like an uninvolved outsider who observes events.

Cultural context or social background
(2003 and 2004 exams)
The setting of a text includes the physical or geographical background, for example the marshes in *Great Expectations*, or the moors in England in the novel *Wuthering Heights*.

Under the heading 'Cultural context or social background' study the text with regard to
- its cultural situation
- social customs, particular traditions or rituals
- national or class differences
- beliefs and values held by characters
- the role of women and men
- the importance of work in the society
- religious beliefs and practices
- power structures and political issues.

Some examples of the cultural context are Nigeria at the beginning of the colonial period in *Things Fall Apart* by Chinua Achebe, and England prior to the Industrial Revolution in the novel *Silas Marner*.

The general vision and viewpoint
(2003 exam only)
You should be able to compare and contrast the different ways of looking at life in the text and see whether there is a coherence, or lack of coherence, between these viewpoints.

ANSWERING A QUESTION ON THE COMPARATIVE STUDY OF TEXTS

1. Know exactly what your three texts for this section are. Take one of these as your main text.
2. Spend time choosing your question. Identify clearly what exactly you are asked in the question: is it a question on themes or issues, or genre, or on cultural context and social background?
3. Begin by working on a rough draft. Work with the main text first. Jot down five or six different points related to the question based on that text. Make sure in each point to have a quotation or reference related to that point.

4. Write out your answer in draft form, using the main text only.
5. Look at the other two texts, and draw in the main points of each text, showing how they compare or contrast. You can do this in two ways: add on some ideas from the two texts to each paragraph, or simply write a separate paragraph on each text, outlining how it is related to the question.
6. All the material from your texts must be tied in to your answer in a fluid and natural way. Don't divide your answer with sub-headings with the title of the texts at the top. The main thing is to link or weave in the texts naturally and to show how they relate to the question, jotting down all points of comparison or contrast between the texts.
7. Organise your points into paragraphs, and make sure you have used quotation or reference from the texts as much as possible.
8. Put priority and order on your points, and make sure each point refers in some way to the question asked.
9. Start writing the answer, and stop at the end of each paragraph to examine what relevance it has to the question.

DRAFT QUESTIONS AND SAMPLE ANSWERS

In the following examples, the method of organising and assembling material for an answer on the comparative question is shown in rough draft form. There are sample questions on *theme or issue* and on *cultural context*. Study the method carefully, and try to apply it to the possible types of questions on the comparative section, which are shown at the end of this chapter.

Sample question on theme or issue
Discuss how the theme or issue of 'love' is treated in the texts you have studied as part of your comparative course.

Stage 1: Identify the texts
   Silas Marner (novel)—the main or anchor text
   The Playboy of the Western World (play)
   On the Waterfront (film)

Stage 2: Analyse the question
This is a question on the issue or theme of 'love' as it is shown in the three texts.

Stage 3: Sketch out the main points from the anchor text
Take the main text (*Silas Marner*), and work out a rough draft on the question, using the whole text. Show how the absence of love destroys Marner. Highlight the negative aspects of a lack of love. Contrast the soul of Marner when he begins to love Eppie.

Stage 4: Sketch the principal points on this theme from the other two texts
Begin to make judgments at this stage about the comparisons and contrasts between the three texts.

Stage 5: Start writing up your answer
Throughout your answer, refer back to the question and draw in all three texts.

Stage 6: Concluding paragraph
Make sure to tie together all the points you have made. At this stage make some evaluations or judgments about the theme and the comparisons and similarities in the texts.

Stage 7: Write out the answer fully, using all texts and references
SAMPLE ANSWER
Each of the three texts—the novel *Silas Marner*, the film *On the Waterfront* and the play *The Playboy of the Western World*—deals with the theme of love in a different way. Love is shown to be central to these texts and to influence the actions and dispositions of the central characters.

In the novel *Silas Marner*, Marner, an old weaver, has been banished by his community from Lantern Yard where he grew up and was educated. This community professed strict Calvinistic beliefs, and rejected him, having drawn lots to decide his culpability. His supposed best friend, William Dane, betrays him by slandering his reputation and marrying his girl.

Marner loses his faith in God and in humankind and proceeds to settle on the outskirts of a small village called Raveloe. Here he becomes a sterile recluse and spends his days weaving for the local villagers and accumulating tons of gold. As he gets richer, his isolation and self-absorption intensify. He is finally rescued from the clutches of this sterile and destructive isolation by love. Love literally crawls up to his door in the form of a small child who is later named Eppie. Marner adopts Eppie and begins to pour out the love that earlier had been poured into his gold. Love redeems him from the stagnant and negative lifestyle that he had slipped into. It opens up new horizons in his soul, 'his large brown eyes seem to have gathered a more answering gaze'.

As the years unfold and Marner is faced with the responsibility for Eppie's education, he is forced to seek help outside himself. A local woman who is kind and generous, called Dolly Winthrop, lends him a hand. She offers him practical advice on how to rear Eppie and advises him to return to the church and have Eppie christened. Through Dolly's intervention and friendly advice, Marner regains his lost faith and begins to practice his religion again. All of this occurs because of his deep, undoubted devotion and love for Eppie.

As the events unfold in the novel, and Eppie becomes a young woman, Marner blossoms also and regains his lost youthfulness and faith in humankind. He begins to see that there is another will which he does not understand, but sees that this is a good will: 'Them as was at the making on us, and knows better and has a better will.'

He achieves his crowning fulfilment when he leads Eppie to the altar rails for her marriage to Aaron Winthrop, Dolly's son. Undoubtedly, all of this has been achieved through the power of love.

Likewise, the theme of love is treated in a dramatically distinct way in the drama entitled *The Playboy of the Western World*. Set in Mayo in the early twentieth century, most of the action takes place within a small pub or shebeen owned by Michael James Flaherty.

The plot centres on the arrival of a dirty young fellow who calls himself Christy Mahon. His arrival in the pub provokes a great deal of curiosity and interest from the locals, among whom figures Pegeen Mike, the fiery daughter of the publican. His story of how he killed his father with 'the blow of a loy' enthralls all of these peasants, who are on the way to a funeral. Hungry for romance, excitement and glamour of any kind, these people, and in particular Pegeen, nourish the illusion of greatness and heroism within Christy to such an extent that, before long, he believes that he really has slit his father with one blow to the belt of his breeches.

Pegeen is a sorry figure, starved as she is of any excitement or romance. She is hungry for a hero in this small and remote place in west Mayo and within minutes her imagination is creating a real hero in the figure of Christy. Initially Christy is surprised at all the attention, but his vanity is flattered, and within a few hours both Pegeen and Christy are declaring their eternal love for one another in heightened romantic language.

Before Christy's arrival, Pegeen had been engaged to Shawn Keogh, a dull but rich farmer. Within a few hours of Christy's arrival, she is renouncing Shawn and declaring she will marry Christy. Now with her image of the new glorified Christy, her imagination takes flight and they both foresee a future filled with unparalleled joy and happiness.

Their love is short-lived, however. It is rudely shattered with the arrival of Christy's father, Old Mahon, who exposes Christy as a liar and 'a dirty stuttering lout'. Within minutes Pegeen's romantic love is no more. The glamorised and heroic image of Christy as a gallant fellow is cruelly shattered. Pegeen banishes him from the house while at the same time lamenting her loss in the words 'I've lost the only playboy of the western world.'

Love in this text has a more tragic conclusion. Built on shaky foundations where the main characters fail to know one another well enough, we bear witness to the grim irony of the conclusion. Pegeen, hungry for love, creates an ideal figure in Christy. In the course of the play he actually does reach this level from his own interaction within this community. She fails to see and understand this growth, however. She only sees the lie at the end and ironically banishes him, to be left alone with the sterile love of Shawn Keogh.

In the film *On the Waterfront* we are given a totally different setting. This time it is on the docklands of New Jersey in the fifties. The story centres on Terry, a young boxer who has been bullied by a criminal gang under Johnny Friendly. Terry feels a failure and an outsider. He is caught in this murky world of corrupt dealings, as his brother Charley is Johnny's right-hand man. Terry meets a girl called Edie and falls in love with her. It so happens that Terry had a hand in her brother's death, unknown to him. Their love grows against the backdrop of violence, bullying of dockers from Friendly's gang and corruption. Terry is clearly frustrated and decides to make a stance. Under the instigation of the local priest Terry decides to tell Edie about his involvement in her brother's death.

This revelation leads his relationship with her to another level. Initially, she is shattered and rejects Terry. Terry now takes a clear stance against Friendly's gang, who control the workers in this area, and decides to inform the police. His brother Charley is brutally murdered by the gang. Terry, now totally enraged, challenges Johnny to a fight and ends up badly beaten. He triumphs, however, at the conclusion, by leading the men to regain their position as workers in the docks and defying Johnny's gang. Love enables him to assert his rights and triumph over corruption.

In all three texts love is seen in different characters and distinct contexts. True self-sacrificing love overcomes the evil and negativity of lives in the novel *Silas Marner*, and in the film *On the Waterfront*. A love that is glamorised and alien from ordinary life is shown to dissipate easily with the exposure of truth in the drama *The Playboy of the Western World*.

Comment

This is a question on one theme or issue in the three texts you have studied for the comparative course.

Identify your texts clearly. The first paragraph answers the question clearly and shows specifically how, in each text, the theme of love is reflected and which characters are involved.

The answer develops by discussing one character from the text *Silas Marner* and underlining how love redeems him from his self-imposed isolation.

A contrast is drawn with the next text, *The Playboy of the Western World*. Here we see how love is based on a flimsy relationship between the two main characters. This answer draws a contrast in the type of love shown and illustrates how this type of love evaporates at the conclusion of the play.

Finally, the answer compares love in the third text. In this case the text chosen is a film. Here again both the background and characters are different. The love however is true and good and succeeds in triumphing over the evil in the world of this film.

The last paragraph makes a statement on the theme as it is dealt with in the three texts. Here you have an opportunity to weigh up and draw various comparisons and contrasts between the three texts. In this case the power of selfless, true love is shown to conquer evil, in contrast with the negative quality of love, which is based only on glamour, romance and stylised speech.

	Love	Characters
Silas Marner	Silas is redeemed from isolation through love	Silas and Eppie Eppie and Aaron
The Playboy of the Western World	Love is idealised and evaporates	Pegeen and Christy Pegeen and Shawn Keogh
On the Waterfront	Love unites people and overcomes corruption	Terry and Edie

Sample question on cultural context

In the three texts you have selected for comparative study, compare the societies from the viewpoint of the degree of personal freedom allowed to their members. Make reference to a key situation in your answer.

Stage 1: Identify texts
    The Remains of the Day (novel)—the main or anchor text
    Macbeth (play)
    My Left Foot (film)

Stage 2: Analyse the question
This is a question on how the various societies in the texts help or hinder the individual freedom of a person.

Stage 3: Sketch out the main points from the anchor text
Identify the type of society in the main text *The Remains of the Day*. Outline how this society contributes or not to the expression of Stevens's sense of freedom. Pick out one key situation which illustrates your stance on the question and shows whether society does or does not help individual freedom. Draw a conclusion on the relationship between the society and the freedom of the individuals as shown in the novel.

Stage 4: Sketch the principal points on this theme from the other two texts
Jot down some points on the other two texts, on the type of society and how this influences the freedom of the people involved. Compare the different types of society and start making judgments about how each one either helps or hinders individual freedom.

Stage 5: Start writing up your answer
Throughout your answer, refer back to the question and draw in all three texts.

Stage 6: Concluding paragraph
Make sure to draw your conclusions together in this final paragraph. At this stage make contrasts and comparisons between the different texts, and evaluate what the three texts say about this question.

Stage 7: Write out the answer fully, using all texts and references
SAMPLE ANSWER
The societies represented in the three texts are noticeably different. The individuals that inhabit these various societies each possess, in their own unique way, a certain degree of personal freedom. In many respects the freedom of these individuals is affected by their particular society or environment.

    The texts I will discuss for this answer are *The Remains of the Day* by Kazuo Ishiguro, the film *My Left Foot* directed by Jim Sheridan and the Shakespearean play *Macbeth*.

    The society that is represented in the novel *The Remains of the Day* is England in the period spanning 1922–56. It is a time when the large old English houses with their lords and ladies flourished. By contrast, the type of society represented in the film *My Left Foot* is working-class Dublin in the early twentieth century. The society which is shown in the play *Macbeth* is war-torn Scotland in the early seventeenth century.

The Remains of the Day, narrated by Stevens, a butler, gives us an insight into life inside a large British house in the early twentieth century. Stevens's life has been contained within the walls of this house. As he frequently states in the novel, he has had the privilege of seeing the best of England from within these walls. Undivided loyalty and service to Lord Darlington is the primary motivating factor for Stevens. He sacrifices everything in order to serve Lord Darlington in the most selfless and absolute way. He considers himself privileged to have the opportunity to serve in such a manner. He also believes that he is fulfilling his purpose in life, and thus exercising his personal freedom to the fullest extent, by sustaining this single-minded commitment to his employer. The key situation that demonstrates this point is when Stevens's father suffers a stroke and dies. Stevens is involved in organising the household in preparation for an important international conference at Darlington Hall. It so happens that Lord Darlington has invited several prestigious political figures in order to win them over to his way of thinking with regard to the situation in Germany. Stevens is aware of all this and is very concerned that the meeting will be successful. When his father becomes seriously ill that night Stevens does not relinquish his duties in any way, but instead arranges for Miss Kenton to call the doctor, and even asks her to lay his father out when he dies later on that night. Stevens then articulates the fact that he felt he had truly come of age as a butler that night, and he recalls the occasion with a profound sense of triumph. Stevens truly believes that he has done the right thing; that he has exercised the highest possible level of personal freedom in sacrificing his family interests for Lord Darlington's cause.

The working class society of Dublin in the fifties forms the background of the story in the film *My Left Foot*. Christy Brown is born into a large family and is forced to live in extremely cramped conditions, in which he has to contend with physical disability in the form of cerebral palsy. He spends much of his early life huddled under the staircase with only a confined space to move around in. However, this limited environment does not prevent him from exercising his personal freedom to the full. Christy manages to transcend the limitations of these cramped conditions and his handicap and attain the status of a famous artist. The bonds of friendship, of warm happy human relationships, are greater than the frustrations of his environment, and enable him to move forward and prove himself as an artist. In addition, the support of all his family, and in particular the strong love of his mother, prove to be a much greater and more enabling support than any material conditions. The key situation that demonstrates the powerful support of his family is when Christy's mother begins to build a room for him, in an effort to rouse his spirits from depression after he is disappointed in his love for his therapist. Christy's depressed spirits are quickly dispelled when he begins to understand the huge capacity for sacrifice in his mother's efforts, and he changes his disposition. He begins to paint again and to express his freedom as an artist.

So, ironically, Christy gains the means to achieve success as a prestigious artist in spite of his apparently very negative circumstances. Even when we witness how he moves on to another social level in his support of Lord Castlewellan's charity event, we are still aware of the undoubted power of these family bonds to consolidate the unique freedom of the individual.

The play *Macbeth* shows us a man who is governed by the unfulfilled ambition to become king. Macbeth earns enormous and undoubted prestige because of his loyalty and valour in serving Scotland as a soldier. However, it is clear that in spite of his success and achievements Macbeth is not free. His mind hungers for kingship. He is married to a ruthless woman who incessantly attacks his lack of manhood because he refuses to commit murder. The key situation, which represents Macbeth tortured with doubts and overcome with fear and anxiety, occurs shortly before he murders Banquo. He tells his wife his mind is full of scorpions because Banquo and Fleance still live. Earlier in this situation we hear Lady Macbeth articulating how restless she also feels even though Duncan is dead: 'Tis safer to be that which we destroy than by destruction dwell in doubtful joy.' This woman who had earlier gloried in her mastery over her husband now finds herself powerless against her own insecurity. Both of these characters have failed to reach the high level of freedom that they thought would come with the crown.

As the play develops and the plot unfolds, kingship only severs the link between these characters and draws them further away from society. They may have attained their heart's desire in gaining the crown, but tragically it has not brought them any happiness nor any internal freedom. They each go their way alone and to their doom.

In three totally different societies governed by very different personalities the question of personal freedom is shown in distinct and unique ways. Of all the societies represented in the texts, the one in *Macbeth* offers more possibilities for happiness and the exercise of personal freedom. Yet ironically this society offers only frustration because of the various motivating factors within the characters. Yet the cramped conditions of the big house in England and of working-class Dublin in the fifties are the backgrounds against which Stevens and Christy attain undoubted satisfaction with their lives. Within these different societies they are able to claim a sense of triumph with their achievements and without question realise the full potential of their freedom.

Comment
This is a question on cultural context. There are three chosen texts—a Shakespearean play, a novel and a film set in working-class Dublin. The answer limits itself to discussing one central character and showing how the environment or the society either hinders or helps that person to realise their full freedom.

The answer begins by discussing the text *The Remains of the Day* and showing how the society in this novel influences the central character, Stevens. The answer then goes on to give a picture of a key situation which highlights this fact. In this situation we see how Stevens achieves a profound degree of internal freedom from within the walls of Darlington Hall.

The answer then moves on to talk about a different type of society in a different text—this time a film. A parallel is drawn between the characters of Christy and Stevens insofar as both succeed in exercising their freedom from within their particular society.

The answer concludes by drawing in the third text, *Macbeth*. In this case a contrast is drawn with the other two texts. The society may have more material advantages, but as the logic of events shows, it fails to offer the necessary degree of personal freedom to the individuals involved.

The answer concludes by summing up the main points made in the world of the three different texts and drawing a contrast between them.

Remember to use your conclusion to weigh up or evaluate the various differences and similarities which you have noticed as you developed your answer.

	Cultural context	Personal Freedom
The Remains of the Day	England 1922–56	Stevens as butler expresses his freedom in Darlington Hall
My Left Foot	Working-class Dublin early twentieth century	Christy Browne attains prestige and freedom in spite of physical disability
Macbeth	Early seventeenth-century Scotland	Neither Macbeth nor his wife attain freedom through kingship

POSSIBLE TYPES OF QUESTIONS ON THE COMPARATIVE STUDY OF TEXTS

Themes or issues
(2003 and 2004 exams)
1. Show how your understanding of a particular theme or issue has been deepend or changed from the study of three different texts on your course.
2. Compare and contrast the issue or theme of self-discovery in any three texts on your course.
3. In three different texts on your course, take one central theme or issue treated by the writer. In the case of each text, show how this theme or issue has been developed or treated by the writer.

Literary genre
(2004 exam only)
1. Take three different texts on your course and show how each writer uses a different method to tell the story.
2. Compare three different texts under one of the following headings:
   tragedy
   social realism
   romance

3. With regard to three different texts on your course, discuss the various methods used by each writer in the opening of their texts. In your answer, concentrate on the relationship between opening and conclusion in each one, and discuss which you consider to be most effective.

Cultural context
(2003 and 2004 exams)
1. With regard to three different texts on your course, show the difference between the value system presented by each writer. State which text you consider to be the most effective, and why.
2. 'Racism forms part of the cultural background of many of the texts on your course.' In the case of three different texts, discuss how this issue is treated.
3. Take one central character from three different texts on your course. In the case of each one, outline how the cultural context of each text has influenced that character. Which text do you consider to be the most effective? Give your reasons why.

General vision or viewpoint
(2003 exam only)
1. Show how the general vision or viewpoint in the texts you have studied as part of your comparative course is related or not to the actual events which occur in the texts.
2. Compare the general vision or viewpoint in the texts you have studied for your comparative course under one of the following headings,
- optimistic
- pessimistic
- unexpected.
3. Identify the general vision in the texts you have studied as part of your comparative course. In your opinion which of these were the most interesting? Give reasons for your answer.

Notes on Some Prescribed Texts

WUTHERING HEIGHTS
Emily Brontë
(2003 and 2004 exams)

Historical and literary background
Wuthering Heights was first published in 1847 in England. The Brontës lived in Haworth, Yorkshire. The novel is set against the background of the wild moors of Yorkshire.

The story
The story is told by two narrators, Nelly Dean, the housekeeper at Wuthering Heights, and Lockwood, who takes over as tenant of the Heights. The story spans three generations and is centred on two main houses, Wuthering Heights and Thrushcross Grange. It begins with Old Earnshaw who has two children, Cathy and Hindley. They live in the Heights. Old Earnshaw returns from Liverpool with a bundle, which turns out to be a boy that he found wandering along the streets. He is called Heathcliff from then on. Hindley and he become bitter enemies. However, Cathy and Heathcliff develop a deep and passionate relationship. These two characters spend their time on the moors. One day they accidentally meet the Lintons who live at Thrushcross Grange. Isabella and her brother Edgar live at the Grange with their parents. Cathy is attacked by their dog and is forced to stay in the Grange until she recovers. Heathcliff is sent home in disgrace.

    Cathy returns after several weeks from the Grange, a changed woman. She is flattered by the attention from the Lintons and in particular Edgar. She develops a double side to her character. She acknowledges to Nelly Dean that it would shame her to marry Heathcliff and he accidentally overhears a part of her conversation. He leaves the Heights for three years and returns when Catherine has been married to Edgar for three years. Heathcliff is changed. He is filled with revenge. He moves into the Heights where Hindley lives alone. He gambles and succeeds in gaining all the property from Hindley, and robs Hareton, Hindley's son, of his lawful inheritance.

Meanwhile Isabella develops an infatuation for Heathcliff and elopes with him. Cathy warns her, but in vain. Isabella escapes from Heathcliff shortly after her marriage when she discovers his true nature, and settles in London. There she gives birth to a young boy who is named Linton. She dies shortly after this. Heathcliff uses young Linton to avenge himself on Edgar and Cathy. Edgar and Cathy also have a child whom they call Cathy. Shortly after giving birth Cathy dies. Heathcliff tricks young Cathy into marrying young Linton and so gains possession of the Heights. Heathcliff dies at the end a tortured soul who is clearly haunted by the presence of the ghostly Catherine. Lockwood buys the Heights from Heathcliff at the conclusion.

Themes or issues
- passion and love
- betrayal and loyalty
- revenge
- the supernatural

Genre
This novel belongs to the genre of romance. In this novel Emily Brontë constantly and vividly parallels inner states and feelings with nature: human emotions, moods, internal states and character development are all mirrored in the natural world and in particular in the wild moors.

Narrative technique
There are two different narrators: Nelly Dean and Lockwood. Nelly Dean is an ordinary woman who is housekeeper for three generations of the Earnshaws and later on the Linton household. Lockwood is a young man from London with plenty of money and time on his hands, who takes over tenancy of the Heights towards the conclusion of the story. Both of these ordinary and readily identifiable narrators tell a story of extraordinary supernatural dimensions. They serve the function of bringing otherwise incredible and unrealistic events within the reader's grasp and understanding. They are used as a means to give this incredible story a foothold in the normal world of everyday affairs.

The narrative technique also makes use of flashback. The first chapter begins at the conclusion and the remainder of the narrative recounts the events of the story through extended flashback. In many respects, the effect of this device in narration is to disorientate the reader and enable them realise that this story is not dealing with normal life.

Style
The style of the novel *Wuthering Heights* is that of a 'poetic prose'. As Charlotte Brontë, Emily's sister, states in her preface to the novel: 'It is rustic all through. It is Moorish

and wild and knotty as the root of heath. Its colouring is of mellow grey and moorland moss clothes; and heath with its blooming bells and balmy fragrance. Her description of natural scenery are what they should be, and all that they should be.'

The novel makes use of many images on a richly symbolic level. Nature is used in a symbolic manner throughout. It can symbolise strife, discord, and moral decay. The storm, thunder and lightning, together with the repeated references to fire, are all used to show the profound depths of violence and heightened passion that dominate the atmosphere.

The actual locations of the two houses mentioned in the novel, Thrushcross Grange and Wuthering Heights, are also used as symbols. The Grange is set in a leafy valley while the Heights is exposed to 'atmospheric tumult' of every kind. The atmosphere within the Heights exudes a profound spiritual degeneration while that in the Grange is civilised and controlled.

Cultural context

The novel is set in nineteenth-century England. We get a vision of two different life-styles in the Heights and the Grange. The life-style in the Heights is wild and uncontrolled. Within the Grange there is rich luxury, 'a splendid place carpeted with crimson, a pure white ceiling bordered by gold, a shower of glass-drops hanging in silver chains from the centre'.

Through the figure of Joseph we gain an insight into the strict harshness of Calvinism. He is a rigid and intransigent figure who spends his time preaching at the children.

Through Nelly Dean we see the role of the housekeeper. In this particular context Nelly is more a mother figure for the children than an actual employee within the house.

General vision or viewpoint

At the conclusion of the novel Heathcliff is ultimately left with power, a power that he finds intolerable and painful. He is consumed with a hell fire, but yet refuses to repent. The heaven of others is entirely unvalued, uncoveted by him. His death is explicitly pagan; he wants no minister, no mourners and no prayers to be said for his soul. In Heathcliff's death, there is a sense that evil has destroyed itself, that the fire of hatred and destruction that eats its way through his system and through the novel has burned itself out. His power for wickedness has been his punishment, just as his passion for Catherine was a curse, not a blessing. He destroys himself throughout the book, thereby showing how true is Isabella's earlier statement that 'treachery and violence are a double-ended spear, which wound the inflictors more than the sufferers.'

The actual conclusion of the novel gives the reader an image of a happy, harmonious and natural human love. The ending shows the happy marriage of Cathy to Hareton; Heathcliff's revenge plans are frustrated; property is restored to its rightful owners and Nelly Dean takes delight in her 'children's happiness'. All of this is cleverly juxtaposed with an image of pain, rapture and ghostly phenomena. Two types of love are simultaneously affirmed at the conclusion; the ghostly vision of Heathcliff and

Catherine as they wander the moors shows us that in some way they too have attained their heaven, while simultaneously we are given the vision of Hareton and young Cathy in a state of blissful union walking in the moors.

AMONGST WOMEN

John McGahern
(2003 and 2004 exams)

Historical and literary background
This novel is set in Ireland in the times following the Irish War of Independence 1919–22.

The story
The narrative starts at the conclusion of the story. Moran is an old Republican who was a guerilla leader in the War of Independence. His wife is dead and he is left to bring up their five children; three girls and two boys. Luke is the oldest and he has gone to work in London because he will not tolerate his father's violent behaviour. Moran can never forget the authority he wielded during the war and tries to behave in the same way within his household. He continually uses the rosary to regain control and power over his family. Moran marries a girl called Rose Brady when he is beginning to get old. Initially Rose is very idealistic about the marriage, but she soon discovers the true nature of Moran and his capacity for violence and dark moods.

Rose is a very selfless person who clearly loves Moran in spite of his strong character and difficult temperament. She encourages the girls to become independent and achieve the best they can in life. Maggie settles in London and eventually marries, as does Sheila. Mona gets a good job in the civil service and remains single. Michael, the youngest, leaves and marries. Luke's refusal to return to Great Meadow, the family home, frustrates and angers Moran greatly. All the rest of the family visit him regularly in spite of the fact that he has been domineering and violent. They are all happy together and have learned to accept Moran's peculiar temperament. Moran dies at the conclusion. Everyone except Luke turns up at his funeral and acclaim him as a truly great and heroic man.

Themes
- power and pride
- the power of the family
- war
- stubbornness

Genre
A social document that is set in Ireland in the period following the War of Independence.

Narrative technique
The story is told in flashback. The opening pages of the novel give a picture of Moran towards the end of his life when his family pay regular visits to Great Meadow. Then the novel is narrated in the third person. There are no formal chapters; the narrative is broken into sections separated by a short space. A lot of the story is told through dialogue, which gives a vivid insight into the various characters.

Cultural context
The background is Ireland in a period following war in the early twentieth century. We hear references to reviving Monaghan Day, which is obviously a tradition of the time. The story is set in the country and outlines the position of the family at that time. Family bonds were strong. The Moran family is united, with the exception of Luke, in spite of their father's erratic temperament.

We also see the faithful practice of the holy rosary. This is a prayer that is said by the family every night. Moran makes use of this means to acquit himself, and refuse to face his own shortcomings. He also uses it as the only way he can exert his power over people, in this case his family.

Women marry securely in this society. Secure jobs such as the civil service are recommended. Study at the university is not financially viable for Sheila. The profession of doctor is also not acceptable within this family because the doctors had emerged as the bigwigs in the country that Moran had fought for during the war.

One of Moran's key fears is being poor. For that reason he is miserly with money and even though he eventually gets two pensions he still exerts a tight control over the finances. He also takes pride in the land he owns. He uses the land as a refuge, many times escaping from the house to work furiously at hay-making or reaping whenever he loses control of himself.

At the conclusion, on his death, Moran is given the typical Republican burial with the tricolor draped over his coffin.

General vision or viewpoint
The implication at the conclusion is that Moran's family is stronger than ever in their love and allegiance to one another. They truly recognise that Moran played a central part in all their lives. Their attendance at his funeral strengthens this bond between them even more. They realise that each one of them, in different ways, has truly imbibed Moran's beliefs and values. They remain loyal to his person and beliefs in spite of everything. Only Luke remains obstinate in his decision not to return home—a reminder that he has inherited a great deal of stubbornness and pride from his own father.

Silas Marner

George Eliot
(2004 exam only)

Historical and literary background
The historical background of this novel is just before the Industrial Revolution in England in the early nineteenth century.

The story
The opening chapter moves from the past to the present by showing us the attitude of the Raveloe people to the profession of the weaver. It also records Marner's treatment by the brethren in Lantern Yard and how he was banished from that community because he was accused of stealing money from an old parishioner. The community in Lantern Yard was a strict Puritan group who judged his guilt on the basis of drawing lots. Marner's best friend, William Dane, a member of this community, betrays him by slandering his reputation and later goes on to marry Marner's girl.

Marner settles on the outskirts of Raveloe, a small village in the heart of England. There he becomes a recluse for fifteen years and spends his time accumulating money by weaving for the local people.

In Raveloe there is a rich family by the name of Cass. Squire Cass is an arrogant man who has two weak and dissolute sons—Godfrey and Dunstan. Godfrey is secretly married to a drug addict and they have a child. Dunstan bribes Godfrey and manages to get his horse. He has an accident outside Marner's cottage and steals his gold. Dunstan later dies when he falls into the quarry near the cottage.

Meanwhile Molly, Godfrey's wife, decides to pay a visit with her child to Raveloe. It is New Year's Eve and Godfrey is having a party to honour Nancy Lammeter whom he hopes to marry. Molly dies on the way and her child accidentally crawls into Silas's cottage while he is having a cataleptic fit. Silas discovers the child and thinks that it is his gold returned. He decides to adopt the child and bring it up as his own. He christens it Eppie. A local woman, Dolly Winthrop, helps him to manage Eppie.

Godfrey marries Nancy. They are unable to have a child. Eppie grows up and becomes engaged to Dolly's son, Aaron Winthrop.

Dunstan's body is discovered in the quarry with the gold of Marner. Godfrey is forced to tell Nancy about his wife and child. They decide to adopt Eppie but she refuses to leave Marner. At the conclusion Eppie marries Aaron.

Themes or issues
- the power of love to redeem
- deception and betrayal
- the strict and rigid nature of Calvinism
- the self-destructive quality of isolation

Genre
The novel *Silas Marner* belongs to the genre of social realism. It gives a realistic insight into rural life in England before the onslaught of the Industrial Revolution. Under this heading also study the following:

The structure of the novel
The first chapter blends past and present, and gives us an insight into the reasons why Marner has settled on the outskirts of the village of Raveloe.

The novel is divided into two parts. There is a time lapse of sixteen years between Part I and Part II. This serves the function of showing the development of the plot: Squire Cass is dead, Nancy is married to Godfrey and Eppie is eighteen years old.

There are two plots: a main plot (Marner's story), and a sub-plot (Godfrey's story). These stories parallel one another.

Eliot makes use of the cataleptic fits to develop the plot. It is significant that, in Part II, when Marner has attained happiness in loving Eppie the fits disappear.

Style
The style of the novel is richly symbolic. The names and locations of places are used as symbols. Raveloe, an easy-going place, lies in the rich central plain of Merry England. Lantern Yard is used ironically. It prides itself on being a strong religious community, yet it is a place that offers no light, and significantly at the conclusion when Eppie and Marner return to look for it, it has disappeared.

Eliot makes use of a didactic or moralistic style to teach or instruct on certain issues such as duty and personal responsibility for one's actions. She also uses this tone to articulate her views on society at that time. For example when Dunstan goes to tell his father, Squire Cass, about the accident with his horse, we are told how 'Fleet the deerhound consumed enough bits of beef to make a poor man's holiday dinner.'

The writer makes use of gold as a symbol of love. There are repeated references to Eppie's golden hair, which is obviously intended to replace the stolen gold. Many fairytale motifs are used—the accumulation of the gold by the miserly weaver, the loss of the gold, the recovery of the loss in the form of a child, the villain, the fairy godmother (Dolly).

Cultural context
We gain an insight into the old English way of life before the Industrial Revolution. The novel is set in the days when spinning wheels hummed busily in farmhouses. It celebrates the integrated sense of neighbourliness that was a hallmark of life before the onset of the Industrial Revolution. The whole story spans thirty years of an era of rapid change in England. The conclusion of the story shows the beginnings of Industrialisation in England.

The story is set in the period of the Napoleonic wars when the price of agricultural goods was high, so farmers were free to farm badly at their ease. This is particularly the case in the highest social class at that time, the Squirarchy. Eliot attacks this particular class through the figure of Squire Cass and his two dissolute sons Dunstan and Godfrey.

Class structures are clearly marked out in the novel. Each person has their own place in society and keeps to it. Godfrey, by marrying below his class, has allowed himself to be dragged into mud and slime.

Calvinism is shown in the portrait of Lantern Yard. The insight given in the novel is dark and negative. They profess a belief in revelation and the drawing of lots. This is how justice is exercised within this community. The beliefs and practices of Lantern Yard are shown to be destructive of human fellowship and human community.

General vision or viewpoint

The general vision at the conclusion is that the old community life as exemplified in Raveloe is slowly vanishing with the onset of industrialisation. The Industrial Revolution is seen negatively. When Marner and Eppie return to pay a visit to Lantern Yard, they find that everyone is in a hurry. Eppie describes it as 'a dark ugly place. How it hides the sky, it's worse than the Workhouse.' We learn about the cramped conditions of life and the bad smell.

One of Eliot's beliefs was 'as you sow so shall you reap'. Marner sows love and kindness and so he reaps happiness in the figure of Eppie, who in turn is united in marriage to Aaron. Godfrey sows deception and selfishness and so he reaps a marriage that turns out to be childless. The general vision is that one must live with the results of one's deeds and take responsibility for one's actions. The power of love to redeem is also evident at the conclusion.

THE REMAINS OF THE DAY

Kazuo Ishiguro
(2003 exam only)

Historical and literary background

The events in this novel take place in the period spanning 1922 to 1956 in England. In 1956 England experienced the Suez crisis, which represented an attack on her colonial powers abroad. The novel deals with the crisis in Europe prior to and including World War II. The Versailles Treaty had been drawn up with strict measures operating against Germany. Lloyd George is the Prime Minister of Britain during the time of this story.

The story

The novel begins in 1956. Stevens, who is a butler in Darlington Hall in England, tells the story. At the beginning of the story, Stevens is working for Mr Farraday, an American gentleman who now owns Darlington Hall. Stevens undertakes a visit to Cornwall. The journey takes six days during which Stevens travels through different parts of England. His purpose is to meet a former employee called Miss Kenton. She is now married and has become Mrs Benn. Her marriage has not been happy, however. Formerly she had worked as housekeeper in the Hall while Lord Darlington was alive.

Stevens hopes that Miss Kenton may rejoin the staff at Darlington Hall, because he is now getting old and needs staff. During the trip Stevens recalls certain vivid incidents from the past through flashback.

Through Stevens's recollections of the past we learn about his father who came to work at Darlington Hall when he was already an old man and a long-serving butler. He died of a stroke in the Hall during an important international conference in 1923. We also learn that Lord Darlington was sympathetic to the Nazi cause—Stevens recalls an incident when Lord Darlington sacked two maidservants who happened to be Jews.

It is clear from Stevens's comments and story that he and Miss Kenton had an attachment for one another. However, Stevens was very committed to his work as a butler and to serving Lord Darlington to the best of his ability. Eventually Miss Kenton leaves the Hall and marries Mr Benn. Several people hint to Stevens that Lord Darlington is mistaken in his political views but Stevens refuses to listen to them. Lord Darlington's efforts to serve the German cause turn out to be misguided and as a result he dies an isolated and broken man. Mr Farraday, an American, buys the Hall. The staff is reduced. Stevens, however, remains in the Hall working as a butler.

Stevens recalls how he met Miss Kenton, now Mrs Benn, on a bench at the pier. She tells him that she has learned to accept the limitations of life and has grown to love her husband after many years. It becomes clear from her conversation that she was truly in love with Stevens. He is heartbroken. Eventually she leaves on a bus.

At the conclusion Stevens meets a retired butler on a bench beside the pier. Stevens tells him that he feels his life has been a waste. The man however advises him to stop looking back at the past and adopt a positive attitude; to enjoy the remains of the day. Stevens decides to do this; to follow the man's advice and stop lamenting the past. The novel concludes as Stevens plans how he can improve his bantering skills in order to surprise his employer, Mr. Farraday, on his return from the States.

Themes or issues
- loyalty and service
- self-deception
- relationships
- professional work

Genre
This novel belongs to the genre of social realism. It gives a realistic insight into the large houses in England in the early twentieth century preceding World War II.

Narrative technique
The novel is told in the first person by Stevens, the central character. This is a limited point of view and therefore has many implications. We are given a very subjective view of events. This is apparent in such things as Stevens's description of the relationship with Miss Kenton. It is clear that Stevens fails to realise the power and depth of her feelings for him. Through this type of narration we gain an insight into the central character, Stevens. We see the underlying motivations governing his decisions about

things. We understand deeply his dreams, desires, shortcomings and blind spots.

The narrative voice could also be described as part-memoir, part-travelogue.

Flashback
During the six-day journey to Cornwall there are various uses of the device of flashback. One effect of the sustained use of flashback in the novel is to highlight the strong link between the past and the present. Stevens is intent on justifying to his reader (but mainly to himself) the motivations for acting as he did throughout his years of service under Lord Darlington.

Much of Stevens's memories cover the period of the nineteen-twenties and nineteen-thirties.

Style
The landscape in the novel is used as a metaphor to parallel the striking sense of calmness and restraint in the English countryside and in Stevens's character.

Cultural context
The cultural setting is that of the great lords and houses in England post-World War II. Dignity and professional competence are primary values for Stevens. Lord Darlington spends a great deal of time engaged in political meetings and entertaining eminent politicians. We gain an insight into the role of the butler in England in the mid-twentieth century. The novel is also narrated in the wake of World War II when Nazism had become a powerful force.

Relationships between men and women are formal and restrained. There is a strong emphasis on sustaining correct social codes of behaviour and etiquette.

General vision and viewpoint
The novel concludes on a positive note. Stevens faces reality fully. He recognises that he has sacrificed a lot by serving Lord Darlington so faithfully. He also recognises that a real attachment existed for Miss Kenton. He acknowledges that Lord Darlington was a tragic victim of circumstances and still forgives him for his errors. Stevens learns to face the limitations of his own life and to stop looking back at the past and lamenting. He decides to adopt a positive attitude and dedicate himself to the task of serving his new employer, Mr Farraday, in the best manner possible. The general vision of this novel is to struggle to make the best of the particular limitations and shortcomings of this life and move out towards other people.

DEATH OF A SALESMAN
Arthur Miller
(2003 exam only)

Historical and literary background
This drama spans a period of forty years from the early twentieth century. This was a

time of dramatic change in lifestyle from an era of abundant job opportunities to one of increasing unemployment because of growing mechanisation. Money and power are primary values in the play.

The story
Willy Loman, the central character of the play, has been a travelling salesman for the Wagner Company for thirty-four years. He is now sixty-three years of age. He is married to a woman called Linda and they have two sons called Biff and Happy. Biff has been living away from home and is unable to sustain a secure job. The relationship between Biff and Willy has been under a strain ever since Biff discovered that his father was unfaithful to his mother. Linda and her two sons are worried about Willy's behaviour. Willy decides to approach Howard Wagner who is the son of the man he worked for thirty-four years ago. Willy wishes to work in New York City, closer to his home. Willy, however, learns that he has no job because he has been a failure while working in New England. Willy is devastated at losing his job and goes to Charley, who is an old friend, to borrow more money in order to pay his insurance premium. Charley offers Willy a job but he refuses out of pride.

When Biff tries to communicate with Willy about his failures in finding work and getting a loan, Willy refuses to listen to him. Later on Biff returns home to find Willy planting seeds and talking to his brother Ben who has been dead for nine months.

At the conclusion, Willy crashes the car and commits suicide. He hopes that he will gain twenty thousand pounds from the insurance. Tragically nobody turns up for Willy's funeral and he dies a forgotten man.

Themes and issues
- family relationships
- self-deception and self-realisation
- personal failure
- work

Genre
The play is a tragedy. The main character, Willy Loman, refuses to face reality and ends by committing suicide, thus destroying any possibility of happiness for himself or his family.

The structure of the play
Under the title of this play the following words are written: 'Certain private conversations in Two Acts and a Requiem.' This play dramatises a mind in turmoil. The structure of the play fluctuates between the past and the present. The time-span of the play is only a twenty-four hour period. There is no logical time sequence in the play. Willy's mind moves to the past twenty years before and focuses in particular on one year—1928.

The style of the play
A lot of the characters, with the exception of Linda, Willy's wife, use clichés and generalisations.

Certain symbols are used, such as the flute, which is connected with Willy's father. The idea of planting seeds suggests that Willy is anxious to reap some fruit in his life; to see something flourish.

Cultural context
The play shows the culture of America in the early twentieth century. This is a period of dramatic changes in society. After World War I there followed an increase in industrial production, but this was accompanied by a slump in the late 1920s, which resulted in high unemployment and the shortage of money. The increase in high-rise apartments in the city of New York is so intense that Willy feels the city is stifling him.

General vision or viewpoint
The general vision of life at the conclusion of this tragedy is grim and pessimistic. The disastrous failure to communicate basic emotions and ideas seems to be the tragic culmination of Willy's life and efforts. This failure destroys his family life and relationships. The basic need for the human being to be loved and understood is evident from Willy's situation. The conclusion dramatises the tragic life-style that results when the individual is unable to feel loved or understood.

A DOLL'S HOUSE

Henrik Ibsen
(2004 exam only)

Historical and literary background
This play's premiere was shown in Copenhagen in 1879 in the Royal Theatre. Ibsen's plays were written for a predominantly middle-class urban audience.

The story
The story centres on a married couple: Torvald Helmer and his wife Nora. They have three children. Nora's husband has been a barrister who has just been made manager of the bank. He treats Nora as a child. He is a perfectionist and cannot tolerate failure. Christine Linde is an old schoolfriend of Nora's who has been a widow for three years.

Nora is a spendthrift but she is also very self-sacrificing towards her husband and family. She has borrowed money in order that they could go on a holiday to Italy because he was sick. In order to do this she forged her father's signature. Unknown to her husband Nora borrows the money from a man called Krogstad, a lawyer who happens to work with Torvald at the bank. He is now a widower and he had a relationship with Christine in the past.

Krogstad is to be dismissed from the bank by Torvald for having committed a small indiscretion. Krogstad is desperate to retain his position in the bank so he tries to persuade Nora to intercede with her husband on his behalf. She refuses and so Krogstad writes a letter to Torvald revealing everything. However, Krogstad changes his mind due to the influence of Christine who consents to marry him. Torvald, however, discovers the letter before he hears about Krogstad's change of mind, and denounces Nora. He decides to cover up the affair and reinstate Krogstad. Just at that moment it is revealed that Krogstad has changed his mind. Torvald decides to forget about everything and go on as usual with life. Nora, however, stands up to him and decides to leave. She does not want to be a wife who is treated like a doll in a doll's house. She leaves her husband and children at the conclusion with the determination to discover who exactly she is and what life is all about. Torvald is the one who has done this for her all her life.

Themes and issues
- self-liberation
- relationships
- deception and dishonesty
- duty and responsibility

Genre
The play belongs to the genre of social realism. The setting is the Helmers' apartment, and the time sequence is about sixty hours' duration. There are three acts.

There is a main plot and a sub-plot which parallel one another. The main plot involves Nora, Helmer and Krogstad, while the sub-plot concerns Mrs Linde and Krogstad.

Style
Both the style and setting are naturalistic. There are seven monologues expressed by Nora. These serve the function of informing us of her inner torment.

The particular language of each character reflects their individual personality. For example, Helmer makes use of a lot of paternalisms such as 'skylark', 'squirrel', 'my little squanderbird' to address his wife.

The setting of the drama is a typical bourgeois drawing room.

Cultural context
The cultural background represented in this play is a middle class family in the nineteenth century.

Marriage between Nora and Helmer is based on a paternal relationship and financial dominance on the part of Helmer. He patronises her while she behaves like a child. Nora represents the middle-class nineteenth century daughter and wife who are protected from the harshness of the outside world.

The nineteenth-century nanny working for a middle class family is shown in the figure of Anne-Marie who looks after Nora's children. While Nora plays with her children and buys them presents, it is Anne-Marie who actually brings them up.

General vision or viewpoint

It is interesting that the play begins with the door opening to let Helmer into the house, and it concludes with Nora slamming the door in his face. Throughout the play a certain number of decisions have been taken and choices made by the characters. For the first time in her life, Nora forces Helmer to face the truth about their marriage. Roles are reversed. She recognises that 'our home has never been anything but a playroom, where we have never exchanged a serious word on a serious subject.'

She leaves him, claiming she needs to be freed from the marriage to educate herself, and to learn to think about life and its issues. Helmer is a tragic figure. He sincerely loved his wife even though he has failed to express it well. He is left abandoned and alone to look after the family and face the ensuing scandal. There is a sense that both people need to readdress certain basic issues in their lives such as the reality of what is involved in marriage.

11
Notes on Shakespeare Drama

In this chapter we will study the main techniques used by Shakespeare in his tragedies. There are also notes on *Othello*, *King Lear* and *Macbeth* under the headings 'Themes and issues', 'Genre', 'Cultural context' and 'General vision and viewpoint'.

TRAGEDY IN SHAKESPEARE

Tragedy in Shakespeare involves a central figure who is an exceptional person, a hero of high stature, whose sufferings are extreme. This person is invested with qualities that raise him above his fellows. In Shakespeare tragedy this situation of loss or catastrophe results in recognition by the hero of the consequences of his mistakes or flaws; this is usually accompanied by a state of moral growth and finally death, which must arouse the sympathy and pity of the audience.

Primary features of Shakespeare tragedy

1. The hero is a person of high status, such as a king or prince or a military leader.
2. This hero is endowed with a fatal flaw, which brings about an exceptional degree of suffering or calamity.
3. The flaw in the character is a form of evil that triggers off the tragic events of the play. These generally lead to the death of the protagonists.
4. Evil in Shakespeare is self-destructive: it annihilates itself.
5. The supernatural forms a part of the structure of his plays, for example the storm in *King Lear*, the witches in *Macbeth*. This element of the supernatural acts only as an agent or catalyst of evil: it never exercises a vital influence on the character. The hero at each stage must face responsibility for his own actions and must act in complete freedom.
6. Chance or accident plays a part in developing the plot. In *Othello*, the coincidental incident of Emilia finding the handkerchief of Desdemona and handing it to her husband Iago, at the same time as Othello is demanding proof of her infidelity is one

example. In *King Lear,* Edgar meets the Earl of Gloucester when he is filled with despair and wants to commit suicide.
7. The conclusions of Shakespeare's plays are distinctive. They always dramatise a qualified form of redemption, with the restoration of good, of harmony and justice; but this is always of a mitigated kind. In other words, it is achieved at the expense of death and destruction of the good. The example of Cordelia in *King Lear,* together with the number of deaths in this play alone, qualifies the complete triumph of good over evil.

To sum up: a Shakespeare tragedy is a story of exceptional suffering experienced by a person of high status and culminating in death.

When you are studying the Shakespeare play,

> (1) examine the central scenes that contribute to the development of the action and plot in the play;
> (2) examine the main features of the central characters or protagonists, and in particular take note of their flaws or shortcomings;
> (3) examine how these flaws or defects contribute to the tragic events that occur in the play;
> (4) study the main characters' recognition of their flaws, and how they grow in self-awareness towards the conclusion of the play;
> (5) examine the soliloquies; remember that soliloquies are an insight into the soul of a character and give us a deep knowledge of what they are thinking and the reasons for their actions.

Examine soliloquies under the following headings:

- Where do they occur?
- What gives rise to them?
- What do they tell us about character?
- What do we learn about the plot?
- What images are used, and why?

Study the summaries of all the soliloquies at the end of the notes on *Macbeth*.

Historical and literary background

The literary and historical background of Shakespeare's plays is late sixteenth-century and early seventeenth-century England. The tragedies *Macbeth, King Lear* and *Othello* were written in the same period, 1600–8.

- This was a time of conflict between a traditional way of life and the new.
- The political framework of sixteenth-century England was hierarchical.
- Rulers at that time—whether king, prince, or general—were regarded as divinely appointed. Usurpation of kingship was considered to be an act of sacrilege.
- The audience came from all strata of society.

MACBETH

(2003 and 2004 exams)

The story

The play is set in Scotland. At the beginning of the play, Duncan is King of Scotland. Scotland is at war with Norway. Macbeth is Captain of the Scottish forces, and possesses the title 'Thane of Glamis'. Lady Macbeth is his wife. Both characters are exceedingly ambitious. Macbeth is rewarded with the title 'Thane of Glamis' because of his valour and personal courage in the battle against Norway. Before he hears of this reward, on his return from the battlefield, he meets three witches. They prophesy to him that he will be king hereafter. They tell Banquo, another general, that he will be father to kings. Macbeth is clearly influenced by these prophecies and it is obvious that he has secretly nourished ambitions for kingship.

Lady Macbeth persuades her husband to murder Duncan, who comes to spend the night in their castle at Inverness. After the murder, Duncan's two sons, Malcolm and Donalbain, escape to England and Ireland respectively. Banquo begins to suspect that Macbeth is the murderer, but he himself is killed shortly before the banquet, which officially inaugurates Macbeth as King. At the Banquet, Banquo's ghost appears to Macbeth to mock him. Lady Macbeth defends Macbeth loyally. Macbeth slaughters Macduff's wife and children because Macduff goes to England for help. In England the king is called Edward. He is a good and saintly man, who offers to help them regain the throne of Scotland and get rid of Macbeth. In England an army of 10,000 men is mobilised and Siward, a general, together with Macduff and Malcolm, resolves to kill Macbeth and restore Malcolm as lawful King of Scotland.

Meanwhile Lady Macbeth, who has committed herself fully to evildoing, now begins to go mad and finally commits suicide. Macbeth pays one last visit to the witches who show him three false visions. He is misled into thinking he will never be killed by any man born of a woman. However Macduff kills him in the end, telling him that he was ripped untimely from his mother's womb. In the end, Malcolm is invested with kingship and order is restored to Scotland.

Themes and issues

Some of the more important themes and issues that are dealt with in the play are:
- evil and deception, false appearance and equivocation
- ambition
- kingship
- loyalty and betrayal
- the supernatural.

Literary genre

The play is from the genre of tragedy. It explores the world of supernatural evil.

The witches represent the metaphysical world of evil spirits. They can be seen as archetypal tempters recreating the original temptation that led to the fall of man.

Structure of the play

The play is divided into five main acts. The final destruction of evil and the triumph of good are shown in the concluding scene. The banquet scene is used ironically. It is supposed to confirm Macbeth's power as king. However, as the events proceed in this scene, Macbeth steadily loses control and the scene concludes in chaos. Furthermore, the conclusion of this scene demonstrates the beginnings of the rift between Lady Macbeth and her husband. She becomes haunted by guilt-ridden fantasies, while he develops into a ruthless, hardened murderer.

The plot revolves around the witches' wicked instigations to tempt Macbeth with thoughts of kingship and the evil consequences that ensue.

Style of the play

There is an abundance of blood-dominated imagery, which serves the function of showing the power of evil and violence in the play.

Irony

Both Macbeth and his wife become victims of irony in this play. This is because their hunger for kingship overrides all moral considerations and turns out to be a disastrous state of being for them. The many references to washing, cleansing and sleeping are all used in a deeply ironic way throughout the play. Both become obsessed with guilt and sleeplessness as a result of their crimes.

Soliloquies

The use of the soliloquy in Shakespeare serves many functions. The three characters that use soliloquies in this play are Macbeth, Lady Macbeth and Banquo. In general, the soliloquy furnishes us with a deeper insight into the mentality of that particular character. We can also gain information about the plot. The images used in a soliloquy usually highlight themes or main features of the character.

Cultural context

Under this heading are the following:

- kingship
- the witches
- the political situation.

The monarch at this time was a sacred figure with divine sanction. No earthly individual had a right to put an end to the rule of a king—this was God's right only. Therefore regicide, or the killing of a king, was no ordinary crime.

The witches represent the supernatural world of evil that was prevalent in Scotland in the early seventeenth century.

The political situation is unstable. The values of order, harmony and stability are shown to be insecure. Scotland under Duncan's rule has been subjected to rebellion from within (the betrayal of Cawdor), and invasion from without (the war with Norway).

General vision and viewpoint

Malcolm's victory restores order and harmony to Scotland. The leafy branches disguising the advance of the troops are symbolic of new life and hope for Scotland. Malcolm is the 'medicine of the sickly weal', who must 'purge Scotland of the evil which Macbeth has reduced it to'. Both Macbeth and Lady Macbeth have betrayed themselves by falling for what is equivocal and illusory. They now find their actions and lives are meaningless. Time, life and death have lost all meaning for both. Macbeth's surrender of himself to evil has brought about nothing but a deep sense of emptiness and the futility of life:

> Tomorrow, and tomorrow, and tomorrow,
> Creeps in this petty pace from day to day,
> To the last syllable of recorded time;
> And all our yesterdays have lighted fools
> The way to dusty death.

In all of Shakespeare's tragedies, evil is shown to be self-destructive. Through the logic of events, Shakespeare shows that there is a universal moral law that one transgresses at one's peril.

Summary of the soliloquies

Macbeth's soliloquies

1. Act I, scene iii, line 128. Macbeth's latent ambition is evident. He shows his vacillating moral outlook: 'cannot be ill, cannot be good'. His references to imaginary fears are ironic in the light of the banquet scene and Lady Macbeth's breakdown.
2. Act I, scene iv, line 48. Duncan's action in nominating his son Malcolm as successor to the throne is ironic. It leads to this soliloquy. Macbeth uses the images of 'black' and 'deep' to show the evil nature of his desires.
3. Act I, scene vii, line 1. This reveals the depths of Macbeth's conscience. It deals with the theme of justice and is a splendid assessment of the virtuous nature of Duncan. There is an acknowledgment by Macbeth of his fatal flaw: 'I have no spur . . .'.
4. Act II, scene i, line 33 (the dagger soliloquy). This reveals the fact that Macbeth's moral sense has become corrupted. Images of evil: 'pale Hecate', 'bloody business', 'on the blade and dudgeon gouts of blood'.
5. Act III, scene i, line 48. Macbeth's assessment of Banquo's qualities shows the threat to Macbeth while Banquo lives. The images show Macbeth's acknowledgment of the immorality of his deed: 'filed my mind', 'mine eternal jewel given to the common enemy of man'.
6. Act IV, scene I, line 144. Macbeth announces his intention of destroying the family of Macduff. He seeks to erase his bitter sense of how meaningless his life has become through this act of gratuitous violence: 'The very firstlings of my heart shall be the firstlings of my hand'.
7. Act V, scene iii, line 20. Macbeth gives us a glimpse of how hollow his life has become. He enumerates all the values he has lost because of his reign as a tyrant.

Lady Macbeth's soliloquies
1. Act I, scene v, line 14. This is Lady Macbeth's assessment of her husband's character. She commits herself to evil to remove the obstacles that stand between him and the kingship. Images used here include 'The golden round' referring to kingship.
2. Act I, scene v, line 39. She calls on evil to denature her (unsex her) in order to be filled with the necessary amount of murderous cruelty. In these soliloquies she suppresses not only her femininity but also her humanity.
3. Act III, scene ii, line 5. This reflects dissatisfaction with kingship. Images here show us the quality of her life, a state of 'doubtful joy'.

Banquo's soliloquy
Act III, scene i, line 1. Banquo's only soliloquy occurs when Macbeth has taken over kingship. It reveals that the virtuous Banquo may have been seduced by temptation and become morally tainted. Images that reflect a latent ambition that the witches' prophecies may come true include 'their speeches shine', 'may they not be my oracles as well and set me up in hope'.

OTHELLO

(2003 exam: comparative studies only)

The story
Othello is a Moor and is the Commander-in-Chief of the Venetian army, which has been commanded to carry out the job of defending Cyprus against the Turks. Cassio has been appointed as his lieutenant. Iago is an 'ancient', or type of adviser to Othello. He is the villain of the play who hates Othello for having promoted Cassio in his stead, and so he plots to revenge himself on Othello. Othello has married Desdemona, daughter to Brabantio, one of the Senators in Venice. Roderigo, a friend of Iago, is being manipulated by Iago into giving him money so that Iago can win the hand of Desdemona for Roderigo.

Iago organises things so that Cassio gets drunk and is expelled from his position in the army. Then he subtly insinuates to Othello that Cassio is having an affair with Desdemona, Othello's wife. Iago uses his own wife, Emilia, to facilitate his plot. She provides Othello with proof that Desdemona has been unfaithful, in the form of a handkerchief which belongs to Desdemona, which was supposedly found in Cassio's apartment. Meanwhile Iago wins the confidence of Cassio and advises him to use Desdemona to intercede on his behalf to regain his position.

Bianca is a prostitute who is having an affair with Cassio. She is used by Iago and is implicated in the attempt to murder Cassio. Iago's plot fails when his attempt to murder Cassio backfires. Iago kills Roderigo because he is afraid of being exposed. Othello yields to the devious suggestion about his wife told to him by Iago and, consumed with rage, he decides to murder his wife. He smothers her in bed. After Desdemona's murder Emilia exposes her husband's villainy. Iago kills her. Othello kills himself. Iago is captured and punished.

Themes and issues
Some of the themes and issues which will be dealt with here are:
- women
- racial prejudice
- dissimulation or false appearance
- jealousy.

The theme of women
All the female characters are unwitting victims of deception, guile and intrigue. They all inadvertently act as instruments of evil. Take, for instance, Bianca's affair with Cassio, Emilia's thoughtlessness in handing over the handkerchief to Iago which furnishes him with proof of Desdemona's supposed infidelity, and Desdemona herself, unable to discern the corrupt plotting undermining her innocence. There is a striking contrast drawn throughout the play between the characters of Desdemona and Emilia. Desdemona's moral rectitude is integral, inviolate and pure. Emilia, on the other hand, is more worldly; her moral reasoning in the face of infidelity is tenuous and weak. She would 'venture purgatory to make her husband a monarch'.

The conversations which take place, in act IV, scene iii, between Desdemona and Emilia about marital infidelity and betrayal on the part of spouses serve the function of confirming and consolidating Desdemona's absolute marital integrity in the eyes of Emilia. This scene also functions to contrast the different standards of values professed by the two women. Emilia has weaker moral standards; standards which are corruptible and more worldly. For this reason, it is fitting that Emilia becomes the woman to stand up and vindicate the purity and integrity of Desdemona's virtue when her husband has murdered her.

It is ironic that Emilia becomes the one to expose the villainy of Iago. Despised repeatedly by her husband for being a strumpet, she emerges at the conclusion of this tragedy as a heroine who vindicates truth and honour. It is the love and loyalty of Emilia, the two virtues which Iago tries to erode in the play, which destroy him finally. Emilia's love and loyalty to Desdemona at the end become the means to reveal the full evil of Iago's manoeuvrings.

The general idea left with us by the play is that 'women must be circumstanced'; they must put up with the state of affairs and do their best with the position of things while men can do what they like.

The theme of racial prejudice
As a Moor from another culture, Othello is an outsider in this society and hence is regarded with suspicion and distrust. His position as a stranger to this culture intensifies his vulnerability and facilitates Iago's devious plot.

From the opening scene we are confronted with the issue of racial prejudice. Iago's resentment and spite rouse Roderigo, who in turn provokes the superstitious Brabantio with the words, 'an old black ram is tupping your white ewe . . .', 'Your fair daughter has been transported to the gross clasps of a lascivious Moor . . .' (act I, scene i). Later that night when Brabantio takes up the issue in the Venetian senate, he condemns

Othello for having 'abused her delicate youth with foul charms . . .' (act I, scene ii). This attack is directed at Othello who, in the words of Brabantio, has bewitched his daughter to such a degree that 'she ran from her guardage to the sooty bosom of such a thing as thou . . .' (act I, scene ii).

Prior to this, Brabantio entertained Othello in his house, paying tribute to him as a high-ranking military general. However, the marriage of his beloved daughter to this Moor—this outsider—is an entirely different matter. It leads him to make the statement to Roderigo, whom in fact he despises, 'O, that you had had her . . .' (act I, scene i).

Othello is deeply insecure because he lacks essential knowledge of issues such as marriage, social relations between men and women and certain customs and traditions peculiar to Venice. It is this lack of knowledge and experience which leaves him an open target for exploitation. Look, for example, at Iago's words in the temptation scene: 'In Venice they do not let God see the pranks, They dare not show their husbands . . .' (act III, scene iii).

Subtly setting his perverted mind to work on Othello's weak nature, Iago suggests that perhaps the cause of Desdemona's infidelity has to do with race and colour:

> Ay, there's the point: as, to be bold with you,
> Not to affect many proposed matches
> Of her own clime, complexion, and degree, . . .
>   one may smell in such, a will most rank,
> Foul disproportion, thoughts unnatural. . . .
>   I may fear
> Her will, recoiling to her better judgement,
> May fail to match you with her country forms
> And happily repent
>
>   (III, iii)

That Iago succeeds in undermining Othello's faith in himself and his own wife becomes saliently clear from his soliloquy, which follows immediately after the above lines.

It is Othello himself who articulates how vulnerable and how defenceless he is because of his colour:

>   Haply, for I am black
> And have not those soft parts of conversation
> That chamberers have . . .
>   (III, iii)

His tragedy lies in the fact that he is unable to transcend these limitations within his own nature and arrive at the real truth. Instead, he consolidates his weaknesses even more by acting on impulse and executing judgment on Desdemona.

There is no doubt that the issue of racism and the underlying prejudice generated by it contribute to the precipitation of a good deal of the tragedy in this play.

Theme of dissimulation or false appearance

This theme of dissimulation finds expression in the character of Iago. Described as a 'demi-devil', he rests confidently on the assurance that people, and in particular Othello, believe him to be honest. He possesses an exterior glitter which is, in reality, sinister, and which misleads everyone in the play.

Cassio turns to him for advice, ironically addressing him as 'Honest Iago', and stating in full sincerity 'I never knew a Florentine more kind and honest' (act III, scene i). When Othello turns on Desdemona in a fit of passion, asking her to produce the handkerchief immediately, she beseeches Iago with the words, 'O, good Iago, good friend . . .'.

Othello repeatedly leans on the 'honesty' of Iago, frequently addressing him as 'Good Iago', 'Honest Iago', 'My life upon her faith: honest Iago'.

Iago handles every situation with tremendous skill and dexterity. He deftly manipulates every person in the play with cynicism and ironic contempt, and speedily turns everything to his own advantage.

Iago's ability to control Othello is supreme. Using several tactics, Iago strategically manages to erode Othello's faith in his own wife. Through this sustained use of devious and ingenious tactics Iago shows how the issue of evil or dissimulation can be compatible with outstanding human powers. His human strengths are potent: a keen energy and vitality, massive or prodigious powers of self-control together with a highly superior intelligence. One of his main weapons is his ability to weigh up all the flaws of the chief characters, which he uses to further his own advantage. It is ironic that in his soliloquies he demonstrates a more astute and correct apprehension of Desdemona's strengths and weaknesses than her own husband.

It is interesting that Iago fools everyone, even his own wife Emilia. While Emilia is projected as a foolish and superficial 'bawd-type' of woman, at no stage is she remotely aware of the depths of evil inherent in Iago's nature. This is because his capacity for dissimulation or duplicity are astounding. In the final scene, her words reveal this fact:

> Disprove this villain . . .
> He says thou told'st him that his wife was false.
> I know thou did'st not, thou'rt not such a villain.
> Speak, for my heart is full.

Shakespeare uses irony to dramatise this theme of false-seeming or dissimulation. Irony is an ideal technique to project such a theme involving, as it does, the discrepancy between what is said or implied and what is really the case. The root of much of the irony in this play lies in the basic misconception by everyone that Iago is 'honest'.

And so a network of ironies, from situational to dramatic to verbal irony, illustrates this theme. For example, when Emilia informs Iago of Othello's attack on Desdemona in the words

> The Moor's abused by some most villanous knave,
> Some base notorious knave, some scurvy fellow . . .
> (IV, ii)

we get a splendid example of irony of situation.

The play abounds in similar examples of the clever use of irony, all of which demonstrate how effective Iago has been in embodying this particular ability to pretend to be something he is not. His ability to deceive everyone triumphs and wreaks havoc as the conflict develops and the events unfold. It is only when Othello has murdered his wife and caused chaos in Venetian society that the full reality underlying Iago's plausible appearance of honesty is finally and ultimately cracked. His smooth veneer of honesty and plausibility is stripped bare by Emilia's staunch defence of the truth and her fearless denunciation of his villainy.

The theme of jealousy

This is an issue which permeates much of the play. There are overtones of jealousy in the opening lines of the play. These stem from the jealous references and disparaging comments that Iago makes about the character of Cassio:

> A fellow almost damn'd in a fair wife;
> That never set a squadron in the field,
> Nor the division of a battle knows
> More than a spinster . . .
>   mere prattle, without practise,
> Is all his soldiership.
>   (I, i)

The root of his envy is anger at Cassio's military expertise and the fact that he has been promoted in lieu of Iago.

Iago's jealousy is pervasive. He himself acknowledges that he is jealous of Cassio:

> He hath a daily beauty in his life
> That makes me ugly.
>   (V, i)

Iago works off this jealousy by creating counter-jealousies. Othello becomes his primary target. Iago announces in an early soliloquy how

>   I will put the Moor
> At least into a jealousy so strong
> That judgment cannot cure . . .
>   (II, i)

He manages to achieve this with consummate success. Othello's concluding words before he dies confirm the truth of this, and the success of Iago's warped intrigues:

> Speak of me . . .
> Of one not easily jealous, but, being wrought . . .
>   (V, ii)

Othello's whole nature is indisposed towards jealousy or envy of any kind, but once it dominates him, it consumes and finally destroys him. The disposition of his temperament is to act rashly and impulsively, to seek immediate proof and resolve his doubts without stopping to reflect on the consequences of his actions. Of course Iago perceives all this thoroughly. Half way through the temptation scene, when he is handed the handkerchief, Iago is able to assess fully the state of Othello's inner nature:

> . . . trifles light as air
> Are to the jealous confirmations strong
> As proofs of Holy Writ.
> (III, iii)

Iago appraises completely that Othello's soul is animated by an uncontrolled, 'an unbookish jealousy'.

It is perhaps significant that both Emilia and Iago provide us with definitions of jealousy in the play.

Iago warns Othello to be wary of jealousy in the temptation scene:

> O! beware, my lord, of jealousy;
> It is the green-ey'd monster which doth mock
> The meat it feeds on.
> (III, iii)

And later on Emilia tells Desdemona that Othello's ill-treatment of her may be due to jealousy, and proceeds to echo her husband's earlier words:

> . . . It is a monster
> Begot upon itself, born on itself.
> (III, iv)

The deliberate echo by both characters of the theme of jealousy could certainly say a great deal about their marriage.

Within the context of this play and the ensuing events, jealousy does turn out to be a monster that breeds on itself, an evil that is self-destructive.

The conclusion of the play dramatises this point only too clearly. Othello destroys the bonds of his marriage, the beautiful Desdemona, and then kills himself.

Iago's destructive plot is overturned and his devilry unmasked at the conclusion.

Literary genre

Othello is a tragedy.

The play is a tragedy of incomprehension. The tragic experience is concerned with a loss of faith. Othello, who is a Moor from another culture, allows himself to be deceived into believing his wife has been unfaithful. His tragedy is rooted in his inexperience of this culture and his unqualified trust in the honesty and loyalty of Iago. He accepts Iago's insinuations as truth, and acts on them by murdering his wife. Only after the murder is the full truth of Iago's wickedness exposed, and Othello then kills himself.

The structure of the play

The plot is the character of Iago in action. This action depends largely on his knowledge of character and in particular the way in which he assesses the vulnerabilities of each of the characters. This plot finds expression in Iago's soliloquies. In these soliloquies he fabricates his plot and outlines reasons for his revenge.

He weighs up each one of his victims' strengths and weaknesses and shows how he will use the weaknesses to further his own evil ends. A great deal of the plot depends on Iago's knowledge of character together with the occurrence of accident or chance. The plot revolves around the image of a net in which people are caught and from which there is no escape. In Iago's own words:

> And out of her own goodness make the net
> That shall enmesh them all.
>
> (II, iii)

The time sequence of the play is very short; the whole play lasts approximately four or five days. In terms of what actually happens, this time-span is incredibly short.

Act I opens on Othello's wedding night. That same night he is dispatched to Cyprus.

Act II opens with the arrival of all the main characters, including Othello, in Cyprus three days later. The night after the arrival in Cyprus Cassio is sacked.

The next day in the temptation scene, act III, scene iii, Iago poisons Othello's mind about his wife's infidelity. That same day, the handkerchief is lost by Desdemona, found by Emilia, given to Iago and planted in Cassio's chamber. Cassio's death is planned to be carried out within the next three days. Othello himself undertakes to kill Desdemona. All of this occurs in one complete scene which is the day after Cassio is dismissed. The time-span is unbelievable.

In act IV Othello is recalled to Venice. Othello humiliates Desdemona publicly by striking her, and later by treating her as a strumpet.

Act V concludes with the conversation between Emilia and Desdemona about marital infidelity. The last scene is the death of the leading protagonists.

The style of the play

Imagery

Imagery reflects some of the major themes in this tragedy. Dramatic contrast forms the pattern for much of the imagery of the play.

Because the play depicts a world of creation set against a world of destruction, contrast lies at the essence of the style. Othello radiates a world of romance, heroic and picturesque adventure. He reflects through his poetic speeches the qualities of soldiership in all its glamour of romantic adventure. On the other hand, Iago is colourless and ugly. He gnaws at the roots and values of this world. With his unfounded suspicions and ambiguous language, he worms his way into its solidity and finally poisons it.

Colour contrast dramatises the difference between certain characters. Desdemona is repeatedly reflected in terms of religious symbolism, for example 'Divine Desdemona', 'white ewe', 'fair devil', 'white sheets'. These are all symbols which show her striking purity, innocence and goodness. On the other hand, dark or black images suggest evil. All the surreptitious manoeuvrings of Iago take place at night. The opening scene is a night scene and serves the function of revealing the dominance of evil, of negation and of malignancy in the atmosphere of the play. This is reinforced by the two concluding scenes, both of which take place at night and have death as their theme.

Another example of contrast in the network of imagery used in the play is in the diabolic and celestial imagery. The use of celestial imagery mainly finds expression in the character of Desdemona. Cassio vehemently declares that the 'grace of Heaven surrounds her'. Her last words have rich religious connotations: 'I never loved Cassio, But with such general warrenty of heaven, As I might love.'

Emilia, in her chastisement of Othello's action, is quick to declare

> O! the more angel she,
> And you the blacker devil . . .
> Thou art rash as fire to say
> That she was false: O! she was heavenly true.

This type of imagery forms a striking contrast to the dark pattern of diabolic and black symbolism which dominates the play.

The pattern of diabolic or demonic imagery is woven about the character of Iago and all his motives, manipulations and manoeuvrings. Iago refers to his own plans as hellish: 'Hell and night, Must bring this monstrous birth to the world's light.' Iago sees himself under the patronage of hell:

> Divinity of Hell!
> When devils will their blackest sins put on,
> They do suggest at first with heavenly shows
> As I do now . . .

This kind of language and imagery is first used by Iago in the play, but as the events proceed and develop, it begins to form the content of much of Othello's language patterns. Othello begins to apply images of hell and damnation to Desdemona: 'Damn her lewd minx, fair devil', 'She is a liar gone to burning hell'.

A significant change occurs in the application of diabolic imagery on Desdemona's death. Emilia, who now realises the full truth, applies this kind of imagery to Othello: 'the more angel she, you the blacker devil'.

Othello, in his sense of retribution and self-chastisement at the wrong action he has committed, cries out the following words of repentance:

> Whip me you devils,
> From the possession of this heavenly sight!
> Blow me about in winds! roast me in sulphur!
> Wash me in steep-down gulfs of liquid fire!
> (V, ii)

Damnation, evil and the subsequent diabolic connotations are all synonymous in this play. The general impression left at the conclusion of Iago's character and operations is that of a nature who is damned and satanic in intent. He is repeatedly referred to as a 'demi-devil', a 'damned slave'. At the conclusion, when Othello, in an overwrought state for what he has done, declares in perplexity

> I look down towards his feet; but that's a fable.
> If that thou be'st a devil, I cannot kill thee.

in many senses these words are a chilling conclusion to Iago's career.

Another type of image used in the play is disease or poison imagery. This is seen in the corrupting effect of Iago's intrigues. Iago himself acknowledges that his plot is 'pestilence in Othello's ear'; that the effort to defame Othello's reputation before Brabantio is 'poison'. Othello refers to the handkerchief as a 'ravan over an infected house'. In his soliloquy, Othello depicts life with an unfaithful wife in terms of 'a forked plague', and 'a horned beast'.

Shakespeare uses a rich variety of images to project his themes. Images also identify certain things about each character as well as showing the gradual deterioration of the moral atmosphere in this play.

Cultural context

Venice and Cyprus are the two areas which are shown in this play. These places have very different value systems. Othello is a Moor and therefore his culture is rooted in North Africa. The predominant culture of this play is rooted in Venice. Venice is seen as a rich and powerful place, with its value system resting firmly on power, possession and control. Control here does not just mean power over people but also the supremacy of reason over emotion and passion. Venice is not just a place, it is an influence. Its mores or standards are implanted firmly in all the characters.

Venetian society has a superficially smooth and civilised veneer, seen in, for example, the noble senator, the competent and well mannered lieutenant, and the conventional gentlewoman.

The Venetian senate

The senate in Venice embodies order, reason, justice and concord. Ancient laws and established customs control violence and ensure the safety and wellbeing of the individual and society. The ideal of this culture is control. In this culture, self-control is desirable and highly valued in soldiers. Othello shows a profound degree of self-control. He is calm and reasonable and knows that his lineage is as royal and as wealthy as any Venetian. Even under threat of attack from Brabantio, he remains serene and in control.

The scene in the senate depicts the values of honour, lawfulness, decorum, knowledge and power. Brabantio's grievances are examined here in a court of law. They are judged by reason and the verdict is enforced by civic power.

Here also in the senate the actions of the Turks are examined, their true purpose is penetrated, sense is made of the frantic and contradictory messages which pour in from the fleet and the necessary defence is arranged.

The two lovers, Desdemona and Othello, are surrounded by the governors of Venice who control passions and enforce law and reason. In this context they are forced to explain how they fell in love and to justify their love for one another.

However, there are anarchic forces at work threatening traditional social forms and relationships. These forces centre on Iago. Iago's discontent with his own rank and his determination to displace Cassio endanger the orderly military hierarchy. Iago's attempts to create civic chaos in Venice are frustrated by Othello's calm management of affairs and by the orderly proceedings of the senate.

Cyprus stands on the frontiers between barbarism, as represented by the Turkish attack, and the city. Cyprus is not the secure fortress that Venice is. It is an outpost far out in the raging ocean; the immediate object of attack by the enemy. Here passions are more explosive than they are in Venice. Cyprus lacks the ancient order and established government of Venice. Othello the Moor is the one man to control violence and defend civilisation. In Cyprus, however, society is less secure and Othello alone is responsible for exposing the truth about things, and for the maintenance of order.

Iago's poison works effectively in this society and he succeeds in manufacturing the riot and chaos that he failed to create in Venice. Disruptions occur both in society and in human relationships. Through his unfounded suspicions of his own wife, he endangers marriage. He tries to subvert the operation of law and justice by stirring up the dark, anarchic passions within Roderigo. The general is set against the officer, husband against wife, Christian against Christian, servant against master. Manners disappear as Othello strikes his wife publicly and, later, treats her as a whore.

Venetians cut one another down in a dark Cyprus street; men are murdered from behind. The quality of life deteriorates.

Another feature of the value system underlying the Venetian culture is the attitude towards women. Not only are women themselves treated with contempt and disdain, but also certain qualities such as loyalty, fidelity and purity are not expected of a woman. Women are largely seen as puppets or pawns to satisfy the male. Women in this culture are trivialised; the bonds of marriage and relationships are abused.

Othello's values are those of the aristocratic Venice, while Iago holds the values of the lower edge of that culture. Iago has contempt for women and all that femininity represents. He believes in control, power, possession and individualism. Significantly he opens the play and dictates the terms of the action throughout. He speaks of money, hate, jealousy and women.

It is Othello's lack of familiarity with this culture which enables Iago to undermine his faith in his wife, Desdemona. Othello is unfamiliar with Venetian customs, in particular the pattern of infidelity and adultery which seem to be rife. Infidelity among the gentry is a commonplace occurrence and it is this particular feature of Venetian culture which erodes Othello's confidence in his wife and makes him a ready tool for exploitation.

General vision and viewpoint

Emilia plays a large part in the vindication of Desdemona's virtue and honour. It is she who heroically defends Desdemona's purity and virtue and steadfastly confirms her innocence. She dies in this act of defence and vindication.

The play concludes with the death of the tragic hero and the restoration of harmony in society. Iago is captured and it is presumed that he will be punished for his crimes. The general impression left to us is that his evil is of an ambiguous nature; the motivation underlying his actions is deliberately left obscure.

The general vision at the conclusion of this play is that evil is punished, but not before it has done a great deal of harm in the play. The power of the woman to change and grow in moral stature and to reveal the underlying corruption within this society can be seen in Emilia's attack on Othello and her corresponding defence of Desdemona.

Othello's repentance together with the execution of judgment on himself is an affirmation of loyalty to Venice.

KING LEAR

(2004 exam: comparative studies only)

The story

Lear is an old man when the play opens. He decides to his divide his kingdom between his three daughters by means of a childish love test based on words. When Cordelia refuses to co-operate she is stripped of her dowry and banished to France. Goneril and Regan, his other two daughters, take over the kingship. They are shrewd operators who have fully assessed Lear's flaws. They plot together so that they will not suffer as a result of his senile unpredictability.

Shortly after Lear abdicates the throne, he moves to Goneril's house with one hundred knights; this was one of the conditions of his agreement. Here he has a violent confrontation with Goneril about the number of knights he actually needs. Regan arrives and the love scene is ironically parodied, the two daughters haggling over the numbers of his knights in a grotesque mimicry of the love test. Lear is thrust out into the storm with his Fool and the Earl of Kent.

The Earl of Gloucester has two sons. One of them, Edmund, is 'illegitimate'. Edmund deceives Gloucester about Edgar, his 'legitimate' son, and convinces him he is a villain who is ready to murder him. Edgar is forced to go on the run and play the role of a mad beggar. He meets with Lear on the heath in a storm, and together they reach some profound insights into human nature. Later Gloucester is blinded by the Duke of Cornwall, the husband of Regan, for helping Lear. Gloucester becomes filled with despair and wanders to Dover to commit suicide. He is saved by Edgar, who discloses his identity to him shortly before Gloucester dies, apparently from a heart attack.

Lear becomes reconciled with Cordelia, who returns to England from France with an army to save him. Both Lear and Cordelia are imprisoned by Edmund, who leads the English army against the King of France. Cordelia is hanged, and Lear dies of a broken heart.

Goneril and Regan become consumed by a passionate lust for Edmund, and they kill one another. Edmund is slain by Edgar. Only the Duke of Albany (Goneril's husband), and Edgar survive to sustain the gory state of England at the conclusion.

Themes and issues

Many different issues and themes are treated in the play *King Lear*:
- blindness to human nature
- the value of suffering and the corresponding growth in insight and moral awareness
- justice
- the child–parent relationship
- good and evil.

Blindness to human nature

The play *King Lear* is a drama of pride. A long life of absolute power, nourished by flattery and blind obedience to his every whim, has made Lear essentially blind to both his own limitations and to the reality of corrupt human nature. Lear has lived the life of an absolute dictator and has therefore generated within himself deeply ingrained faults 'of long engraffed condition'.

Choleric and mercurial in temperament he is characterised by a presumptuous self-will with absolutely no self-control: 'full of changes his age is', 'unconstant starts', 'he slenderly knows himself'. All of these defects are cynically assessed by his two daughters Regan and Goneril immediately after they have received the power of kingship. Lear arrogantly refuses to listen to Kent when he tries to get him to see the true natures of Goneril, Regan and Cordelia. Instead he banishes both Kent and Cordelia and hands over the kingdom to his two daughters, Goneril and Regan, who later betray him.

Similarly, in the sub-plot, Gloucester, who is gullible and also blind to the reality of human nature, is deceived by Edmund into believing his legitimate son, Edgar, is a villain.

It is only at the conclusion of the tragedy that both characters grow in insight and moral awareness and learn the real nature of their children.

Suffering and growth in moral awareness

The world of the play *King Lear* is a world of suffering. This is brought home to us many times in the play, for instance, Lear's rage and loss of sanity in the storm scenes, together with the violence inherent in the blinding of Gloucester. There are numerous images of suffering and cruelty.

Yet this suffering is shown to have a positive purpose. It is through suffering that both Lear and Gloucester attain insight. Many times their insights echo one another, which reinforces the deliberate parallel that Shakespeare draws between the main plot and the sub-plot.

Both of them recognise their own responsibility for their predicament; Lear's words that his suffering is a 'judicious punishment' are a direct echo of Gloucester's words 'O my follies'. They come to understand the true natures of their children. Lear describes Goneril and Regan as 'Two pernicious daughters', and speaking about Cordelia he acknowledges that 'I did her wrong'.

When Gloucester is blinded by Cornwall and Regan flaunts the truth about Edmund and Edgar before him, Gloucester cries out 'Then Edgar was abused'. They both grow in self-knowledge. Lear realises in the storm scenes that he is 'an infirm, weak and despised old man'; Gloucester declares that 'I stumbled when I saw'.

Their high status had allowed them to become blind to the reality of the world around them; stripped of their status they are stripped of their delusions: 'Yet you see how this world goes' Lear states, and Gloucester replies 'I see it feelingly'.

Both men achieve moral growth and develop new qualities within themselves. Shortly after he is blinded Gloucester wanders across the heath in despair and meets with Edgar who brings him to Dover. At this stage his horizons have been broadened through extreme suffering and, for the first time in his life, he becomes aware of the plight of other people. He speaks about justice and the unequal distribution of wealth in the lines

> So distribution should undo excess,
> And each man have enough.
>
> (IV, i)

Earlier Lear had come to a similar conclusion and had realised he had paid too little attention to the poverty around him:

> I have ta'en too little care of this,
> . . .
> That thou mayst shake the superflux to them,
> And show the heavens more just.
>
> (III, iv)

Lear's central experience is his growth in moral awareness under the impact of suffering; profound agony on the heath together with the loss of everything, both physical and spiritual, free his heart from the bondage of selfish self-absorption. He loses everything in the world, but gains an apprehension of his own soul and of human nature. He learns the real nature of humility, endurance, love and understanding. His path is not straightforward; he moves from an unweening pride and arrogance, through rebellious anger bordering on despair, to an eventual patience and humility of soul.

Lear's arrival at truth is by means of a paradox, by means of 'reason in madness'. In other words he has to lose his sanity to gain insight and self-awareness, and moreover many of the most profound lessons that he learns in the play are through the medium of the professionally mad Fool.

Shakespeare clearly means to show us through this tragedy that 'he was a man more sinned against than sinning'. His sufferings are out of proportion to his original fault.

Likewise Gloucester grows to be a better man towards the conclusion of this tragedy by means of suffering. Gloucester's nature at the beginning of the play is self-indulgent, he is over-sensual and so he suffers the punishment of being blinded. His blindness precedes Lear's madness. We see the first stage of his moral growth when he undertakes to stand by Lear and give him support even at the risk of his own life. This act of going to 'relieve' Lear out on the heath and offer him consolation and comfort costs him his eyes. Afterwards, when Gloucester realises that it is Edmund who betrays him, he immediately prays to the gods for forgiveness and that Edgar will prosper:

> Kind Gods, forgive me that, and prosper him!
> (III, vii)

Both men suffer because of their weakness and both grow to be better men morally through this suffering.

Lear's fault is one of pride, or an intellectual fault. He fails to judge character and action. He loses his reason and goes mad. At the height of his madness he achieves his deepest insights into human nature and grows both morally and spiritually. The first manifestation of the moral growth is his plea to the Fool to go into the hovel before him:

> In, boy; go first . . .
> poor Fool I have one part of my heart that's sorry for thee yet, . . .
> I'll pray and then I'll sleep.
> (III, iv)

This manifestation of a concern for other people, this profound growth in humility, this attitude of praying is all very striking evidence of a profound change in Lear's nature, and is shown to be particularly evident at the conclusion when he becomes reconciled with Cordelia. He kneels down and begs forgiveness from Cordelia with the words 'if you have poison for me I will drink it.' He allies himself with Cordelia as 'God's spies', and claims that he will take on the 'mystery of things'.

All his earlier pride, arrogance, bad temper and impatience are now supplanted by a deep and sincere repentance. When he meets Cordelia he kneels down and begs her forgiveness. He tells Cordelia,

> Thou art a soul in bliss; but I am bound
> Upon a wheel of fire, that mine own tears
> Do scald like molten lead.
> (IV, vii)

So while the play shows us a cruel world of suffering it also illustrates the positive aspects of this suffering. Lear and Gloucester both die better men as a result of their experiences.

Justice

When the play opens, Lear, as King of England, is justice.

The play is structured upon the consequences of a grave error and abuse of justice by a king within whose powers justice lies. When Lear relinquishes his crown to Goneril and Regan and abdicates his right to dispense justice, for the first time in his life he becomes subject to justice. Lear in this position is better able to assess human systems of justice, the full reality of his kingdom and of power as he himself has wielded it for so many years.

The entire play shows the corruption and hypocrisy inherent in human systems of justice in the England of Lear's reign. The mock trial scene in act III, scene vi analyses and exposes the whole system of justice and kingship in the kingdom.

The mock trial is conducted by Lear who is completely mad, the Fool whose job it is to act like a madman, and the simulated or pretended madness of Edgar. The whole scene is an ironic comment on how depraved and perverted are the existing systems of human justice.

The scene also confronts the problem of evil. Lear asks the fundamental question 'Is there any cause in nature that make these Hard-hearts?' (act III, scene vi). The scene is positioned or structured in a striking manner to reinforce these two themes or issues: evil and injustice.

Immediately after this scene Gloucester is put on trial in a grossly unjust manner. Cornwall acknowledges immediately before he punishes Gloucester that,

> we may not pass upon his life
> Without the form of justice.
> (III, vii)

Yet he maintains that 'our power shall do a court's to our wrath which men may blame but not control'.

In other words, Cornwall is perfectly capable of manipulating and perverting justice in order to satisfy his own revenge. Ironically in this act of injustice he meets with his own death at the hands of a servant.

There is another trenchant image of justice given to us in act IV scene vi. Here we are exposed to the great image of authority in the farmer's dog who barks at a beggar. Even 'a dog's obeyed in office' is the implication of such ideas; in other words those who wield authority are corrupt. Here, justice is useless and ineffective.

The storm symbolises divine justice. However, there is no consistent statement made on the theme or issue of divine justice. In the death of the bad characters Albany sees the judgment of the heavens at work. When he hears that Cornwall dies in the act of plucking Gloucester's eyes out Albany cries out

> This shows you are above,
> You justicers, that these our nether crimes
> So speedily can venge!
> (IV, ii)

Edgar repeats this type of sentiment when he tells Edmund in the final scene

> The gods are just, and of our pleasant vices
> Make instruments to plague us.
> (V, iii)

The play does not reflect justice in every character's fate. Cordelia is hanged and Lear dies afterwards of a broken heart. There is no coherent or unifying conclusion drawn in the play about the impact of divine justice.

The overall impression left to us about the human system of justice is one of the power and strength of corruption, unbridled evil and general abuse within the system.

The child–parent relationship
One of the central issues dealt with in this play is that of the relationship between parents and their children. This issue or theme is reflected both in the main plot and the sub-plot.

Lear, out of a foolish mixture of both tenderness and blindness, gives everything away to two daughters and banishes the third. He does this through a fatal error involving love and language. He believes that true love is expressed in words and hyperboles and so he is deceived by the meaningless and empty platitudes of Regan and Goneril. Likewise, he interprets Cordelia's silence as a lack of love.

At the same time as Lear is suffering from the cold ingratitude of his two daughters, Edgar falls from the rank to which his birth entitled him. This happens because of his father Gloucester's blindness and his brother Edmund's devious plots. Edgar is forced to assume the shape of a beggar tormented by evil spirits in order to survive detection. Both characters are driven out onto the heath where they endure a most profound degree of suffering and degradation.

In some ways Lear and Edgar have a share of the blame in the tragedy which befalls them. Lear confuses his royal function with his parental role. Expecting his daughters to flatter him like his courtiers he will reward them with land in return. It is the King of France who has to remind him that this is wrong in the words 'love's not love, when it is mingled with regards that stands Aloof from th'entire point.'

Edgar is naive and gullible and allows himself to be deceived by his own brother, Edmund. He accepts Edmund's story about Gloucester's anger without a moment's questioning and for the rest of the play adopts the role of a disguised runaway.

The evil which happened to both Lear and Edgar may be a mixture of their own flawed natures plus their treatment by their families. Lear is treated with gross injustice by Regan and Goneril. He is thrust out of the palace and forced to survive the storms. The two sisters are then left to deal with their unadulterated lust for Edmund. This eventually consumes them both and they end up destroying one another. In fact Albany, husband of Goneril, predicts this fact when he condemns his wife for her treatment of her father:

> Tigers, not daughters, what have you perform'd?
> A father, and a gracious aged man, . . .
> Most barbarous, most degenerate! have you madded . . .
> If that the heavens do not their visible spirits
> Send quickly down to these vile offences,
> It will come,
> Humanity must perforce prey on itself,
> Like monsters of the deep.
>
> (IV, ii)

This is in fact what actually occurs in the story of both sisters; destroyed by their jealous passion for Edmund, they end up killing one another.

In contrast, Cordelia continues to love her father in exile. Together with her husband, the King of France, she organises an army to save her father, Lear. At the play's conclusion, her love remains steadfast and Lear is able to anticipate a life in prison with pleasure now that he has her presence with him:

> . . . Come, let's away to prison;
> We two alone will sing like birds i' the cage.
> (V, iii)

Likewise, Edgar performs a similar function in the sub-plot. He prevents his father from committing suicide and it is through him that Gloucester learns the value of endurance:

> Men must endure
> Their going hence, even as their coming hither.
> (V, ii)

Throughout the story of Regan and Goneril there is the recurrent idea that the breaking of human ties, especially those of blood and loyalty, are both abnormal and unnatural. On the other hand, the qualities of love and endurance, which are each manifested in different ways by Edgar and Cordelia, are shown to be binding and positive forces in this play.

Good and evil
One of the central questions asked in this play is what is the cause of evil: 'Let them anatomise Regan and see what breeds around her heart. Is there any cause in nature that makes these hard hearts?'

The play shows the release of evil and the subsequent course of evil. It dramatises the conflict between good and evil and this conflict may be summed up as follows: evil may triumph for a short time but ultimately good asserts itself and emerges victorious at the conclusion. However the cost of this victory results in the destruction of much that is good. And the evil in the play turns out to be self-destructive.

This can be illustrated in the following way. In the stories of Edmund, Goneril and Regan we see the evil that was rooted in both Lear and Gloucester set free in the world. When Lear divides up his kingdom he introduces a principle of calculation or measurement which both Regan and Goneril adopt and carry to an extreme. He also makes a fatal error of understanding. When he introduces this spirit of calculation he is ruthless in his punishment of those who fail to conform to this principle. His daughters both succeed to power. What comes to power with them is this spirit of calculation. One by one they dispose (or plan to) of their enemies. In the final ironic twist this jealousy consumes them both, and they turn on and dispose of each other. This is a magnificent expression of the self-destructive capacity of this world of evil.

Similarly Edmund's wicked nature stems from Gloucester's weaknesses. Gloucester wants to do as the world does, to forget morality, to be comfortable. Likewise Edmund wants to have what the world has: 'lands by wit', to 'grow' and 'prosper'. Edmund's worldliness stems from Gloucester's attitudes.

On the other hand, Edgar and Cordelia, who both symbolise goodness, endure and continue to love their fathers while they are exiled, and give themselves selflessly in order to redeem them.

The final act exposes the ultimate showdown between both sets of characters, and the good emerges victorious.

However there is a certain qualification to this good when we bear witness to the deaths of the leading protagonists; Lear, Cordelia and Gloucester. In other words, good triumphs but at a price.

Literary genre

King Lear is a tragedy. The general sequence of a tragic work follows the story of a hero or a central protagonist who is endowed with a fatal flaw. This flaw causes suffering, the loss of everything and finally death.

In the context of this play, Lear's main flaw consists of an overweening pride and blindness to human nature. Shortly after he has abdicated his kingship he suffers a violent confrontation with Goneril and Regan, and he is forced to accept their terms or face humiliation and poverty out on the heath.

In an extreme state of degradation and suffering throughout the storm scenes he learns the meaning of life, and grows in humility and self-knowledge. All of this occurs with the help of his Fool, who plays a key role here.

Likewise Gloucester is blind to the reality of human nature and fails to see through the wickedness of his son, Edmund. Ironically, it is only when he is physically blinded that he attains a real insight into the truth.

Both characters acknowledge their earlier flaws, and both develop and grow to see the real truth about people and about themselves.

Structure of the play
Plots and parallel meanings

This play is made up of two plots that echo one another in theme. The deliberate parallels that are set up between the two plots serve the function of realism; to give credibility to a play where the characters and events would otherwise be incredible.

Another effect of this deliberate repetition is to universalise and broaden the themes, such as filial ingratitude and evil.

The story and theme of the sub-plot are repeated in the main plot. Two credulous fathers are betrayed by selfish and unscrupulous children. Both are victims of false appearance. Both are weak, gullible and poor judges of character. Both lack sound judgment, both are old men. The Fool teaches Lear while Edgar teaches Gloucester.

The Fool plays a central role in the structure of the play. This role is primarily paradoxical: the supposedly wise King is being taught lessons in wisdom and folly by a fool. We see this mainly in the storm scenes. The Fool is a foil for Lear and also a form of relief. He counters the madness of Lear. He is used almost like a chorus, as he harps all the time on Lear's transgressions. His role forms a curious mixture of faithful service and severe condemnation. He offers relief to the gloom of the tragedy.

The Fool represents the voice of reality for Lear. He appears in act I scene iv, when Kent has just manifested his loyalty for Lear by attacking Oswald, Goneril's cunning servant. Lear is about to pay Kent for his action when the Fool enters and mockingly offers Kent his coxcomb. The implication here is that Lear is a fool if he thinks he can repay people with money now that he has handed over everything to his wicked children. The play is full of comments like this, where the Fool mocks Lear's self-deceit, and essential blindness to human nature. The Fool is not only Lear's teacher but also echoes Lear's conscience. It is significant that Lear is given few soliloquies in the play; the implication could be that the Fool articulates all his insights; that it is against the backdrop of the storm scenes and the Fool's whirling and sometimes ambiguous statements that Lear achieves his moral growth. The whirling ambiguities of the Fool are reflected in the sequence of events.

The relationship between Lear and his Fool is part of the tragic movement of the play; the movement downwards towards the ultimate exposure and defeat when the King is degraded to the status of the meanest of his servants. We watch the royal sufferer being progressively stripped first of extraordinary power, then of ordinary human dignity, then of the very necessities of life when he is more helpless and abject than any animal. However there is a more dreadful consummation than this reduction to physical nakedness. Lear hardly feels the storm because he is struggling to retain his mental integrity, his knowledge and his reason, which for him are the essential marks of humanity itself. From the time when his agony begins and he feels his sanity threatened, he gradually becomes aware of the sufferings of others: 'Poor Fool I have one part of my heart that's sorry for thee yet'. His sympathies are aroused and broadened; he realises that all men are one in pain: 'take physic pomp expose thyself to feel . . .'

In the role of the Fool we are confronted with the paradoxical reversal of wisdom and folly. At the beginning of the play Lear and Gloucester are both blind fools; when Lear loses his sanity his vision is enlarged, as his wits begin to leave him he begins to see the truth about himself, when they are wholly gone he begins to have spasmodic flashes of insight in which he sees the truth about the world. The Fool prophetically exclaims that he would make a good fool. When he loses everything—his kingdom, his sanity and his honour—when he becomes an outcast from society, he attains truth. What is this truth which he attains?

This truth is linked to the idea of suffering and attaining a strong and firm endurance through suffering: 'give me patience', he prays, and later on he tells Gloucester to be patient: 'thou must be patient, we come crying hither'.

In the hour of Lear's helplessness during the storm on the heath, King and Fool, master and slave as they have been so far, become something different—the bond between them grows closer. In the process of madness we become aware of a deep relation of contraries (opposites)—that of wise man and fool. The essence of this relationship consists in a reversal of accepted values: the supposedly wise man of the opening scenes, the Lear who was in a position to have his slave whipped and exercise his own will without contradiction, has become the fool, as his own acts have shown.

Through his behaviour and language, the Fool offers advice, all of which is based on practical wisdom.

The Fool is an all-powerful auxiliary for both the main plot and the sub-plot.

When the Fool leaves the play in the last storm scene, act IV scene vi, we can assume that Lear has grown in moral awareness and it remains for him to be reconciled with Cordelia.

Soliloquy

The soliloquy is a fundamental part of the structure of a Shakespearean tragedy. Shakespeare uses both the public and the private soliloquy in his plays. Each type has a different function. Many of Lear's soliloquies are public, where he articulates his condemnation of humankind. In the storm scene, act III, scene iv, he becomes aware for the first time in his life of the full reality of poverty within his kingdom, and acknowledges that he has done nothing to remedy the situation. Likewise Edgar, Edmund and Kent use the public soliloquy to give reasons for the way they are acting. Edmund is the character who has the most soliloquies and these serve the function of showing how he will manipulate events and use opportunities to his own advantage. All of his soliloquies show him to be exceptionally intelligent, cynical and unprincipled.

Edgar's three soliloquies serve different functions. He gives us an insight into the quality of life in the kingdom as it existed under Lear, the Bedlam beggar who was pelted in the villages and looked upon as mad. He also plays the role of moraliser, or preacher of good and evil, in his soliloquies, for example in the speech where he compares his role to Lear's:

> When that which makes me bend makes the king bow;
> He childed as I fathered . . .
> (III, vi)

Style and language

Shakespeare's style is richly poetic. In his plays the important characters speak in verse, while the minor characters use prose. Language and imagery become an avenue of understanding in the plays of Shakespeare. There is a very wide variety of images and language patterns used in this play. Much of this serves the function of communicating the central message and themes of the playwright.

Nature and the storm scenes

The five storm scenes are symbolic of moral discord. The storm dovetails personal conflict and external convulsion well. The storm which has broken out in Lear's mind is admirably fused with the description of the warring elements. The external storm is itself a projection of his inner state which is expressed in the form of a single poetic reality. Thus related to the action of the elements, Lear assumes a stature which is more than merely personal. Throughout the storm scenes Lear bears the main weight of suffering. He is surrounded by human beings each of whom is used in a different way to illuminate some aspect of his predicament. The Fool, Kent and Edgar bear some of his tragic burden: they show an insight into some of his tragic situation.

Gloucester, who joins him, shows a parallel in his suffering and fall in fortunes.

Lear's first appearance in the storm shows him in a state of hostile condemnation and rebellion. He calls upon the storm to destroy the entire universe and the whole world of nature:

> And thou, all-shaking thunder,
> Strike flat the thick rotundity o' the world!
> Crack nature's moulds, all germens spill at once
> That make ingrateful man!
> (III, ii)

The cause of his anger is still self-love and self-pity, a sense of outrage that he, Lear, King of England, could suffer such a degree of humiliation.

The Fool is the character who points out to him the deeper causes of his tragedy. He does this mainly through his language. Much of his language is made up of puns, riddles, word play and ironic speeches where he teaches Lear to adopt a self-interested and calculating attitude. The irony of speeches like this is that he fails repeatedly to follow his own advice; he insists on following Lear, who has nothing.

In the following lines the Fool reminds Lear that they both have a small amount of wit:

> He that has a little tiny wit,
> With heigh-ho, the wind and the rain,
> Must make content with his fortunes fit,
> Though the rain it raineth every day.
> (III, ii)

There is a profound sense of man's infirmity together with a strong feeling of power and greatness during the storm.

It is within the storm scenes in the company of three different types of mad people that Lear penetrates through to the essential truth of human nature, stripped of the false trappings of sophistication, and he finds in the half-naked Edgar the image of 'unaccommodated man'.

It can certainly be stated that the storm scenes are the most dramatic in the play. The Fool leaves the play in the storm scenes; Lear goes mad in the storm scenes. The paradox of the play, 'reason in madness', is enacted in the storm scenes.

Gloucester's first stage in moral growth occurs when he goes out into the storm to offer comfort and consolation to Lear. It is this action which costs him his eyes.

Animal or bestial imagery
There is a recurrent idea in the play of animals preying upon one another like monsters in the deep. The animal or bestial imagery suggests one human exploiting and destroying another for his own wicked ends.

Men and women are continually referred to as beasts or monsters. Goneril is referred to as a 'sea monster', a 'serpent', a 'wolf', a 'vulture' and a 'kite'. In act III, scene iv, Lear refers to the sisters as 'pelican daughters' feeding on their father's blood. Edgar calls his brother a 'toad spotted villain'.

All of this imagery serves the function of depicting the bestial level reached by man when evil possesses him.

Images of sight and blindness

Much of the symbolism or imagery reflect two of the central ideas in the play: the idea of sight and blindness. Since both protagonists begin in a state of moral blindness to the full reality of their children and of human nature, this imagery plays an important symbolic role in the play.

Because this play concerns itself with two old men who are blind to the reality of their own lives and blind to the nature of other people, Shakespeare makes use of irony to dramatise these ideas.

Irony serves several functions in the play. It illustrates the profound discrepancy between the real nature of things and their mere appearance. Shakespeare uses irony as a technique to show blindness in characters. Certain characters, such as Gloucester, Lear, and Edgar, are essentially blind to the truth about themselves and others. So as Lear banishes Kent, his loyal servant and the only one who will tell him the truth, he ironically prays to Apollo, the god of light.

Edmund uses a false letter to frame his brother, then adopts the role of confidante to Edgar by advising him to stay out of Gloucester's way. Edgar is blind to evil and corruption in nature, and particularly in his brother Edmund's nature, and we hear him ironically telling Edmund how 'some villain has done me wrong' (act I, scene ii).

The play is full of ironic reversals. Gloucester gains full insight only after he has been physically blinded. Lear, King of England, learns his wisest lessons on human nature and on life in the context of extreme degradation and in the company of the Fool.

Irony functions as a moral commentary on the wicked characters and is another means of illustrating in a graphic manner the profoundly self-destructive quality of evil.

Cultural context

England and the medieval court form the primary cultural background of *King Lear*. The play deals with the culture of kingship and monarchy at that time. The characters are drawn from the aristocracy or nobility. They are public figures whose actions and subsequent sufferings become universalised.

The plot of the play deals with inter-family relationships and ensuing intrigue, rivalry and conflict. Lear makes a fatal error regarding the nature of kingship: at the beginning of the play he believes he can abdicate the duties of king and retain merely 'the name and all th'addition to a King' (act I, scene i).

Lear has been King of England for many years; he has no male heir and so roles change and he hands over his authority to Goneril, Regan and their husbands. In this act of abdication Lear disrupts the social order and causes general anarchy in his kingdom.

The blinding of Gloucester is a barbaric act, which co-exists with Christian insights expressed by Lear in some of the storm scenes and at the conclusion of the play. In prison with Cordelia he sees them both as 'God's spies', taking upon themselves the mystery of things.

The play deals with particular matters, such as clothes and courtly deference, which are an inherent part of this cultural environment. Lear sheds these symbols of wealth, rich clothes and fine speech in his movement towards truth. The play shows the human being reaching truth when stripped of these false adornments of culture. Lear finally sheds his sanity and descends to a state of physical and emotional nakedness.

General vision or viewpoint

At the conclusion of this play there is a certain sense of reconciliation, harmony and justice. Love is not a victory in the play; the victory at the conclusion brings with it much tragedy.

The play presents a world of extreme suffering and many characters express negative philosophies. This suffering, however, brings the benefit of knowledge and awareness. There is an element of justice in the world, but it is not absolute; evil is punished, but good is not always rewarded. The play illustrates the value of endurance and love in the face of cruelty and evil.

The conclusion, therefore, is neither completely pessimistic nor optimistic; people are not shown as mere playthings of a blind or capricious power. The world is not given over wholly to darkness either. There is a blending of loss and sorrow, but also a certain peace at the exposure of evil. There is a certain awe and apprehension in the face of the unfathomable mystery of evil.

In the figures of Albany and Edgar there is a sense of stability and a realistic note in the words

> All friends shall taste
> The wages of their virtue, and all foes
> The cup of their deservings.
> (V, iii, line 306–8)

The general vision or viewpoint offered to us at the conclusion of this tragedy is that life is grim and tough, but people can survive it.

12
Notes on Films

CHARACTERISTICS OF FILMS

This chapter contains some guidelines that can be used in answering questions in the 'comparative study' section. There are also notes on all the films on the prescribed syllabus for Higher level:

The Third Man (2003 exam)
My Left Foot (2003 exam)
A Room with a View (2004 exam)
The Dead (2004 exam)
Cinema Paradiso (2003 and 2004 exams)
Strictly Ballroom (2003 and 2004 exams)
On the Waterfront (2003 and 2004 exams)
Richard III (2003 and 2004 exams)

A film is about people, places, and situations. The way they are shown, and the reason they are shown in a particular way, varies greatly. A film is a narrative: it tells a story. Being able to say what a film is about, or what the meaning of the story is, is another way of identifying the themes or issues treated.

It is important to understand what particular values or view of life are represented in a film. A film can promote or criticise certain issues, depending on the stance taken by the director on the themes or issues being presented.

Examine what values or understanding of life the film emphasises or criticises. Ask yourself the following questions:

- Is there a coherent message or moral in the film?
- If not, why not?
- How does the film leave you at the end? Depressed? Sad? Happy? Why?

Film genres

A film-maker structures the story or narrative in a particular way. In other words, the viewpoint adopted by the film-maker in relation to the subject is what constitutes the film's genre. Film genres include detective story or thriller, western, romance, biography, and social realism.

Features of the film genre
Films are made up of images that are photographed within a particular *frame,* the rectangle that contains the image. The camera frame controls what the audience see and how they see it. According to what the film-maker is trying to say, this frame can control certain actions and eliminate others, or it can direct attention in a particular direction, either towards an object or person or away from them.

Understanding the genre of a film means being able to ask and answer certain questions:

- Is there a pattern of striking camera movements, long shots, or abrupt transitions?
- Why does the film end on this image?
- Why does the film start in the way it does?
- When was the film made?
- What does the title mean in relation to the story?
- Why are the credits presented in this particular way? Why are they presented against a particular background?

Every film uses patterns of repetition that are contrasted with certain important moments. One of the first steps in analysing the meaning of a film is recognising these patterns and understanding why they are important.

THE THIRD MAN

(2003 exam only)
Written by Graham Greene; directed by Carol Reed.

Genre
The Third Man is in the category of *film noir,* with features of the thriller. Film noir (literally 'dark film') is characterised by high-contrast black-and-white photography with low-key lighting, which creates a moody effect and gives a suspenseful quality to the story. The world portrayed by film noir has a dark look about it and generally shows the dark side of life.

The stock character in this type of film is the private detective, working in a world that conspires against him. In *The Third Man* Holly Martins is the detective who undertakes the investigation of the death of his friend Harry Lime. There is also a sense of entrapment or imprisonment by the individual; this is achieved by images of people pictured behind bars.

Another feature of this genre is the presence of a *'femme fatale.'* In *The Third Man* we have Anna, the woman torn between her love for Lime, her corrupt lover, and her duty to what is right.

Historical and literary background
The background of this film is Vienna just after the Second World War. Post-war Vienna was divided by the Allies into four occupation zones: the American, Soviet, English and French zones. The film is set against the background of general devastation and demoralisation in the wake of war. It was a time of corruption and illegal dealings on the black market. The background is typical of wartime: moral and spiritual destitution, poverty and corruption, desolation and anxiety, distrust, and confusion of values.

Cultural context
The Third Man is set in post-war Vienna. The opening sequence contains newsreel film that speaks about the black market and the moral decadence that often follows in the wake of war. War in the film is seen as something to be capitalised on; this gives the film a realistic edge. The culture depicted in Vienna is a civilised and educated one. The military officer is seen as a moral compass in this world: he is a force that represents law and order, is shrewd and worldly-wise, with no illusions. Vienna is suffering from the effects of war: tea is scarce, clothes are shabby, buildings are derelict, and people in general are depressed.

The story
Holly Martins, a writer of pulp fiction, comes to Vienna to meet an old friend, Harry Lime, who has promised him a job. When he arrives he learns of the death of Lime in a car accident. He attends the funeral, where he meets Major Calloway, who is suspicious about Lime's activities. Martins undertakes to investigate the circumstances of Lime's death. He meets Anna, Lime's former girl-friend, who is working illegally in Vienna. Martins learns from Calloway that Lime was involved in dealings on the black market involving penicillin, causing a great number of deaths as a result.

Meanwhile he has discovered that Lime is not dead; and he tries to meet him. He finally tricks him into a meeting, which gives rise to a chase through the sewers of Vienna, a chase that culminates in Martins shooting and killing Lime.

The story is told by means of a voice-over narration, which is the voice of Holly Martins. The plot revolves around the activities of Harry Lime in Vienna and his supposed death in a traffic accident. It develops through the medium of Holly Martins and his attempts to uncover the truth surrounding Lime's death. Various events occur to contribute to the tension, such as the appearance of Lime hidden in an archway outside Anna's flat one night, and the information given by Major Calloway about Lime's sleazy manoeuvrings. The falsification of Anna's passport consolidates Lime's guilt. The plot culminates in a magnificent scene in the sewers underneath the streets of Vienna, with Martins and Lime at the centre.

Themes or issues
War
War is a central issue in *The Third Man,* and the brutal effect of war on civilisation is shown throughout the film. It is shown on the surface level of society through the

images of burnt-out buildings, crumbling structures, and general devastation. On another level the tragic effect of war is shown in the lives of the citizens. There are images of distrust and fear, a sense of helplessness and hopelessness in the aftermath of a catastrophe. These images percolate through the film and generate an atmosphere of distrust and suspicion. People are shown to be insecure and wary; camera angles suggest the fear and the suspicion in this society.

Finally, this corruption seeps through to the inner person. The black market mirrors the degeneration of humankind because of the corrupting effects of the war. The profound effects of Lime's actions are shown in the sick children at the hospital and are pitifully registered in the reaction of Martins, who up to now has compromised with Lime's evil doings. Lime allows himself to become completely cynical about life and people as he speaks to Martins in the carnival scene. War and all its evil effects are a strong element in this film.

Loyalty
This theme is a strong element in *The Third Man*. The character of Holly Martins, who alone tries to find out the truth about his friend, embodies this theme. He refuses to accept the fact that Lime is a dealer in black-market medicine, and he even gets himself embroiled in a fight in defending Lime's innocence.

Anna, Lime's girl-friend, also steadfastly adheres to her memory of him and will not accept the reality of his criminal nature. Right to the end Anna remains determined to uphold Lime's reputation. The long concluding sequence demonstrates in a vivid manner how strong her loyalty is. She is pictured walking down a long avenue filled with falling leaves while Martins remains standing on the roadside watching her. This image suggests that in spite of all that has happened, Lime still means everything to her.

Moral corruption
This theme is generally a corollary of war. The disastrous effects of war usually reveal in some way the particular taintings of moral corruption. Early on in the film there are images of dealings in stolen watches, of a dead body in the Vienna sewers, of racketeering and crime. According to Lime, corruption and double-dealing are the only way to survive and to deal successfully with life. As he preaches to his friend Martins in the fairground, 'in Italy for thirty years under the Borgias they had warfare, terror, murder, and bloodshed, yet they produced Michaelangelo, Leonardo da Vinci, and the Renaissance; yet in Switzerland, with brotherly love, five hundred years of democracy and peace, all they produced was the cuckoo clock.' According to this cynical view, corruption is an essential part of the way we survive in this world. However, this corruption backfires on Lime and his associates as Martins' conscience becomes more enlightened about the nature and consequences of Lime's evil doings. Lime is exposed at the conclusion and finally destroyed.

Structure and style
Visual images and photography
The film depicts imposing architecture, which creates an image of a rich, ornate background. It makes distinct use of many oblique shots. These tilted angles suggest a world caught off balance, a world that has lost its direction. The camera also focuses on different aspects of the characters in the film. A series of close-ups registers some ambiguous movements of people and facial expressions that are deliberately enigmatic. We notice, for example, the picture of the Austrian at the funeral in the beginning of the film with sly, furtive eyes registering the activities of Martins in the graveyard.

Much of the lighting is dark and shadowy, in keeping with this genre and that of the thriller. Movements are eerie and ominous; many images show figures in doorways looking out stealthily, or pictures of people behind bars, as if in prison. There are many cul-de-sacs, mainly shown at night. Much of the effect of the lighting and direction comes from the use of black-and-white photography.

Language
The various accents give a distinct tone to this film. When Martins arrives in Vienna he meets a porter who communicates the news of Lime's accident in broken English and a smattering of German. Much of the dialogue is sharp and tense, particularly that of Lime, whom we meet for the first time in the carnival scene. Here his language is short and clipped, suggesting that he is trying to deal with an awkward situation. Calloway's accent is upper-class English and long drawn out, in contrast with Martins, who speaks laconically, like the characters he writes about in his pulp fiction.

Sound
The main sound in the film is the background music, played on a zither, a traditional stringed instrument, which gives an eerie atmosphere to the film. For the most part the music creates tension: there is no joy in it. After the funeral of Lime the music is long drawn out and creates a distinctly ominous atmosphere.

Symbols
There are many references to animals, to cats and budgies, all of which could suggest the theme of exploitation and abuse. The architecture of the house is of a heavy baroque type, which is rich in symbolic resonance. At the beginning, when Martins arrives in Vienna, we see him walking under a ladder outside a grand building decorated with an elaborate façade. Then the image is sharply undercut by the use of dramatic shadow, which gives the whole atmosphere of the film a distinctive symbolic resonance. The scene is set for a story involving crime and the underworld.

General vision or viewpoint
The film concludes cleverly on two different scenes that are skilfully juxtaposed. The first takes place in the sewer, with Lime at the centre of the police chase. The second takes place after Lime's funeral, as Anna walks in the long-drawn-out shot away from the grave and down the avenue of trees, with Martins standing beside the road. For this reason there are different statements or visions in the conclusion of the film. The general vision is that evil is punished. The wickedness and evil manoeuvrings of Lime catch up on him in the sewer: he is caught like a rat in his own trap. This image is significant. Lime has caused a great deal of suffering to innocent children and to people in general through his greed and selfishness. Martins experiences a moral trauma and confusion throughout the film. His dilemma springs on the one hand from his loyalty to his unscrupulous friend Lime and on the other hand from his duty to what he knows is right and just. It is only at the hospital, when he becomes fully exposed to the brutal suffering caused by Lime's illegal trafficking in penicillin, that he is convinced of Lime's guilt. Shortly after this, he shoots Lime in the sewer.

As Anna continues to walk slowly out of the graveyard after the real burial of Lime, we bear witness to the astonishing loyalty of her love in spite of everything. The power of love is strong, and it can even blind one to evil. This seems to be implicit in the long shot at the conclusion as Anna, overwhelmed by grief, ignores Martins and walks on. Truth triumphs at the conclusion, but at a price.

MY LEFT FOOT

(2003 exam only)
Based on the book by Christy Brown; directed by Jim Sheridan.

Genre
Biography.

Historical and literary background

The background of this film is working-class Dublin in the nineteen-thirties, a time of poverty and hardship.

Cultural context

The cultural background of this film is working-class Dublin in the early twentieth century, a time of relative poverty. Families are large but united, and traditional hospitality and neighbourliness still exist. We see this in the frequent offers of neighbourly help, the street games organised by local teenagers, and the family meals. The Catholic faith is a strong feature of life in this society, evident in the many religious images. The local pub is an important focal point in the life of the community. Significantly, when Christy writes his first words on the slate, his father carries him down to the pub for his first pint of stout. Christy is being initiated into manhood.

The story

My Left Foot is based on the autobiography of Christy Brown, a writer and painter who was born with cerebral palsy into an impoverished family. The film begins with the mature Christy arriving at the house of Lord Castlewellan to participate in a presentation for charity. It then develops by means of flashback as it recalls Christy's attempts to overcome the limitations imposed by his condition. He is a strong and determined character who comes from a tough social background in which a person is expected to make out for himself.

Poverty is a central feature in the lives of the characters. Christy's father fluctuates in his moods, as he finds it hard to accept Christy's limited ability. His mother, on the other hand, is a stalwart figure who quietly perseveres and patiently encourages Christy through all his vicissitudes. All his family unite to encourage him in his attempts at painting. It is significant that the first word he writes is 'Mother'. His mother is an indispensable agent in his growth; she continually sacrifices herself so that he will get all the help and encouragement he needs.

Later, Christy's father dies as he tries to build a room where Christy can carry out his work undisturbed. Christy falls in love with his therapist, who helps him to develop his talents. At the conclusion he marries the nurse, Mary, who is seen with him during the reception in the house of Lord Castlewellan.

Themes or issues
The principal theme of this film is courage in the face of adversity, seen in the life of Christy Brown and his family. The superhuman struggle to overcome the personal limitations imposed by cerebral palsy and the corresponding courage that is shown by the characters triumph at the conclusion of the film.

Family
The power of the family is another theme of *My Left Foot*. We see how the support of his family generates a positive attitude in Christy. The mother is a central figure of power and unity.

Love
The theme of love and the need for emotional security features strongly. It is seen as a powerful emotional force that transcends personal limitations and builds up the person.

Class
We get an insight into the class structure of society in this film. Christy belongs to the working class, while Lord Castlewellan's background is the Anglo-Irish ascendancy class; this is shown through such symbols as the big car, the butler, and the long avenue lined with trees.

Structure and style
Visual images and photography
Close-ups are used to focus our attention on Christy's attempts to communicate, to show his frustrations or simply give expression to his feelings. Close-ups of the mother portray her anguish and suffering, while those of the father show his perplexity and confusion with the whole situation.

The streets are long and dark, suggesting the poverty of working-class Dublin. When Christy becomes famous the lighting significantly becomes brighter, and there are more open spaces. Money has enlarged his possibilities.

Sound
The music is intense and dramatic, underlining the frustrations and tensions of the story.

Language
The language used is the Dublin working-class dialect of English.

General vision or viewpoint
The general vision of this film is positive. The impression we are left with at the conclusion is the importance of struggle and optimism in the face of difficulties. The power of the mother is a central facet in consolidating unity and strength within Christy, in spite of all the odds; she is a continuous source of hope and optimism.

Christy's own tenacity is evident also, not only in the way he develops his talents to an outstanding degree but in the strength with which he deals with people. This is evident at the conclusion, when he nags the nurse to such a degree that she agrees to meet him that night. Later on he marries her.

A ROOM WITH A VIEW

(2004 exam only)
Based on the book by E. M. Forster; directed by James Ivory.

Genre
Romance.

Historical and literary background
The film is based on the novel by E. M. Forster, first published in 1908. This was a time when England was a colonial power.

Cultural context
Two contrasting cultural backgrounds are depicted in this film: upper-class England and Florence. Bourgeois England is restrained and rigid. Great importance is attached to certain codes of behaviour. Women are not allowed to travel alone but have to be chaperoned. The style of life is stiff and formal; this is shown in dress, speech, movement, and social behaviour.

The culture of Florence is rich and flamboyant. The atmosphere is open and bright; the streets are exciting and fascinating. We see open, airy streets and squares, impressive monuments, and striking architecture. The Italians are a colourful and varied people; they have no problem with chatting to foreigners or even engaging in a violent street fight. The social codes are radically different.

The story
Lucy Honeychurch, a young Englishwoman, is on a visit to Florence, chaperoned by

her cousin, Charlotte Bartlett. They have been led to believe that they will have a wonderful view at the Pensione Bertolini, but they are disappointed when they arrive. An English father and son overhear them when they express their dissatisfaction and promptly offer to exchange rooms. Charlotte, for her young cousin's sake, is offended at this presumption, especially when the young man is dangerously attractive. However, the rector of Lucy's parish in England, Mr Beebe, happens to be staying here as well; he offers to act as an intermediary, and the rooms are exchanged without further ado.

The next morning Charlotte tours the city with Eleanor Lavish, a novelist, whom she met at dinner the night before. Lucy goes for a walk alone, and she witnesses a violent street fight, in which a young man is seriously injured. She becomes weak and faints from the shock of what she has seen. Luckily, George Emerson, the young man she had met in the *pensione* (guesthouse), is there to help her back to her lodgings.

The following day all the English visitors arrange to go sightseeing as a group, and the Emersons belong to the party. George and Lucy become separated from the others, and in a cornfield he kisses her. Charlotte witnesses what happens, and after they return to the city she arranges for them to leave their rooms the next day. The women agree not to tell anyone what has happened to Lucy.

Back in England, Lucy accepts a proposal of marriage from Cecil Vyse, a pompous and arrogant snob. By chance, the Emersons take a house in the village of Summer Street, close to the Honeychurch residence. Mr Beebe and Lucy's brother, Freddy, invite George to go swimming in a nearby pond on his first day in the village. The men are very high-spirited, and naked, and they chase each other around the pond. Unfortunately, this occurs at the same time that the ladies are taking their afternoon walk in the woods, and they come upon the men in all their naked glory.

Freddy befriends George, and he is invited to the Honeychurch home regularly to play tennis. Lucy is perturbed by George's renewed proximity; the contrast between George and the stuffy Cecil is very obvious, and this unsettles Lucy.

When Charlotte comes to stay with the family, she is concerned for Lucy, fearing that the presence of George will do harm to her engagement to Cecil. One day Cecil is reading aloud and criticising what he considers to be a dreadful novel, and both Lucy and George are listening. The book happens to be by Eleanor Lavish, the woman who stayed in the same *pensione,* and is set in Florence; and Cecil reads a paragraph describing exactly the scene where George kissed Lucy. On the way back into the house, out of sight of the others, George repeats the performance.

Lucy is upset by this, and hurt that Charlotte told Eleanor Lavish, after they had agreed not to tell anyone about what had happened in Italy. In the presence of Charlotte, she asks George to leave. George gives a passionate account of his love for her, and tries to make her see that Cecil cares for her only as he would a prize possession. Lucy denies the fact that she may love George; but all the same she breaks off her engagement with Cecil soon afterwards.

When George sees that Lucy will not have him, he decides to leave Summer Street, as he cannot bear to be near her. Lucy is surprised and shocked to see the furniture being removed from the house. Mr Emerson talks to her and makes a heartfelt plea to her to stop denying the truth. Realisation dawns on her that she does love George after all; and the film ends with the two lovers on their honeymoon in the same *pensione* in Florence, where they kiss at the window of the 'room with a view'.

Themes or issues
Love
A Room with a View is essentially a love story with a happy ending. Within the first ten minutes Lucy exchanges glances with George Emerson across the dinner table, and we know that something is going to happen. Even Charlotte Bartlett can see this. She senses danger immediately, and she is extremely protective of Lucy.

The relationship develops the next day when George catches Lucy as she faints with horror at the sight of blood after a street fight. Lucy is naturally wary of him and gives the distinct impression that she does not trust her own feelings where he is concerned. On the way back to the *pensione* they pause for a while looking down on the river, and George simply says, 'Something tremendous has happened.'

Unlike Lucy, who is unsure of her feelings, George knows that he is attracted to her, and he acts on his instincts. He takes the opportunity to kiss her a second time after Cecil has read the paragraph based on their first encounter in Italy. He is more spontaneous when he acts like this, though he is very reserved in company.

It is clear to the viewer that Lucy is attracted to George, but class barriers prevent her from admitting to her love for him. It is only when her refusal to accept his love drives him away that she is jolted into the realisation that she does love him after all and cannot bear the thought of losing him.

The story draws a contrast between the idea of love and real love as it is evinced in everyday life. Cecil Vyse proposes to Lucy because he desires a wife who is suitable to his needs. Lucy comes from a suitable family, she is attractive, and she plays the piano very well. Cecil is emotionally shallow, but Lucy refuses to acknowledge that their relationship will be hollow and insincere. It is only when George arrives and passionately declares his love for her that Lucy realises what true love is.

Self-deception and self-realisation
It is obvious from the start that Lucy deceives herself about her feelings for George. On the day they meet, George's father is intrusive, pushy, and generous almost to the point of rudeness. This emphasises the fact that they are from different classes. Charlotte is horrified at his manner, and Lucy knows unconsciously that a relationship between herself and George would be unacceptable to her family.

On her return to England she is courted by Cecil Vyse, a man from the highest social class. This fact underlines the gap between herself and George. Lucy accepts Cecil's proposal of marriage, because it seems the right thing to do. Cecil is neither physically nor emotionally attractive to her, and as the story unfolds she finds him more unbearable, particularly when compared with George.

The plot is based on the fact that Lucy is lying not only to everyone else but to herself as well. Finally, realising that she cannot suppress her feelings any longer, she transcends the social barriers that separate her from her lover. Much of the viewer's enjoyment of this film comes from observing Lucy's struggle to admit her true feelings to herself, and watching her succumb to them in the end.

Class
To the English upper and middle classes at the turn of the century, social position was crucial. In *A Room with a View*, snobbery and pretentiousness and the accompanying hypocrisy are glaringly exposed. Charlotte's attitude towards Mr Emerson in the *pensione* is a striking example of this. The Miss Alans, an elderly couple, also illustrate this when they sympathise with Charlotte and Lucy for having to endure Mr Emerson's insistence on exchanging rooms.

Cecil Vyse is an insufferable snob, who sneers at everything that does not match his standards. In fact he shows how social standing and gentility do not necessarily go together: he is quite rude about Lucy's brother, Freddy, because he is not an academic; he also makes Lucy's mother feel that she is not good enough for him.

It is Cecil who unwittingly organises the letting of the cottage in Summer Street to the Emersons. This is not done out of good will but to get the better of the owner and to punish him for being (in Cecil's opinion) a snob. It doesn't occur to him that George Emerson will be invited to socialise with people as genteel as the Honeychurch family.

It is because of her position in society that Lucy accepts Cecil's proposal and refuses to consider George's advances. There is too much at stake for her to contemplate disgracing herself and her family; the fact that Cecil continuously reminds her of the difference between his position and George's reinforces the point. It is Cecil who precipitates his own downfall through this approach, as Lucy begins to see that he is more in love with the idea of who he is than with giving himself to her selflessly in a loving relationship.

In the end, Lucy has the courage to overcome the social barriers that divide her and George and to follow her instincts. Much of the film concentrates on Lucy's emancipation from the restrictions imposed on her by her family and the society that surrounds her.

Structure and style
Visual images and photography
The Florentine scene, with the view as the main focus, is a striking feature of the film. Art is an important topic, as the architecture of Florence illustrates. The stone carvings on the streets and the inside of a church are examined; paintings in the art gallery in London feature too, and Cecil compares Lucy to a Leonardo painting. The lovers kiss in a beautiful cornfield and later on in a green countryside. The colour green is evident everywhere; the lush landscape of England is seen in the swimming episode and in the tennis parties.

There are no significant changes in the lighting at any point in the film. Italy and England in the summer are both awash with light. England indoors is often in shadow, and this sometimes varies according to the scene. When Lucy is refusing George, the room is particularly dark. Most of this shadowy lighting reflects their relationship.

Language
The accents of the actors are clearly drawn. Cecil Vyse in particular has what he considers to be a superior accent. His speeches are in a haughty tone, and this is more exaggerated when he is criticising or demeaning someone. His language makes him sound and look ridiculous. Mr Emerson speaks with a plain and unadorned accent. He comes across as a more honest character, who speaks as he feels, and he stands out in contrast to Cecil, and in particular to the company he meets in Florence and England.

Symbols
The piano is a symbol in the film. Lucy plays it regularly, expressing her strongest emotions through her playing. It is Mr Beebe who is struck by the fact that her personality does not match the way she plays. He makes the point that if Lucy lives as she plays, 'it will be very exciting for us, and for her.' He suspects that she will break out some day and that 'one day music and life will mingle.'

General vision or viewpoint
The general vision or viewpoint seems to be ambivalent about the England the film portrays. In one way it could be seen as a lightly critical satire of Edwardian society; on another level it could be an affectionately observed comedy of manners.

The Dead

(2004 exam only)
Directed by John Huston.

Historical and literary background

The film is an adaptation of James Joyce's short story 'The Dead' in *Dubliners*. The film is set in Dublin in 1904.

The story

Two elderly sisters, Miss Kate and Miss Julia Morkan, hold their annual dinner party for their friends and relatives. They invite various people including their nephew Gabriel and his wife Gretta. Mary Jane is the niece of the two Miss Morkans, and plays the organ. They invite a lot of young couples. They spend the evening dancing and engaging in friendly conversation. Aunt Julia sings an old song called 'Arrayed for the Bridal'.

Freddy Malins turns up drunk, and his mother is disgusted. Mr Browne is an older man and a friend of the two aunts who belongs to 'the other persuasion' and enjoys his drink. The party is formal and polite, except for the frequent interruptions from Freddy who continues to make irrelevant remarks. Most of the conversation revolves around music and the past. Aunt Kate talks in animated tones about how the top gallery of the Old Theatre Royal used to be packed in their day. Mrs Malins mentions that Freddy is off to Mount Melleray at the weekend. This gives rise to a conversation about the religious practices of the monks. Mr Browne thinks that repentance and indulgences are great things: a type of 'free insurance'. They make allusions to how the monks sleep in their coffins to remind them of their last end.

Gabriel gives a speech after they have had dinner. It is filled with references to the people who have gone before, and to the responsibility of all to enjoy the present times. He reminds them of their duties and loving affections for those who are alive. He makes a toast to his two aunts who are sincerely moved.

As Gabriel and his wife take their leave and cross the Liffey on O'Connell Street Bridge, Gabriel notices that his wife is deeply moved by the song 'The Lass of Aughrim'. On their way home in the carriage Gabriel makes some attempts to engage his wife in conversation, but it is clear that she is distracted and removed from him. He feels a deep disquiet.

Back in the bedroom of the guesthouse where they are staying for the night, Gabriel tries to find out from his wife, Gretta, what is the matter. He then discovers that she is lamenting the death of a young man called Michael Furey, who died of a broken heart because of her. Gabriel questions her a few times about whether or not she loved him. It is clear she has never forgotten Michael in all her years married to Gabriel. As she falls asleep on the bed, crying profusely, Gabriel moves to the window and, looking out through the net curtains at the countryside, he sees snow falling.

The film concludes with the voice of Gabriel speaking about how small a part he has played in his wife's life, and how he has never known what it is to really love. In flashback, Aunt Julia is shown laid out on her bed while Gabriel struggles to express his sympathy to Aunt Kate. Gabriel's voice continues to speak about the fact that soon everyone will be only shades, and will die. He notes that the snow is falling and that he too will be like everyone else from the past: he will dwindle and dissolve just like the snow.

Themes or issues
- relationships
- memories
- mortality
- love

Genre
The genre of this film is social realism. It is set in a specific time in Dublin in the early twentieth century, and gives us a deep insight into the different types of relationship between people.

The film is told mainly through dialogue, and there is a long monologue at the conclusion spoken by Gabriel, the central character.

Camera angles
There are many shots of dark buildings from the outside, and shadowy halls and rooms.

The camera focuses equally on every character during dinner and enables the viewer to gain an insight into the personality of each one. There are several shots of Gabriel alone, obviously fretting over his feelings of inadequacy.

Flashback
The director makes use of flashback only once in the film. This occurs at the conclusion when Gabriel is reflecting from the window about the imminent death of Aunt Julia, and he looks into the future and sees her laid out on the bed with the rosary beads twined between her fingers. The use of flashback here highlights the theme of death which is particularly evident in the concluding sequence.

Cultural context
The culture is that of Dublin in the early twentieth century. Behaviour is formal and polite. There are frequent scenes of the cab, which is an old black carriage drawn by a horse and driver. The large lamps on the streets and the candles and paraffin lamps seen from within the house clearly set the time period.

Clothes are distinctive of this time: the men wear large black bowler hats while the women have long gowns to the ground. The style of clothes is rich and elegant.
There are many images of photographs and mementos on the table, which suggests that the past is important in the lives of these people.

General vision or viewpoint
Gretta's disclosures about her love for Michael Furey in the past leads to the long monologue from Gabriel as he contemplates the snow falling outside his bedroom window. It is clear that although these two people have been married for some time, they still do not know each other very well. Gabriel has never fully experienced what it is to really love someone, while his wife has lived in the past and has sustained a schoolgirl love for someone who died when he was seventeen years old. The disclosure from his wife leads to Gabriel's contemplations about the future, and the fact that all people will die; they will be merely shades.

The general vision at the conclusion is negative and depressing. There are many scenes of bleak, empty graveyards and snowy countryside. It is as if the world of nature will obliterate humankind's efforts, and everything will be brought to nothingness.

CINEMA PARADISO

(2003 and 2004 exams)
Written and directed by Giuseppe Tornatore.

Genre
Social realism.

Historical and literary background
Cinema Paradiso begins in a small Sicilian town in the nineteen-forties, shortly after the Second World War. This was a time when the cinema was just developing. It made a huge impact on the people of Sicily, who in many ways were isolated from the cultural developments of mainland Italy.

Cultural context
The cultural context of this film is Sicily during a period from just after the war to about thirty years later. There is a strong emphasis on the changes that take place in the Sicilian style of life during this period. At first the people are simple, ignorant of urban life, and they worship the world of the cinema with awe. The projectionist, Alfredo, is a representative of this type of community—a simple man, who cannot read or write. The power of the priest in the community is evident in the way he censors unsuitable material in the films.

As the life-style changes, however, the people become more sophisticated and less satisfied with the films shown. The ownership of the cinema changes hands, and the priest no longer exercises control over the films shown. The old and rather tame romances are gone and more vibrant genres take their place: people are now watching westerns, thrillers, and passionate love stories. Economic change brings about the eventual closure of the cinema to make way for a car park.

The story
The story deals with Salvatore de Gito, a successful film director, who hears about the death of Alfredo. A flashback recalls Salvatore's youth and adolescence in a small Sicilian town and shows his relationship with Alfredo, the local film projectionist, who becomes a father figure for him, as Salvatore's father has disappeared. Salvatore is fascinated by the local cinema and spends most of his youth there, helping Alfredo. He falls in love with the daughter of a banker, but they separate, and she leaves the town.

Eventually Alfredo persuades Salvatore to leave and get a better job, as he will never do anything worthwhile otherwise. The cinema is bought by a new owner, and the style changes. Formerly the local priest could censor many things: now images are more permissive. The cinema is burnt down, and a car park is put there instead. Salvatore returns after thirty years for Alfredo's funeral. It is clear that he has not found real love in his life.

Themes or issues
Love and relationships
One of the most powerful and endearing issues treated in this film is that of relationships. The relationship between the child Salvatore and Alfredo is perhaps the most tender and poignant. Alfredo is child-like in his nature and treats Salvatore almost as his own child. This relationship is strengthened when Salvatore saves Alfredo's life when the cinema catches fire. This relationship remains strongly embedded in the memory of the mature Salvatore years after he leaves the town.

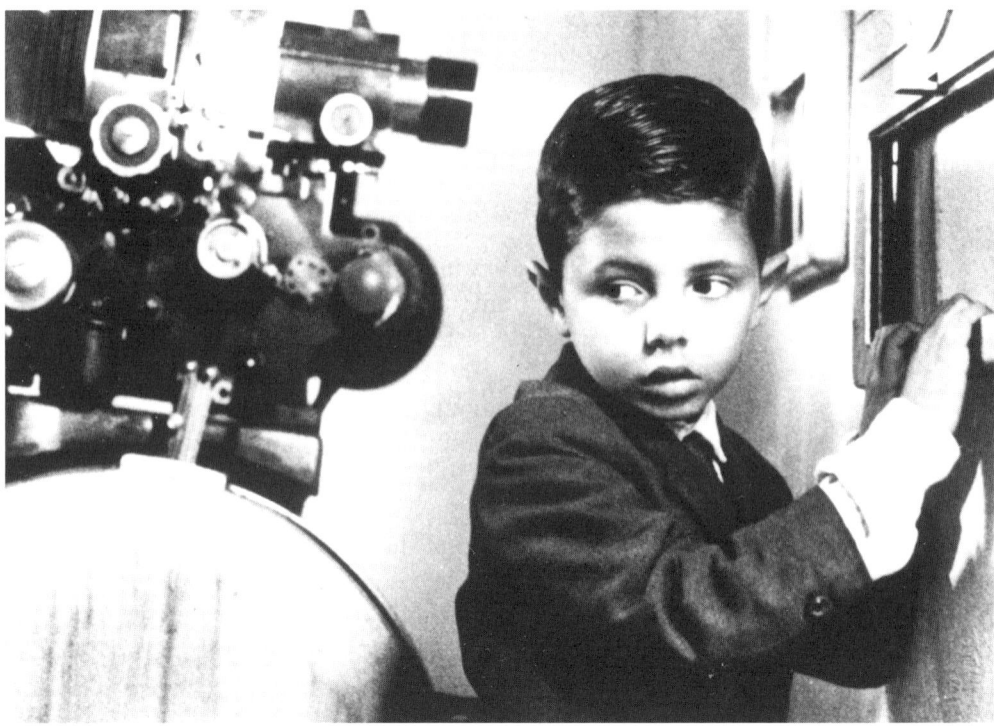

The fascination of the cinema
The town community are characterised by their utter simplicity of nature. For them, the cinema is another world, which is filled with entertainment and excitement. Through the eyes of the child Salvatore we bear witness to the immense wonder filling these simple people as the screen reveals yet more images from another world. We also see the power of the local priest in the community to maintain moral standards, as he ruthlessly cuts any scenes that are morally offensive.

Change comes, however; and when a new owner takes over the cinema, the style of things becomes different. Censorship is less strict; but the cinema is closed to make way for a car park.

Structure and style
Visual images and photography
A variety of camera angles is used in the film. At the end of the film the technique of superimposing one picture over another is used, and this is done brilliantly, giving the effect of a reflection in a car window as Salvatore looks out on the countryside.

There is a clever variation at the funeral, when the shot is taken from inside the hearse, looking out at the mourners. The picture resembles a television screen, surrounded by the rear window of the hearse. The camera techniques are more varied here at the end, showing the viewers that things have really changed since Salvatore left thirty or more years ago, and now everything is presented differently.

Language
The film is in the Sicilian dialect of Italian; it is also issued with English sub-titles. Much of the richness of the language and the meaning will be lost on the non-Italian viewer. However, the facial expressions of Toto as a child and the tender expressions of Salvatore are all the more meaningful.

General vision or viewpoint
The general vision of this film is an overview of the rapid changes in Sicily and, by inference, throughout much of Europe over a forty-year period after the Second World War. The narrator does not seem to like these changes, yet there is a sense of inevitability about it all. At the end, as Toto gazes at the old square he knew as a boy, now filled with cars and noise, there is a definite sadness. The message is to be one of disappointment that life has changed in such a way.

The most shocking part is when the cinema is knocked down to make room for a car park. That says it all. The cinema, which stood for the old cultural values, is gone.

STRICTLY BALLROOM

(2003 and 2004 exams)
Directed by Baz Luhrman.

Historical and literary background
This film is set in Australia during the 1970s.

The story
The story centres on the main character, Scott Hastings, and his attempts to win the Australian Pan Pacific Dancing Competition. The film opens with Scott taking part in the Waratah Dance Championships. Barry Fife controls these competitions and will not allow dancers to change their style or steps. Scott, however, wants to dance his own steps, and this brings him into conflict with Barry Fife and his own mother Shirley, who is determined that he shall win. Initially, Liz is Scott's dancing partner, but she refuses to dance with him because of his efforts to be innovative in his dancing style.

Scott's mother spends a great deal of time convincing him to conform to the rules of the Dancing Federation. Scott refuses and meets Fran, whose family are Spanish in origin. Fran lives with her grandmother and father at the back of a small bar. Fran and Scott spend a lot of time practising how to dance and secretly improve their steps, unknown to anyone.

Meanwhile we learn more about Scott's father, Doug. We see him surreptitiously putting on records and dancing on his own a lot. It is clear that his wife outwardly despises him, as he is not a very assertive character. We also learn, as the story develops, how Doug had the potential to be a prestigious dancer, but had tried to dance his own steps and was banned by the Federation.

Finally, Scott and Fran enter the Pan Pacific Competition even though they are opposed by all the members of Scott's family and receive threats from Fife. The final sequence plays the music of 'Love in the Air', and everyone in the hall moves onto the dance-floor in spite of Barry Fife's protestations, and dances their own individual style. Fife's corrupt manoeuvrings are defeated at the conclusion.

Themes or issues

- power and corruption
- deception
- self-expression and individuality
- love and romance

Genre

This film belongs to the genre of romance. There are touches of absurd humour throughout. The director makes use of caricature to mock, as is seen in Barry Fife's capacity to bully people.

There are also comic touches in the documentary-style interventions from Shirley, who is intent on trying to explain to the viewer how her son must become a champion.

Camera angles

A variety of camera angles is used, mainly of different styles of dancing and of the various events.

Flashback

The film opens with a flashback to the Waratah Championships, which establishes the competitive atmosphere of the film. It also introduces the leading characters that will govern the plot of the story.

Cultural context

There are different social classes represented in the film. The culture is that of Australia. It is restricted to dancing events and competitors.

We gain an insight into a contrasting cultural world through Fran's story. Her background represents a more traditional way of life than the flashy ballroom scenes. The Spanish culture is represented through the figure of her father and his friends and the flamboyant style of dancing which we see in their house.

General vision or viewpoint
The defeat of Barry Fife's wicked manoeuvrings and the success attained by Scott and Fran in dancing in an individual style represent a change in the traditional system, which has obviously operated in this federation for years. The fact that Doug Scott's father was considered a failure, when in reality he was trying to perfect his art, made him appear weak in his own family. With the introduction of a new style of dancing, expressed by Scott and Fran, not only is the corrupt system of Fife exposed and destroyed, but Doug's status as a dancer is restored and he is vindicated before his family.

The values of love and selflessness are made apparent in the sincere union of Scott and Fran.

ON THE WATERFRONT
(2003 and 2004 exams)
Directed by Elia Kazan.

Historical and literary background
This film was shot on location in Hoboken, New Jersey in 1954.

The story
Terry is a young worker on the docks. He has been a boxer, but has now stopped boxing. Terry looks after a flock of pigeons on the roofs of the houses. A man called Johnny Friendly controls the docklands and the workers there. He is the one that decides who gets works and who does not. He is a bully and a criminal. Terry's brother Charley is Johnny's right-hand man. Terry also works for Johnny. Under Johnny's instigation, Terry sets a trap for Joey, a fellow worker on the docks, who is going to testify against Friendly's behaviour in the courts. Terry is not fully aware of the implications of this trap. It turns out that Johnny kills this man. After this, Terry meets Edie, the sister of the dead man. They fall in love. The local Catholic priest, Barry, is outraged at the behaviour of Friendly's gang and the fear that he is spreading among the workers, and so he begins to mobilise them to fight against injustice and form a union. The priest organises a meeting in the church, but Johnny's men beat up those who attend and smash the windows of the church. Johnny's men kill a worker on the docklands, named K. O. Doogan, because he tries to stand up to him and get his rights.

Terry talks to the priest, and decides to tell Edie about his involvement in the death of her brother. She is heartbroken. Terry decides to give testimony against Johnny Friendly.

Friendly challenges Charley to straighten Terry out and get him to say nothing. Terry refuses, and Johnny's gang kills Charley. Terry testifies in the courtroom against Friendly. Friendly is given a warning and allowed out on parole. Terry's friends kill all the pigeons on the roof as punishment for his action. Terry decides to go down to the waterfront and get his rights. He has a fight with Johnny and is badly beaten up by his men. All the workers including the priest gather round him and challenge him to walk along the docks in defiance of Friendly's gang. Terry leads the men and they regain their rights over Friendly's gang. Friendly is beaten at the conclusion.

Themes or issues

- oppression and violence
- loyalty and betrayal
- redemption through love
- human rights

Genre
The film is set along the docklands of New York. The black and white photography makes the time of the film realistic.

Dialogue
Dialogue between the characters is realistic and highlights the features of New Yorkers at that time.

Music
The soundtrack includes music by Bernstein.

Symbols

The pigeon becomes a symbol of Terry's plight as he is caught between his love for Edie and Friendly's gang. Terry tells Edie at one stage that 'the city is full of hawks, they spot a pigeon and they are down on top of them'. He goes on to tell her that pigeons are very faithful; they get married and stay that way. He proves this at the end by boldly confronting Friendly and his gang.

Fences, gates and wiring are used to show the imprisonment experienced by these people.

Camera angles

A wide variety of camera angles is used in the film.

A lot of scenes are shot from a point high above, showing how people are merely pawns in this system.

Cultural context

This film deals with the culture of America and the docklands during the fifties. The workers are set in conflict with Friendly's gang, who operate as a type of Mafia. The landscape is bleak, dark and clearly depressed. These workers are pawns in the hands of Friendly, who knows they need the money to buy food.

The church becomes a vehicle for the workers to unite against oppression.

Edie represents the situation of women in these times. She is being educated in a convent by nuns. She is clearly an innocent girl who has been protected from the evil and corruption of the world.

General vision or viewpoint

Terry's valiant struggle to overcome his previous failure in boxing is shown in his fight against Friendly, and in the courage with which he challenges him to fight.

The final scene is dramatic, showing the injured and almost blind Terry struggling to walk and regain control of his body, in a heroic fight against the gang of criminals. He is triumphant against the evil syndicate of Friendly, and so he is able to enlist the help of the other men along the docks. His heroic fight against oppression enables them to overcome their fear and cowardice and to take a clear stance against the bullying and corruption of Friendly's gang. The workers regain their rights and their control over the workplace at the conclusion. Justice and harmony are re-established. Friendly is defeated and has to answer to the law.

RICHARD III

(2003 and 2004 exams)
Directed by Robert Loncraine.

Historical and literary background

The film *Richard III* is based on the historic War of the Roses, which took place between the House of Lancaster and the House of York. The film begins with the coronation of Edward, who is of the House of York, settled on the throne of England; King Henry, his predecessor, was murdered by Edward's brother Richard.

The story

In the opening sequence of this film we are told that civil war reigns in England, because the king is under attack from the rebel York family, who are fighting to put their eldest son on the throne. His youngest brother, Richard of Gloucester, leads Edward's army. Richard's tanks break down the walls of Tewkesbury and Henry and his father are shot.

Edward becomes King of England. He is married to Elizabeth and they have two sons, and a daughter also called Elizabeth. At the coronation ceremony of Edward, Richard gives the welcoming speech. Rivers, Queen Elizabeth's brother, who is an enemy of Richard's, arrives for Edward's coronation. Buckingham is an ally of Richard. He is a leading statesman who conspires with Richard at all stages.

Shortly after this Richard seduces Lady Anne, widow of Tewkesbury, whom he has murdered earlier. Richard announces to the audience that since he cannot prove himself as a lover because of his deformed shape, he is determined to prove himself as a villain. He frames Clarence, his brother, and has him committed to the Tower of London. Richard then suggests that Elizabeth has done this.

Richard then hires a man called Tyrell to murder Clarence, which he does while he is taking a bath, and drowns him in his own blood. Richard proceeds to inform Edward of this death as Edward is in the process of making peace between the various statesmen. On hearing the news Edward has a stroke and dies shortly afterwards. Richard murders Rivers.

Elizabeth's son is brought to London to be crowned King. Both he and his young brother are kept in the tower until the coronation ceremony. Hastings is Prime Minister. There is a meeting with the archbishop, Hastings, Buckingham and Richard, who is now the Lord Protector. Richard accuses Hastings of treachery and Tyrell executes him.

Both Richard and Buckingham then justify this execution to the Lord Mayor by claiming that Hastings plotted to kill Richard and Buckingham. Richard also insinuates that the two princes in the tower are bastard children who have no legitimate right to the throne.

The Lord Mayor wishes to crown Richard as King. Richard adopts a false show of piety and reluctance to take on responsibilities of kingship. Eventually he succumbs and is crowned King in a ceremony closely resembling a Nazi meeting.

After this ceremony Richmond is advised by the archbishop to flee to England for safety. There he mobilises an army to fight Richard.

Richard asks Buckingham to murder the two princes in the tower. Buckingham hesitates and reminds him of his earlier pledge to give him the earldom of Hereford. Richard replies that he is not in the giving mood. Buckingham, knowing his life is in danger, flees to France to join Richmond. Tyrell murders the two princes in the tower. Richard now plans to get rid of Anne and marry Elizabeth, the sister of the two young princes. Elizabeth's mother flees to England and young Elizabeth is married to Richmond shortly before the battle. Buckingham is captured by Richard's army, tortured and brutally murdered by Tyrell.

Richard's own mother has cursed him and prophesies that his end will be bloody and says that she will pray for Richmond's success in battle. Richard is tormented by nightmares on the night before the battle.

The battle takes place in daytime with tanks and modern military weapons. Richmond drives an army tank through the battlefield, intent on killing Richard. At the conclusion, Richmond and Richard are standing on the top of a dilapidated building. Richard challenges Richmond to come to hell with him, and offers him his hand. Before Richmond shoots him, Richard falls backwards into a sea of fire.

Themes or issues
- kingship
- violence, murder and corruption
- betrayal

Genre
The genre of this film is tragedy. It gives a vivid account of Richard's murderous movements both before and after he becomes king.

Soliloquy
This film makes frequent use of the traditional soliloquy. Richard, the villain of the film, engages in soliloquy frequently in the film. He announces his plot and justifies his behaviour through the use of soliloquy.

Music
Jazz music and the music of the nineteen-twenties forms the main background of this film. In particular, violence and violent actions are accompanied by strong jazz undertones.

Flashback

There is only one flashback in the film. This occurs when Tyrell informs Richard that the two princes are dead. We then see how they were smothered with a piece of red material.

Cultural context

The cultural setting of this film is England in the nineteen-thirties. It is a distinct modern setting for a film that is based on a king who ruled in England in the fifteenth century.

The coronation of Richard is almost Nazi-style. The red flag that is unfolded behind the grandstand and the red flags waved by the people who are gathered all resemble the swastika.

Close associations are drawn between the figure of Richard and that of Hitler. The dress is predominantly military-style uniforms that also resemble Nazi style.

The culture is rich and ornate: luxurious chandeliers, expensive carpets and paintings, large lobbies, elegant photographs and clothes are a hallmark of the atmosphere in this film.

General vision or viewpoint

The battle at the conclusion takes place during the day. The place is filled with army tanks and soldiers marching to their deaths. On the night before the battle Richard has nightmares and is haunted by his mother's last words, which condemned his actions. It is clear that he feels guilty, but suppresses his conscience and continues to justify his actions. In the morning of the battle, he mobilises his troops by preaching about the fact that conscience is a word cowards use.

Richmond is clearly intent on murdering Richard himself. He resolutely sets out in a military tank to kill him. Richard is finally trapped at the top of a dilapidated building and has lost the battle. Everyone around him is dead. He has murdered all his family and has no friends left. He fails to repent and instead recklessly challenges Richmond by offering him his hand with the words 'hand in hand to hell'. His drop into the sea of fire is symbolic of the fact that he has damned himself by his actions and refuses to repent. The accompanying music 'I'm sitting on top of the world', is an ironic way of highlighting how Richmond has defeated the evil in Britain. Richmond is victorious. Heir to the house of Lancaster and married to Elizabeth, heir to the house of York, Richmond is the first of the Tudor line to rule England as Henry VII.

13
Unseen Poetry

APPROACHING THE UNSEEN POEM

The first thing you must do when tackling an unseen poem is try to understand its meaning. The tone and the choice of words will help to convey the poem's meaning. You will find that the more times you read the poem the more the meaning will become clear to you.

Some modern poetry has no clear and unequivocal meaning, and in fact is not meant to have a definite meaning. In many instances the meaning can be very obscure; so don't worry about understanding the meaning immediately.

Remember, a poem can have many different interpretations. It is important to take risks when reading and to try to understand a poem's meaning.

A poem is based on communicating some emotion or emotions to the reader through a particular choice of words and structure. To understand more deeply what the content or meaning of a particular poem is, we need to examine the following:

- ideas: the content or subject matter
- persona
- language.

Ideas

1. State the idea or attitude expressed in each component part or in each verse.
2. Are there key words or word repetitions strategically placed in order to express the main ideas? (Remember, poetry is emotion and may communicate through syntax, repetition, or image association, rather than logic.)
3. See why the verses are structured in the particular way they are.
4. Try to understand the relationship between the different parts of a poem; this will help to reveal its structure.
5. The theme or themes can be elicited or drawn out from grasping how the particular ideas or responses are developed in the poem.

Person
1. Who is speaking in the poem? Is it the poet, or is the poet pretending to be someone else?
2. To whom is the poet speaking—to a particular person, or to a general audience?
3. What do we learn about the poet from the poem?

Language
When you analyse the style of a poem—that is, the language, tone, point of view and techniques used—it will help towards gaining a deeper understanding and interpretation of the poem.

The particular way in which language is used in a poem helps to give a shape and structure to the poem's thought and meaning.

The language of poetry is made up of

- imagery
- words
- sound
- rhyme
- grammar
- alliteration
- metre
- onomatopoeia.

Imagery
Imagery is any form of descriptive writing. Imagery focuses the meaning of the poem as a whole; it can also function to create atmosphere and establish a certain pattern within a poem. A poet can make use of language in many different ways to create imagery or word pictures. Don't just identify imagery but be able to say what its function in poetry is.

Imagery creates atmosphere and establishes a pattern within a poem. Imagery is effective when it is central to the poem's meaning.

When studying imagery in a poem, know how to identify the following:

- metaphor
- simile
- symbol.

Both metaphor and simile compare one thing with another. In a metaphor this similarity is implied, while a simile shows the comparison through the use of the words 'like' or 'as'. Similes are closer to ordinary speech; metaphors are more condensed and economical.

Simile: 'The fog descended like a blanket.'
Metaphor: 'The blanket of fog descended.'

A symbol is a word that stands for or points to a reality beyond itself. For example, flowers can symbolise the shortness of life. Some other examples:

- sunrise: a new beginning
- water: purity
- a river: life
- the sea: eternity
- a garden: order
- spring: new life and energy
- autumn: maturity, fulfilment
- winter: old age and death

When you are examining symbols, an act of imagination is required before the meaning becomes fully clear. Aim at capturing the way in which a symbol glows or echoes with meaning. The statement or ideas that are being made do not make sense on the surface level: the sense or meaning of symbols must be inferred from some association, comparison, contrast or inversion of images and ideas used in the poem.

Take, for example, the following lines from T. S. Eliot's poem 'The Waste Land':

Unreal City,
Under the brown fog of a winter dawn,
A crowd flowed over London Bridge, so many,
I had not thought death had undone so many.

The fog and the winter dawn have many different meanings; they could refer to the spiritual apathy and stagnation that were a feature of the time when Eliot was writing the poem.

With regard to imagery in poetry, ask yourself the following questions:

What does it say?
Why is it used?
Has it got connotations or sound effects?
Does it fit into the context?
How well does it do its task?

Words
Examine the way words work within a poem.

Appropriateness
Are the words that are used poetic, colloquial, or abstract? If so, why?

Associations
Have the words got connotations or associations?

Green waters of the canal pouring redemption for me.

Kavanagh here is suggesting religious renewal.

> Fleeing from the foreign faces and the foreign swords

This suggests fear and violence.

Allusions
An allusion is a reference to another book, event, person, or place. The allusion may be implied or hinted; sometimes the effect of an allusion may be to make something that is being said more significant, more ambiguous, or more amusing.

Collocation
This occurs through an explosive, unexpected or sometimes contradictory combination of words, such as 'dense din,' 'tremendous silence.'

> As I was green and carefree, famous among the barns
> About the happy yard and singing as the farm was home.

Repetition
Repetition of a key word or phrase at different points can give emphasis to the power of the poem:

> And indeed there will be time ... there will be time, time to descend the stair, time for you and time for me ...

> I am tired with my own life and the lives of those after me,
> I am dying in my own death and the deaths of those after me.

Rhythm
Rhythm can be used in poetry to add to the mood or atmosphere, and therefore it can contribute to conveying the meaning more clearly. Effective rhythm is one where the stress falls on the crucial or important word. In the best poetry the rhythm and meaning of the words appear as one and not two things. Ask yourself whether it is significant that these thoughts and feelings have been expressed in this particular rhythm.

Internal rhyme occurs when a word in one line rhymes with another word in the same line:

> He found the forest track and brought back
> This beak.

The internal rhyme serves to emphasise a sense of movement:

> The grains beyond age, the dark veins of her mother.

The internal rhyme between 'grains' and 'veins' underlines the finality of death. Internal rhyme can serve the function of surprising the reader and quickening the pace of a line.

A line can be *end-stopped,* with an *end rhyme*; or it can run on into another line in a flow of thought. End rhyme occurs when two consecutive lines rhyme, or alternate lines rhyme. Look at the following lines, which are an example of end rhyme:

If I were a dead leaf thou mightest bear, [a]
If I were swift cloud to fly with thee; [b]
A wave to pant beneath thy power, and share [a]

The impulse of thy strength, only less free [b]
Than thou, O uncontrollable! If even [c]
I were as in my boyhood, and could be [b]

The comrade of thy wanderings over Heaven, [c]
As then, when to outstrip thy skiey speed [d]
Scarce seemed a vision; I would ne'er have striven [c]

As thus with thee in prayer in my sore need. [d]
(Percy Bysshe Shelley, 'Ode to the West Wind')

Rhythm sometimes exists to link words and ideas. It can also be used to suggest speed, calm, anger, or monotony. Definite rhythm can make a particular point; for example:

Only thin smoke without flame
From the heaps of couch-grass
Yet this will go onward the same
Though Dynasties pass.

The absence of rhythm can suggest fear, worry, or aimlessness. Uneven rhythm is also used for a particular purpose; for example:

How the old Mountains drip with Sunset
How the Hemlocks burn—
How the Dun Brake is draped in Cinder
By the Wizard Sun—

How the old Steeples hand the Scarlet
Till the Ball is full—
Have I the lip of the Flamingo
That I dare to tell?

These lines are taken from a poem by Emily Dickinson. The uneven rhythm serves the purpose of building up an atmosphere in nature before the poet herself intrudes into the poem.

Alliteration
This is the repetition of the initial consonant. When you are dealing with an unseen poem, discuss the effect of alliteration: don't just give examples. Ask yourself whether or not it produces a distinctive tone and whether or not it is regularly spaced:

> I caught this morning morning's minion king-
> dom of daylight's dauphin, dapple-dawn-drawn Falcon, in …

The alliteration of the *m* and *d* sounds here serves the function of conjuring up a sense of richness, majesty, and power.

> I should hear him fly with the high fields and wake up to the farm forever fled from the childless land

The idea of time passing is expressed here in the alliteration of the *f* sound.

> O wild west wind, thou breadth of Autumn's being …

The *w* alliteration here enacts the poet's awe in the presence of such a mighty force.

Assonance

This is the repetition of identical vowel sounds. Look, for example, at the effect of assonance in the following lines from Tennyson:

> Lo! in the middle of the wood,
> the folded leaf is woo'd from out the bud
> Sun steep'd at noon, and in the moon
> Nightly dew-fed; and turning yellow
> Falls, and floats adown the air.

The combined effect of the assonance of the *a* sound creates an impression of rich abundance in nature.

Onomatopoeia

This is where the word conjures up the sound: 'wheeze', 'buzz', 'splash'.

> watch the crisping ripples on the beach
> Liplapping of Galilee.

Ambiguity

Ambiguity in poetry means the use of words to mean two or more different things. Many times a poet can enrich the meaning of a poem by using words that are ambiguous. Ambiguity can emphasise the many nuances or levels of meaning that can be found in poetic language.

Look at the following line:

> Dapple-dawn-drawn Falcon

Does it mean that the falcon is etched against the landscape of the sky? Or does it mean that the falcon has been drawn out by the dawn into the sky?

> My heart in hiding
> Stirred for a bird …

Does this mean that his heart is in hiding because he is a priest and therefore detached from the world? Or does it mean that he is literally hiding as he watches the bird in the sky?

> Fathering and all humbling darkness
> Tells with silence the last light breaking …

What exactly is meant by the term 'humbling darkness'? Does it mean that death will humble humankind, including the poet? Does it mean that darkness is death? If so, why 'humbling'?

All these examples illustrate the power of ambiguity in poetry.

Effects of sound
Don't just give examples: show the effect.
Harshness can be conveyed by the use of consonants: *b, t, k*:

> Blight and famine, plague and earthquake, roaring deeps
>
> Clanging fights, and flaming towns, and sinking ships.

A sense of smoothness can be conveyed by the use of certain vowels and also by the *s* sound:

> There is sweet music here that softer falls.

Grammar
Consider some of the grammatical devices used in poetry.
- The omission of 'and', verbs, or commas. Ask yourself why.
- Adding 'and', commas, verbs, or capital letters when not usual. Ask why.
- Short sentences. What is their purpose?
- Long sentences. Anger? Boredom? Movement?
- Unusual syntax. Look at the purpose.
- Word compounds: 'world sorrow', 'blue-bleak', 'leafy-with-love'. What are they saying? Why are they used?
- Word compression—using the smallest number of words to achieve maximum intensity. This can be used to convey a dense or intense meaning, or it can be deliberately ambiguous.
- The unusual use of words: 'Pitched past pitch of grief,' 'More pangs will, schooled at forepangs, wilder wring.'
- Nouns made into verbs. Why?
- Coining of words. Why?

Metre
A very short line can express emotion: joy, anger, hatred.
A very long line—what effect has it?
Run-on lines can express movement, speed, growth, or development.

Method of answering questions on an unseen poem

Remember that a poem is made up of content or subject matter. This content is shaped in a particular way and adds up to what is known as the structure or form.

1. Aim first of all to give a general summary of what the poem is about and the different stages in the poem.
2. Read the poem through several times to grasp some idea of the meaning.
3. Examine the title of the poem, and see what relation it may have to the content.
4. Assess what type of poem it is. Is it narrative, an argument, a philosophical insight into life, an ode, a lyric, a sonnet?
5. If the poem is a narrative, understand the main events. When you understand why the events follow one another in a particular way you will understand how the poem is designed. There are three elements common to poems that tell stories: expectation, surprise, and reversal.
6. If the poem is a meditation on life, get the general meaning of what is being said.
7. If the poem is an argument, follow the main stages. Ask yourself why the argument moves from that stage to this. Look at the conclusion of the argument. Is it logical? Is it effective? Has it achieved what it set out to do? Am I convinced? Identify the main points and the different stages of the argument.
8. Look at the words and see whether they carry symbolic or emotive meaning. Ask yourself why this is so. Look for a particular *tone*—this is the voice, mood or outlook of the poet.
9. Show how figures of speech contribute to the poem. Remember, figures of speech can be metaphors, symbols, personification, similes, etc. Many times poems convey their meaning by implication, suggestion, word connotations or associations, and not through explicit statement.
10. Be aware of your reaction to the poem. What thoughts or feelings do the words stir up in me? Remember that a poem does not have to make complete sense. Many times the power of poetry comes from its ability to establish or suggest many different levels of meaning and many possibilities.

Questions and sample answers

Attempt your own answers first, then compare them with the sample answers given.

Epitaph on a Tyrant
W. H. Auden

> Perfection, of a kind, was what he was after,
> And the poetry he invented was easy to understand;
> He knew human folly like the back of his hand,
> And was greatly interested in armies and fleets;
> When he laughed, respectable senators burst with laughter,
> And when he cried the little children died in the street.

1. Write a short note on the structure of this poem.
2. What is the tone of the poem?
3. Comment on the poet's use of language.

Sample answers

1. The structure of this poem consists of one stanza. The poem is called "Epitaph on a Tyrant", and for that reason the poet expresses neatly and compactly his tribute to this tyrant in six short sentences. There are no run-on lines; instead the poet uses end rhyme, in the words "fleet" and "street", "after" and "laughter", "understand" and "hand". The function of this rhyming scheme is to convey an ironic vision of a man whose life yielded destruction.

> Perfection, of a kind, was what he was after [a]
> And the poetry he invented was easy to understand; [b]
> He knew human folly like the back of his hand, [b]
> And was greatly interested in armies and fleets; [c]
> When he laughed, respectable senators burst with laughter, [a]
> And when he cried the little children died in the street. [c]

2. The tone of the poem is satirical: the poet is mocking or satirising the tyrant. In the second line he suggests that this tyrant's poetry was easy to understand: in other words, his deeds and life were motivated by selfish interests, such as trying to dominate people and murdering them. For example, when he cried the little children died in the street. The effect of the whole poem is sobering.

3. The language used is restrained and terse. The poet seems to be wary of expressing himself in too much language. This poem is a portrait of a man who wielded power through bullying and brute force. The poet wishes to paint a graphic picture of this tyrant, and for that reason he uses images that are arresting and dramatic. The poem is made up of one stanza, which says it all. The poet does not repeat himself; and therefore the effect is much more dramatic and intense.

The Hippopotamus
T. S. Eliot

> The broad-backed hippopotamus
> Rests on his belly in the mud;
> Although he seems so firm to us
> He is merely flesh and blood.
>
> Flesh and blood is weak and frail
> Susceptible to nervous shock;
> While the True Church can never fail
> For it is based upon a rock.

The hippo's feeble steps may err
In compassing material ends,
While the True Church need never stir
To gather in its dividends.

The 'potamus can never reach
The mango on the mango-tree;
But fruits of pomegranate and peach
Refresh the Church from over sea.

At mating time the hippo's voice
Betrays inflections hoarse and odd,
But every week we hear rejoice
The Church, at being one with God.

The hippopotamus's day
Is passed in sleep; at night he hunts;
God works in a mysterious way—
The Church can sleep and feed at once.

I saw the 'potamus take wing
Ascending from the damp savannas,
And quiring angels round him sing
The praise of God, in loud hosannas.

Blood of the Lamb shall wash him clean
And him shall heavenly arms enfold,
Among the saints he shall be seen
Performing on a harp of gold.

He shall be washed as white as snow,
By all the martyr'd virgins kist,
While the True Church remains below
Wrapt in the old miasmal mist.

1. Discuss the use of contrast in this poem.
2. Comment on how the form of the poem develops the theme.
3. Examine the images in the poem, and show how they contribute to the particular vision presented in the poem.

Sample answers

1. The poet develops his thoughts by drawing a contrast between the image of the hippopotamus and the church. There is a striking contrast between the two images: the

broad-backed hippopotamus resting in the mud on his belly, and the image presented to us of the church that can never fail, based, as it is, 'upon a rock'. The poet seems to be illustrating the difference between the impermanence of material things, as shown through his symbol of the hippopotamus, and the permanence and power of the spiritual, as evinced in the images of the church. Each stanza develops this contrast. As the poem develops we bear witness to the growing power of the church, while simultaneously witnessing the weakness of material things. Images such as 'the 'potamus can never reach | The mango on the mango-tree' show the failure of material things to achieve permanence.

On the other hand, the poet may be illustrating the continuity and permanence of the church in such lines as the following: 'But fruits of pomegranate and peach | Refresh the Church from over sea.'

At the conclusion of the poem, the poet skilfully fuses this contrast. The hippopotamus is surrounded by singing angels; he is seen among the saints, and washed clean by the blood of the Lamb. Perhaps the poet is painting an image of the fate of those who are faithful to the church.

2. The poem is structured in a series of nine stanzas, all of the same length. Each of the stanzas is structured in the same manner—four lines of verse—which makes subtle use of end rhyme. Look, for example, at the effect of the rhyme between the following words in the last three stanzas:

> I saw the 'potamus take wing [a]
> Ascending from the damp savannas, [b]
> And quiring angels round him sing [a]
> The praise of God, in loud hosannas. [b]
>
> Blood of the Lamb shall wash him clean [a]
> And him shall heavenly arms enfold, [b]
> Among the saints he shall be seen [a]
> Performing on a harp of gold. [b]
>
> He shall be washed as white as snow, [a]
> By all the martyr'd virgins kist, [b]
> While the True Church remains below [a]
> Wrapt in the old miasmal mist. [b]

The poet's use of rhyme between words such as 'wing' and 'sing', 'savannas' and 'hosannas', illustrates the striking contrast between the material and the spiritual worlds. He also makes effective use of repetition: for example, 'enfold' and 'gold' paint an image of triumph and glory at the conclusion.

3. The poet makes use of the unusual image of a hippopotamus to put forward his theme of the power of the church. The images that describe the hippopotamus are earthy and real: resting in the mud on his belly, the vivid image of his broad back, his

voice betraying inflections hoarse and odd at mating time. These are images that are related to the earth, to earthly things. On the other hand, the images that describe the church's activity are more positive and unified, such as 'While the True Church need never stir | To gather in its dividends' and 'The Church can sleep and feed at once' suggest an internal harmony and sense of oneness. The poet's use throughout the poem of emphatic repetition in phrases such as 'the True Church' intensifies this dramatic power of the church.

Exposure
Wilfred Owen

> Our brains ache, in the merciless iced east winds that knive us …
> Wearied we keep awake because the night is silent …
> Low, drooping flares confuse our memory of the salient …
> Worried by silence, sentries whisper, curious, nervous,
> But nothing happens.
>
> Watching we hear the mad gusts tugging on the wire,
> Like twitching agonies of men among its brambles.
> Northward, incessantly, the flickering gunnery rumbles,
> Far off, like a dull rumour of some other war.
> What are we doing here?
>
> The poignant misery of dawn begins to grow …
> We only know war lasts, rain soaks, and clouds sag stormy,
> Dawn massing in the east her melancholy army
> Attacks once more in ranks on shivering ranks of grey,
> But nothing happens.
>
> Sudden successive flights of bullets streak the silence.
> Less deadly than the air that shudders black with snow,
> With sidelong flowing flakes that flock, pause and renew,
> We watch them wandering up and down the wind's nonchalance,
> But nothing happens.
>
> Pale flakes with fingering stealth come feeling for our faces—
> We cringe in holes, back on forgotten dreams, and stare, snow-dazed,
> Deep into grassier ditches. So we drowse sun-dozed.
> Littered with blossoms trickling where the blackbird fusses.
> Is it that we are dying?
>
> Slowly our ghosts drag home: glimpsing the sunk fires, glozed
> With crusted dark-red jewels; crickets jingle there;
> For hours the innocent mice rejoice: the house is theirs;

Shutters and doors, all closed: on us the doors are closed—
We turn back to our dying.

Since we believe not otherwise can kind fires burn;
Nor ever suns smile true on child, or field or fruit.
For God's invincible spring, our love is made afraid;
Therefore, not loath, we lie out here; therefore were born,
For love of God seems dying.

Tonight, His frosty will fasten on this mud and us,
Shrivelling many hands, puckering foreheads crisp.
The burying-party, picks and shovels in their shaking grasp,
Pause over half-known faces. All their eyes are ice,
But nothing happens.

1. This poem is a powerful comment on the effects of war. Identify the main feelings expressed in the poem. Show how these feelings are conveyed through the language and imagery.
2. Show how the poet has structured his thought in the poem and what the effect of such a structure is.
3. Identify the particular tone and attitude towards life in the speaker.

Sample answers
1. The poem opens with an image of men worn out and fearful as they struggle to keep awake on a bitterly cold night. There is a feeling of tension in the last line of the first stanza, which is underlined by the poet's use of sibilance: 'Worried by silence, sentries whisper, curious, nervous.' The whole feeling is one of fearful apprehension about what is going to happen. These feelings are given added momentum and intensity by the reiterated use of the short, terse line 'But nothing happens.' The poet paints some very vivid images of fear and dread and builds the reader up to an expectation of something momentous and dreadful. Then the line 'But nothing happens' serves the function of emphasising this anxiety even more.

There is a strong feeling throughout the poem of the futility and waste of war. This is achieved by the use of the rhetorical question in the concluding line of the second stanza: 'What are we doing here?' In a sense the poet answers this question in the next stanza, in the grim line 'We only know war lasts, rain soaks, and clouds sag stormy.' The brutal impact of war is registered vividly in these images.

As the poem develops, the feelings within the poet change. In the fifth stanza the poet asks, 'Is it that we are dying?' This leads him on to some nostalgic reminiscences about his past life, the reality of life at home, and his loved ones. But these images are brutal and grim. The only reality of his former family life is mirrored in images such as 'sunk fires … Shutters and doors, all closed: on us the doors are closed …' The only reality is death.

Towards the end of the poem the feelings of the poet become almost hopeless as he continues to depict the devastation caused by war. The sixth stanza is gloomy and shows how the poet's dreams have been killed by war to such an extent that even his love is gone:

Our love is made afraid;

> Therefore, not loath, we lie out here; therefore were born,
> For love of God seems dying.

There are undertones of hopelessness and near-despair in these lines. The conclusion of the poem is filled with some chilling images:

> The burying-party, picks and shovels in their shaking grasp,
> Pause over half-known faces. All their eyes are ice …

The poet seems to be saying, with these images of frost and snow, how war robs people of feeling. The men's faces are only 'half-known': war has generated indifference and unfeeling attitudes.

2. The poem is structured in seven stanzas, of equal length. Each stanza concludes on a short emphatic statement or question, which underlines the futility of war. In each stanza the poet has drawn a parallel between the world of nature and the plight of these men who are hiding in the trenches. The images from nature are wild and savage: 'the merciless iced east winds that knive us … the mad gusts tugging on the wire, | Like twitching agonies of men among its brambles … The poignant misery of dawn.' The function of such imagery is to emphasise the brutality experienced by these men because of the war.

The structure is coherent and compact. The particular effect of such a structure is to illustrate the real impact caused by war on the lives of people and how it wreaks devastation.

3. The tone of this poem is deeply dispiriting and negative. The speaker seems to lose faith in life as the poem develops and progresses. In the opening stanza he is caught in a situation of extreme suffering, surrounded by icy winds and a fearful apprehension and confusion about what is happening, 'worried by silence … drooping flares confuse our memory of the salient …' This sense of bewilderment and confusion on the part of the speaker is given an added intensity by the concluding line of each stanza: 'But nothing happens.' 'What are we doing here?'

The tone of the poem reaches a climax of suffering as the men cringe in holes. The poet tries to escape from this anguish in the trenches by recalling images of home and loved ones. But these efforts only conjure up more images of death and loss, and so the tone intensifies in its dark, pessimistic strain. This gives way to some sobering reflections on life, war, and love. The poet concludes that he finds it hard to accept that 'kind fires burn; | Nor ever suns smile true on child, or field or fruit.' The alliteration here underlines the dark, negative aspect of the speaker's vision of things. The pointlessness of war and the loss of everything, including one's identity, are given striking expression in the concluding stanza, as the dead bodies are only half known to the people who come to bury them.

You're
Sylvia Plath

> Clownlike, happiest on your hands,
> Feet to the stars, and moon-skulled,
> Gilled like a fish. A common-sense
> Thumbs-down on the dodo's mode.
> Wrapped up in yourself like a spool,
> Trawling your dark as owls do.
> Mute as a turnip from the Fourth
> Of July to All Fools' Day,
> O high-riser, my little loaf.
>
> Vague as fog and looked for like mail.
> Farther off than Australia.
> Bent-backed Atlas, our travelled prawn.
> Snug as a bud and at home
> Like a sprat in a pickle jug.
> A creel of eels, all ripples.
> Jumpy as a Mexican bean.
> Right, like a well-done sum.
> A clean slate, with your own face on.

1. What particular vision of things is given in this poem? Take into account the poet's unusual use of words.
2. Comment on the language used in this poem, and how it communicates the ideas.
3. Write a short comment on the tone of the poem.

Sample answers

1. The title of the poem is 'You're'. The poem gives us an image of a certain type of character, who is happy as they act like a clown with their feet to the stars. As the poem develops, we get an insight into the type of character represented in the poem's title, 'wrapped in yourself like a spool'. There are implications of an isolated and deep character, 'trawling your dark as owls do'. The poet makes sustained use of simile to paint some vivid images for us of this unusual character: 'gilled like a fish', 'mute as a turnip', 'like a sprat, snug as a bud'. The general effect of the lines is of an impenetrable and inaccessible character, 'vague as fog and looked for like mail. | Farther off than Australia.'

   This portrait is varied. The character represented is as jumpy as a Mexican bean, yet right like a well-done sum. The poet uses a large variety of imagery to paint this highly original portrait of a most interesting character.

2. The writer uses language in a highly original way. Much of the effect of this poem comes from the writer's striking use of simile. Almost every image is structured on some

clever similes: 'Gilled like a fish,' 'Wrapped up in yourself like a spool,' 'Right, like a well-done sum.' The use of the image 'feet to the stars' in the opening lines is cleverly juxtaposed with the metaphor 'high-riser' in the concluding line of the first stanza. The poet uses alliteration of the *r* sound to conjure up a sense of comfort and ease—'like a sprat in a pickle jug, | A creel of eels, all ripples.' The effect is intensified by the use of assonance in 'creel of eels, all ripples.'

3. The tone of this poem is detached and factual. The poet is painting a vivid picture of different features of a character, and she does this through recording a series of clear, factual images in an objective tone:

> Clownlike, happiest on your hands,
> Feet to the stars, and moon-skulled.

14
Prescribed Poetry

In this chapter there are some sample questions on the prescribed poetry. A method of organising and assembling material for an answer on prescribed poetry is given. Study this method carefully, and apply it to the questions on the prescribed poetry at the end of this chapter.

APPROACHING THE QUESTION

1. Rephrase or rewrite the question
2. Take a stance on the question. Decide to agree, disagree, or partly agree.
3. Begin a draft of your answer. Write down seven or eight points that will form the framework of your answer. These points must be on different aspects of the question and must contain quotations or references. Besides, these points will form the basis of each of the paragraphs of your answer. The graph illustrates these points more clearly.

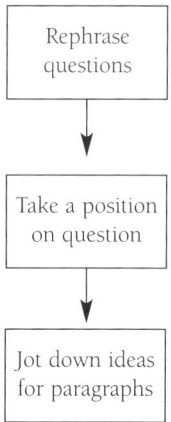

Remember, a good Higher level answer must be structured in paragraphs, and all must develop the question asked. The concluding paragraph must tie up all your ideas and refer back to the question. In addition, a good conclusion makes a definitive statement on the question.

QUESTIONS AND SAMPLE ANSWERS

Study the following questions and draft answers on the two poets, Séamus Heaney and Elizabeth Bishop. Follow the method given in answering questions like these. It can help to rewrite these questions fully as a first step. In your answers, always use quotations to or references from the poems.

There is a complete answer on Gerard Manley Hopkins following the two draft answers.

Question I
'The value of tradition and a keen sense of the past are strong issues dealt with in the poetry of Séamus Heaney.' Discuss this statement with reference to or quotation from the poetry of Heaney on your course.

Stage I: Rephrase the question
Séamus Heaney's poetry deals with the past and with tradition or old customs and folklore. Discuss.

Sample opening paragraph
This statement is true. Séamus Heaney has written a variety of different types of poems. In many of these poems he is concerned with the influence of the past on the present state of the country. In addition, he makes use of his poetry to show certain traditions, such as the blacksmith's work in an ordinary forge, or the simple rural lifestyle in Ireland long ago, and to celebrate the skills that sustained the farming community.

Paragraph 2
Heaney believes that we need to become more aware of our tradition in order to possess a true sense of identity. Show how Heaney celebrates certain traditional practices in skills such as bread-making in the poem 'Sunlight', or making horseshoes in the forge. Develop points about the real values manifested in the two central characters, the blacksmith and his aunt, in both poems.

Paragraph 3
Develop Heaney's own point about how 'our sense of the past, our sense of the land and perhaps even our sense of identity are inextricably interwoven'. Make reference to poems such as 'The Harvest Bow', 'A Constable Calls' and 'Sunlight' to develop these points and show how these ideas are reflected in the poems.

Paragraph 4
Discuss how Heaney speaks about Irish culture and the rich inheritance of the past in the poem 'Bogland'. Develop your answer by talking about the various aspects of bogland represented in the poem. Make reference to the rich and original metaphors that are used here.

Concluding paragraph
Sum up Heaney's attitude to tradition and the past in the poems you have discussed. Draw together the main points and reflections on both tradition and the past from the five poems you have discussed.

Show how Heaney has expressed these insights effectively and has given clear, coherent expression to his ideas through a variety of techniques, such as the original use of metaphor, symbolism and contrast. Show how the voice of Heaney percolates through so many of these poems.

Question 2
'Elizabeth Bishop's poems move from description towards moments of discovery, which can be joyful or devastating.' In your reading of Elizabeth Bishop's poetry, did you find this statement to be true? Support your answer by quotation from or reference to the poems on your course.

Stage 1: Rephrase the question
Would you agree with the statement that the poetry of Elizabeth Bishop moves from describing or drawing pictures to revealing moments of insight, which can be either happy or traumatic?

Sample opening paragraph
This statement is true. Bishop's poems move from describing and evoking certain moments of profound illumination and insight towards the revelation of a situation that can be either joyful or devastating. She is a highly subjective poet. Most of her topics spring from her own experience. The poems I propose to discuss are 'The Fish', 'At the Fishhouses', and 'In the Waiting Room'.

Paragraph 1
Discuss her descriptions in 'The Fish' and in particular her meticulous use of sharply observed detail.

Pay attention to her use of colour and small details in lines such as

> He was speckled with barnacles,
> fine rosettes of lime,
> and infested
> with tiny white sea-lice ...

Show how the fish becomes an objective symbol almost of the poet's own problems in the image of the rainbow (line 75): 'until everything was rainbow, rainbow, rainbow!'

Discuss this central moment of illumination, and show how this discovery is positive, a source of joy and added wisdom.

Paragraph 2
Discuss 'At the Fishhouses', and look at how she uses a succession of vivid details in her description:

an old man sits netting,
his net, in the gloaming almost invisible,
a dark purple-brown,
and his shuttle worn and polished.

Describe and discuss how all these details conjure up a distinct atmosphere of seafaring people.

Comment on her use of small details in lines such as

The five fishhouses have steeply peaked roofs
and narrow, cleated gangplanks slant up
to storerooms in the gables
for the wheelbarrows to be pushed up and down on.

Discuss how the change comes in this poem (lines 45 onwards) and how the poet achieves this through her use of images that are now cold and deep. Discuss the reason for the repetition of certain images, how the colours change:

The water seems suspended
above the rounded grey and blue-grey stones.

The mode of discovery in the poem is gradual, deep, reflective, and sobering. Discuss the fact that while this vision is neither joyful nor devastating, it certainly is a moving and emotional experience for the poet.

Perhaps it is a wisdom that comes to her from her background—a neurotic mother and her own abandonment as a child.

Show how her vision at the conclusion is sobering, that this experience is unalterable:

It is like what we imagine knowledge to be:
dark, salt, clear, moving, utterly free,
drawn from the cold hard mouth
of the world, derived from the rocky breasts
forever, flowing and drawn, and since
our knowledge is historical, flowing and flown.

Paragraph 3
Show how 'In the Waiting Room' takes a simple situation and uses a descriptive and narrative approach to probe, on a deeper level, the meaning of her own sex.

Discuss the originality of approach, how on the basis of a simple descriptive narrative the poet merges the vision of herself with that of her aunt.

Show how she experiences a crisis of identity in the context of ordinary banal images encountered in a waiting room:

The waiting room
was full of grown-up people,
artics and overcoats,
lamps and magazines.

Note her emphasis on the colour and movement of the volcano spilling over in rivulets of fire:

> the inside of a volcano,
> black, and full of ashes;
> then it was spilling over
> in rivulets of fire.

Note the description of the black women:

> black, naked women with necks
> wound round and round with wire
> like the necks of light bulbs.

Comment on how she reacts to these images with fear and disgust.

Paragraph 4
Discuss 'Sestina' and how it is structured on some graphic domestic imagery. Comment on how it depicts a child seated at a kitchen table watching her grandmother preparing tea.

Discuss how the poet juxtaposes the image of the kettle boiling with the recurrent reference to 'drops of tears'. Show how these images change and develop in the poem to reveal a moment of insight that is sorrowful.

Develop the idea of how the whole notion of sorrow is firmly implanted in the child's mind by the conclusion of the poem.

Show how the reference to the child drawing 'another inscrutable house' underlines this unfathomable aspect of life and domestic bliss, which is a strong feature in her poetry.

Concluding paragraph
Discuss how all four poems operate on the level of simple, vivid and keen descriptive detail.

Show how this vision differs in each of her poems, revealing either joy or heartache. Conclude by showing how these various illuminations or insights display different aspects of the poet's life.

Sample answer

The following is a complete sample answer on a question about the poetry of Gerard Manley Hopkins. Read the question and pay particular attention to the detailed commentary that follows the answer.

'The poetry of Hopkins is filled with not only a deeply personal but also a passionate response to the world and its creator.' Test the truth of this statement from your reading of the poems of Hopkins on your course.

Answer
Hopkins is primarily a nature poet. His appreciation of nature led him to see the glory of God reflected in and through nature and natural things. In this respect he went beyond the philosophy of the Pre-Raphaelites who professed the idea of art for art's sake. Hopkins found God's presence in the form of energy, beauty and the ultimate order and pattern that lay behind the apparent randomness of the world. The aim of all his affirmative poetry is to praise God, to show his glory through the whole of creation. His work undoubtedly reflects a profoundly personal and passionate expression of his experience of God and the world he has created.

Hopkins favoured the use of the sonnet form in his poetry. This imposed a discipline on him and enabled him to force thought and emotion into a structured fusion. In the sonnet 'God's Grandeur', he shows the whole world of nature as 'charged with the grandeur of God'. God's presence permeates the world of nature. Hopkins' poetry was written to be read with the ears. He was one of the most original of all English poets and his response was not only unique but intensely passionate. He created a new terminology to describe his creative processes. 'Inscape' was the effort made on the part of the poet to penetrate the outer layer of things in order to express the real richness of truth and beauty that lay within. For Hopkins the finding of inscapes in the world was a visionary experience. Underlining his own theory of inscapes (belief in the unique selfhood or individuality of created things) lay his heartfelt belief that the loveliness of the created world is a reflection of the love of God.

The sonnet 'God's Grandeur' illustrates in a vivid manner how God's greatness manifests itself in the world. Sometimes it flames out, catching our attention in a flash like the light coming from foil that catches the rays of the sun when it is shaken. Hopkins shows us how the intrusion of humankind in the universe tarnishes God's brilliant attempts at creation:

> Generations have trod, have trod, have trod;
> And all is seared with trade, bleared, smeared with toil;

The implication here is that man's will and God's will are in conflict. In spite of the fact that humankind has destroyed the earth, it will still perpetually renew itself. The thought in the sestet is both clear and positive. Hopkins makes reference to the power of the Holy Spirit in the world. He draws an analogy between a bird protecting its fledgling and the Holy Spirit's presence protecting this world. We see Hopkins' passion and excitement in the last lines of this dramatic sonnet in his use of the exclamations 'Oh!' and 'Ah!'. There is a heartfelt confidence that God's power will be perpetual in creation.

Similarly, in certain poems such as 'Spring' and 'Pied Beauty', Hopkins expresses his breathless excitement for the wonder of God's creation. 'Spring' is a beautiful sonnet which overflows with a rush of energy as he tells us how there is nothing so beautiful as spring. He is an expert at exploring all the resources of the English language. The strength of his verse is its rich variety. The images here appeal to the senses of sight and touch, 'glassy peartree leaves and blooms, the descending blue, that blue is all in a rush with richness'. There is a striking fusion in this sonnet of description and reflection.

The sestet makes use of a rhetorical question to ask what all this beauty and richness is about. Hopkins wants Christ to capture the world in its momentarily perfect state and preserve it at this level. He does not want to have it 'sour with sinning'. His voice is sincere and heartfelt here.

Hopkins had a fascination with the language of trades and occupations. In his poem 'Pied Beauty' he praises 'fold, fallow and plough | And all trades, their gear and tackle and trim'. The whole poem 'Pied Beauty' is a song of praise about the wonder and variety in God's created world. Beauty for Hopkins was to be found in what is wild in nature. In this poem the rich variety of contrast highlights the beauty of creation in a special way: sweet/sour, adazzle/dim, swift/slow. The implication underlining this distinct use of contrast is that while God himself is not subject to change, he has created a world that is in a state of constant flux and change. The sustained presence of this infinite variety is only one more reason why this world reflects the glory of God.

Hopkins called 'The Windhover' 'the best thing I ever wrote'. A poem that he specifically dedicated to Christ our Lord, he writes it in a mood of excited wonder and awe. As Hopkins registers the movement of the windhover in the sky one morning, and his mastery in the universe, he is led to think of Christ's mastery in the world. Hopkins moves here from vividly apprehending the bird one beautiful morning towards a deep state of religious insight. By the time he exclaims 'O my chevalier!' in the sestet, Hopkins is addressing Christ. He no longer sees the bird, but Christ's majesty flaming out; his grandeur a million times lovelier and more dangerous. Perhaps he is hinting about the danger of too much devotion to mortal beauty.

In the last lines of the sestet, Hopkins concludes this poem with some rich and original paradoxes: the idea of the shiny plough emerging from the dull plod and the dark earth, and also the embers dying in the fire revealing a gold-vermilion. Again, as in all of Hopkins' poems these paradoxes can only by understood in a profoundly spiritual context. The dreary, mundane ploughing of the soil produces the shiny plough; sacrifice and effort produce richness and fruit. The crackling embers reveal a rich colour, likewise the sacrifice of Christ involved suffering and pain but it yielded the fruits of the redemption. In Hopkins' case, the dull, mundane life of the priest and his suffering will yield the gold-vermilion of grace and the increased richness of the love of God.

There is no doubt that Hopkins' poetry was motivated and filled with an intense and passionate love for the world and its creation. All his poetry is innovative and charged with an energy and wonder in the joy of the created world. All his affirmative poems are joyous assertions of the divine purpose and pattern of the life of humankind and the created world.

Comment
This question has two aspects to it: to show the personal and the passionate response of Hopkins to the world and creation.

Note how the answer limits itself to discussing poems that deal with the ordinary world of nature but go on to demonstrate the glory of God, through the particular poetic methods used by Hopkins.

The answer begins by discussing Hopkins' purpose in writing poetry—to reflect the glory of God in the whole of creation—and then relates this purpose to the question.

The answer then develops by discussing the distinct and unique techniques used by Hopkins to express his deeply ardent approach to the world.

Note how the answer limits itself to discussing four different poems by Hopkins. Remember that you will not have time to go into a lot of detail in your answer, so limit yourself to discussing no more than five poems.

POSSIBLE TYPES OF QUESTIONS ON PRESCRIBED POETRY

1. 'Séamus Heaney is essentially a poet of rural Ireland.' Discuss this statement, relating it to the imagery and language he uses in his poetry. Support your answer by reference to the poems on your course.
2. 'Robert Frost makes use of nature and natural images to delineate human emotions and to create a particular atmosphere in his poetry.' Test the truth of this statement with reference to the poems you have studied for your course.
3. Examine how relevant the poetry of Sylvia Plath is for a modern reader. In your answer take into account the particular techniques she uses to communicate her themes.
4. 'The insights given to us in Elizabeth Bishop's poetry have a universal aspect, and they are given a very particular location and time setting.' In the case of any two poems by Bishop on your course, discuss this statement. Support your answer by quotation from or reference to the poems you have studied.
5. 'Hopkins is a unique and original poet whose poetry is compelling and timeless.' Would you agree with this estimation of Hopkins' poetry? Support your answer by reference to the poems you have studied.
6. 'Yeats explores complex issues that are highly relevant to modern society.' Would you agree with this statement? Make reference to the poems by Yeats on your course in your answer.
7. Write an essay in which you outline your reasons for liking or disliking the poetry of Derek Mahon. Support your points by reference to the poetry of Mahon that you have studied.
8. 'John Donne's poetry offers the reader some valuable insights on both the poet himself and his world.' Would you agree with this statement about the poetry of Donne? Support your answer by reference to the poems of Donne that you have studied.

More detailed information on prescribed poetry is available in *New Explorations Critical Notes* (edited by John G. Fahey)

Separate revisions of these notes are available for the 2003 and 2004 exams.

15 Answers

Answers to question 1 (page 23)

(a) When you look at the house from the outside it seems to have about twenty rooms.

(b) The writer makes use of short, terse sentences with both humour and sarcasm in order to maintain the reader's interest in the passage.

(c) Boyle, who is filled with self-delusion, sees himself as the man of the house.

(d) Many teenagers of this type come from homes where the parents are unable to control them properly, or where the mother is at work and hasn't enough time for her children.

(e) I would be delighted if you would reply and let me know whether or not you are available, and the possible times.

(f) The writer means by this statement that people usually make a place what it is by their presence there.

Answers to question 2 (page 23)

(a) When he states his arguments he gives a balanced account of both sides.

(b) This can be found in a magazine bought by rich people. It would not be likely to feature in a newspaper, as there are too many photographs.

(c) The house is not the usual type, as it is old and enormous and appears to have been restored.

(d) The environment surrounding a person can usually tell you a lot about that person. If, for instance, you were in an untidy house you would presume that the owner was an easy-going type of character.

(e) The impression I get of Oprah from her programme gives me some indication of the type of person she is and of her life-style. I think her home would also tell me a lot about her.

(f) The picture of the mirror and the woman with the pearls suggests that this family has a luxurious life-style.

Answers to question 3 (page 23)

(a) The play is filled with examples of both jealousy and betrayal. This is evident, for example, in the figure of Iago.

(b) University students consistently analyse their actions, for they may upset a friend or a teacher.

(c) I wish to inform you of the type of photographs and images that I would like included in my gallery.

(d) The difference between the cost price and the selling price rose.

(e) Trade fairs are a common commercial activity nowadays, many of them held in export markets.

(f) I believe the writer expresses himself and his observations of human motivations very well.

Answers to question 4 (page 23)

(a) I find myself struggling to retain my popularity.

(b) A time-and-motion study in this section would improve output.

(c) I am stuck in this claustrophobic condition, with no-one knowing either the despair or the loneliness I am experiencing.

(d) We regret to inform you that the Boxhead golf clubs you ordered on 15 July are not in stock.

(e) The 15:20 train that runs on weekdays in summer will not run on Sundays in either winter or summer.

(f) These people soldier on, living on very little as they struggle for success.

16 Past Examination Papers

AN ROINN OIDEACHAIS AGUS EOLAÍOCHTA
LEAVING CERTIFICATE EXAMINATION, 2001

English – Higher Level – Paper 1

Total Marks: 200

Wednesday, 6th June – Morning, 9.30 – 12.20

- This paper is divided into two sections, Section I COMPREHENDING and Section II COMPOSING.
- The paper contains **four** texts on the general theme of IRISHNESS.
- Candidates should familiarise themselves with each of the texts before beginning their answers.

- Both sections of this paper (COMPREHENDING and COMPOSING) must be attempted.
- Each section carries 100 marks.

SECTION I — COMPREHENDING

- Two Questions, A and B, follow each text.
- Candidates must answer a Question A on one text and a Question B on a different text. Candidates must answer only one Question A and only one Question B.
- **N.B.** Candidates may NOT answer a Question A and a Question B on the same text.

SECTION II — COMPOSING

- Candidates must write on **one** of the compositions 1–7.

Section I
COMPREHENDING (100 marks)

TEXT 1
BEING IRISH

The following extracts are adapted from the book, *Being Irish*, in which a number of contributors give their responses to the question 'What does it mean to be Irish today?' The book was published in 2000, and its editor is Paddy Logue.

Jennifer Johnston *is a writer and was born in Dublin in 1930.*
I have never found another country in which I would rather live and die. I feel great pride when we do things right and a great anger when we get things horribly wrong. All my bondings have happened in this country, with my family and the past, my city, and the whole landscape of the island, to the language we use and the way we have moulded it and made it different and vital, the stories we tell and the songs we sing and all the people with whom I have learned and worked and played. I feel comfortable here; the shoes of Irishness fit me well. What more can I say?

Polly Devlin *is a writer, broadcaster and conservationist. She lives in London.*
When I went to London at age nineteen my Irishness became something new in my life – something much less local but not quite real. My being Irish was used as an explanatory sort of fond shorthand among my English peers. The way 'she's Irish' or 'that's very Irish' was said seemed different from how 'she's French' was said. It seemed to me that there was a lot less baggage to being French in England. My nationality seemed more of a personal matter, as though it would account for any unpredictability in my nature. I was both flattered and resentful and, perhaps, being young and isolated, played up to it.

Seán McCague *is President of the Gaelic Athletic Association.*
The modern Ireland is a thriving economic entity that has still managed to treasure most of its traditions. Our rich cultural heritage has been protected while at the same time we welcome the world onto our shores. There is a unity of mind in being Irish. Our games, our heritage, our music, dance and our built and green heritage are all part of what we are.

Brian Kennedy is a singer from Belfast.
Songs are a safe place to visit how you really feel, regardless of the intensity. In trying to explain being Irish, I would say it's like taking a picture of the word 'sadness' and then taking another picture of the word 'joy'. When the film comes back from the chemist, it has been double-exposed and the two words have become superimposed like some strange hybrid. Someone told me they could hear this in my voice, especially when I sang an old Irish song.

Patricia Harty, a native of Tipperary, is Editor-in-Chief of Irish America *magazine.*
My heart lights up when I see another Irish person. I love Irish music, and there are more Irish *seisiúns* in New York than anywhere else. I believe I can tell an Irishman from the way he walks, the way he holds his head. With Irish people so much is left unsaid, or is said with a nod or a wink or an unspoken gesture. Like all people who have faced danger together, the Irish have a highly developed intuitive sense of each other.

Martin Mansergh is a special adviser to the Taoiseach on Northern Ireland, Economic and Social Matters.
To be Irish today is something to be proud of. It is to be part of a stunningly beautiful country that is a success story on many fronts, the peace process, an economy driven by technological innovation, as well as much cultural and sporting achievement. The resources exist at last to tackle outstanding social problems. Our young people look outwards.

N.B. Candidates may NOT answer Question A and Question B on the same text. Questions A and B carry 50 marks each.

Question A

(i) What aspects of Irishness emerge most strongly for you from the above extracts?
(20)
(ii) In your opinion, which one of the writers expresses his or her sense of Irishness best? Give reasons for your answer supporting it by reference to your chosen extract.
(15)
(iii) Choose **one** of the people in the above text and, based on the views he or she has expressed, write a short account of the kind of person you imagine him or her to be.
(15)

Question B

Imagine your job is to welcome a group of foreign students to Ireland. Write out the text of a short talk (150–200 words) in which you advise them how best to get along with the Irish people they will meet. (50)

TEXT 2
A NEW IRELAND

The following text is adapted from the inauguration speech of President Mary Robinson, the first woman to hold the office of President of Ireland. The speech was delivered on December 3rd, 1990.

Citizens of Ireland, mná na hÉireann agus fir na hÉireann, you have chosen me to represent you and I am humbled by and grateful for your trust.

The Ireland I will be representing is a new Ireland, open, tolerant, inclusive. Many of you who voted for me did so without sharing all my views. This, I believe, is a significant signal of change, a sign, however modest, that we have already passed the threshold to a new, pluralist Ireland. The recent revival of an old concept of the Fifth Province expresses this emerging Ireland of tolerance and empathy. The Fifth Province is not anywhere here or there, north or south, east or west. It is a place within each of us – that place that is open to the other, that swinging door which allows us to venture out and others to venture in. If I am a symbol of anything, I would like to be a symbol of this reconciling and healing Fifth Province.

My primary role as President will be to represent this state. But the state is not the only model of community with which Irish people can and do identify. Beyond our state there is a vast community of Irish emigrants extending not only across our neighbouring island but also throughout the continents of North America, Australia, and of course Europe itself. There are over seventy million people living on this globe who claim Irish descent. I will be proud to represent them.

There is another level of community which I will represent. Not just the national, not just the global, but the local community. Within our state there are a growing number of local and regional communities determined to express their own creativity, identity, heritage and initiative in new and exciting ways. In my travels around Ireland I have found local community groups thriving on a new sense of self-confidence and self-empowerment. Whether it was groups concerned with adult education, employment initiative, women's support, local history and heritage, environmental concern or community culture, one of the most enriching discoveries was to witness the extent of this local empowerment at work. As President I will seek to the best of my abilities to promote this growing sense of local participatory democracy, this emerging movement of self-development and self-expression which is surfacing more and more at grassroots level. This is the face of modern Ireland.

The best way we can contribute to a new and integrated Europe is by having a confident sense of our Irishness. Here again we must play to our strengths – take full advantage of our vibrant cultural resources in music, art, drama, literature, and film; value the role of our educators, promote and preserve our unique environmental and geographical resources of relatively pollution-free lakes, rivers, landscapes and seas; encourage, and publicly support local initiative projects in aquaculture, forestry, fishing, alternative energy and small-scale technology.

I want this Presidency to promote the telling of stories – stories of celebration through the arts and stories of conscience and of social justice. As a woman, I want women who have felt themselves outside history to be written back into history. May I have the fortune to preside over an Ireland at a time of exciting transformation, when we can enter a new Europe where old wounds can be healed, a time when, in the words of Séamus Heaney, 'hope and history rhyme'.

N.B. Candidates may NOT answer Question A and Question B on the same text. Questions A and B carry 50 marks each.

Question A

(i) Basing your answer on the text of the above speech, how do you think Mary Robinson views her role as President of Ireland? Outline your views in 150 to 200 words, supporting your points by reference to the text. (30)

(ii) To what extent would you find yourself in agreement or disagreement with her view of the role of President? Support your point of view by reference to the text. (20)

Question B

In the above text, Mary Robinson refers to the importance of 'the local community'. Write a short article (150–200 words) about a project or activity in your local community, which you admire or condemn. (50)

TEXT 3
AN IRISH SENSE OF HUMOUR

The following text is a narrative (in abridged form) taken from the poet Ciaran Carson's book *The Star Factory* which tells the story of Ulster and its people. The author tells us he received this story from his father. The book was first published in 1997.

Johnny McQueen and Agnes Reed were married during the war. Times were hard for them and they wished for nothing better than a home of their own. One morning Johnny spotted a little cottage that was up for rent in Mullaghbawn, with half an acre attached. The pair wasted no time and the next day they were installed in their own little house.

One night, as he was sitting by the fire contentedly smoking his pipe, Johnny announced that he would go to Newry to buy a spade or a shovel to 'do something with that half-acre out there'.

Next day Johnny went into Newry town and brought back what he needed. He was no sooner home than he went out the back and started to dig. A couple of hours went by and when Agnes looked out she couldn't see Johnny at all, he was down in this great hole, digging for all he was worth. So out she goes, and says:

'What in God's name are you at, at all?'

Johnny emerges from the hole and stands looking at it proudly.

'By God,' says he, 'isn't that a beautiful hole?'

'What use is it? What can you do with it?' says Agnes.

'I know what I can do with it,' says Johnny, 'I can put it in the paper and sell it, that's what I'll do.'

The next day Paddy Murphy was eating his breakfast and reading the *Frontier Sentinel* in his house in Newry town.

'Listen to this, Kathleen,' he says to his wife, 'here's the most peculiar ad I've seen in a long while: SUPERLATIVE HOLE FOR SALE; ALL ENQUIRIES TO 'FOUR WINDS', MULLAGHBAWN, CO. ARMAGH. I think I'll take a run over there right now and see what it's all about.'

It wasn't long till Paddy stood outside McQueen's. He knocked on the door and Johnny came out.

'Are you the man that has the hole?' says Paddy.

'I am,' says McQueen, 'are you interested?'

He took Paddy out and showed him the hole.

'By God,' says Paddy, 'I never saw such a hole in my life. She must be thirty foot deep.'

'She is,' says Johnny, 'and maybe more. Are you for buying?'

'I am, surely,' says Paddy, 'how much are you looking?'

'Well, she's worth twenty pound, for she took me the guts of a whole day digging her, but seeing I'm a Newry man myself, I'll let her go for ten.'

'Fair enough,' says Murphy, 'it's a deal. But how will I get her home to Newry?'

'Well,' says Johnny, 'there's always the Ulster Transport Authority.'

So Paddy landed at the UTA depot in Newry and he said to the clerk: 'I'm just after buying this hole beyond in Mullaghbawn, and I'd like to hire a lorry and six men to bring her back to Newry.'

'That's all in order,' says the clerk, 'I'll have a lorry and a gang of men out there in no time, and you should have the hole some time tomorrow afternoon.'

Next day Paddy spent the whole afternoon pacing the floor waiting for the hole to arrive. Night came and there was no word of the hole. So, next morning he went to the UTA office and demanded to speak to the manager.

'It's like this,' says Paddy, 'I bought a hole beyond in Mullaghbawn, and I was looking forward to having her installed in the front garden, and I hired a lorry and six men in this very office for the job, and damn the hole I've seen yet. What kind of service do you call that?'

'You're right,' says the manager, 'this won't do at all.' And he called over to the clerk for an explanation.

'Oh,' says the clerk, 'are you the man that bought the hole? Well, I sent out a lorry and a gang of men, and after struggling with the hole for seven hours, they eventually succeeded in placing her on the back of the vehicle; but there's a wild steep incline between Mullaghbawn and Newry, and the hole fell off the back of the lorry. The men were trying their level best to get the hole back on, when the lorry fell into the hole. The men then tried to haul the lorry out of the hole, but fell in themselves, and we haven't seen sight nor hair of them since!'

N.B. Candidates may NOT answer Question A and Question B on the same text. Questions A and B carry 50 marks each.

Question A
(i) Where in this story, did it first strike you it was going to be a funny tale? Account for your answer. (10)
(ii) In the remainder of the story, what are the signals that let you know it is intended to be a humorous story? (20)
(iii) Write a paragraph (100–150 words) in which you comment on the appropriateness of the title, 'An Irish Sense of Humour'.

Question B
Imagine your local radio station is producing a programme entitled *COMIC MOMENTS*

in which a person from the community introduces his/her favourite comic moment from the world of radio, television, or live performance. Write the text (150–200 words) of the presentation you would like to make. (50)

TEXT 4
IMAGES OF IRELAND

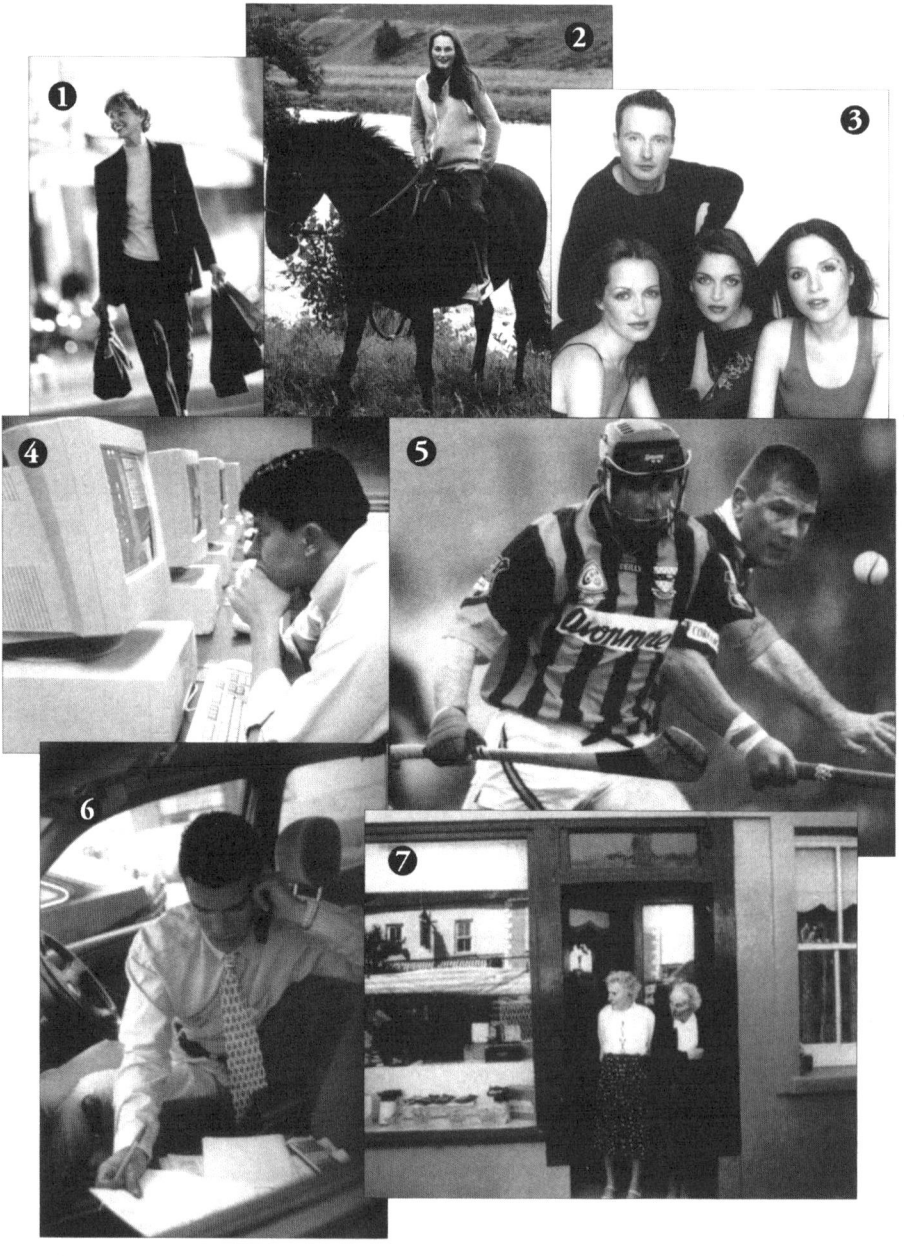

N.B. Candidates may NOT answer Question A and Question B on the same text.
Questions A and B carry 50 marks each.

Question A

(i) Taking all of the above images into account, in your opinion what overall picture of Ireland is projected in this visual text? Outline your views in 150–200 words, supporting your points by reference to the images. (20)

(ii) (a) Imagine this series of images is to be used in a brochure whose objective it is to promote Ireland abroad. Which one of the images would you choose for its front cover? Justify your choice. (15)

(b) You are the editor of the brochure mentioned in part (a). Which one of the images would you judge to be **least representative** of the Ireland you wish to promote? Justify your choice. (15)

Question B

A Day in the Life

Choose **one** of the people pictured in TEXT 4 and write **four** short diary entries that your chosen person might write on **one important day** in his/her life. You should indicate clearly the person you have chosen and you should write the diary entries as though you were that person. (50)

SECTION II
COMPOSING (100 marks)

Write a composition on **any one** of the following.
Each composition carries 100 marks.
The composition assignments below are intended to reflect language study in the areas of information, argument, persuasion, narration, and the aesthetic use of language.

1. 'Citizens of Ireland . . . you have chosen me to represent you . . .' (TEXT 2)
   You have been elected President of Ireland. Write the first speech you would make to the Irish people.
2. 'The shoes of Irishness fit me well.' (Jennifer Johnston, TEXT 1)
   Write a personal essay in which you explore your sense of what it means to be Irish.
3. 'Our games are . . . part of what we are.' (Seán McCague, TEXT 1)
   Write an article intended for inclusion in the sports pages of a newspaper in which you attempt to persuade your readers of the value of sport in our lives.
4. 'Songs are a safe place to visit how you really feel.' (Brian Kennedy, TEXT 1)
   Write an article for your school or local magazine in which you explore your feelings about the place of music and/or songs in your life.

5. 'Our young people look outwards.' (Martin Mansergh, TEXT 1)
   Write a letter to Martin Mansergh in which you outline your response to his view of young Irish people.
6. 'An Irish Sense of Humour.' (TEXT 3)
   Write a narrative similar in style to the story told in TEXT 3.
7. Write a short story prompted by one or more of the images in TEXT 4.

AN ROINN OIDEACHAIS AGUS EOLAÍOCHTA
LEAVING CERTIFICATE EXAMINATION, 2001

English – Higher Level – Paper 2

Total Marks: 200

Wednesday, 6th June – Afternoon, 1.30 – 4.50

Candidates must attempt the following:
- **ONE** question from SECTION I—The Single Text
- **ONE** question from SECTION II—The Comparative Study
- **THE QUESTIONS** on the Unseen Poem from SECTION III—Poetry
- **ONE** question on Prescribed Poetry from SECTION III—Poetry

N.B. Candidates must answer on Shakespearean Drama.
They may do so in SECTION I, The Single Text (*King Lear, Hamlet*)
Or in SECTION II, The Comparative Study (*Hamlet, Henry V, King Lear, Othello*)

INDEX OF SINGLE TEXTS	
Jane Eyre	—page 2
Great Expectations	—page 2
Far from the Madding Crowd	—page 2
King Lear	—page 3
Hamlet	—page 3
Antigone	—page 3

SECTION I
THE SINGLE TEXT (60 MARKS)

Candidates must answer **one** question from this section (**A–F**).

A *Jane Eyre*—Charlotte Brontë

  (i) "Despite great changes in her life's circumstances, Jane Eyre remains true to herself."

  Do you agree with this view of Jane? Support your answer by reference to the novel.

OR

  (ii) "Injustice is a major feature of the world of Charlotte Brontë's *Jane Eyre*."

  Discuss this view of the novel, supporting your answer by reference to the text.

B *Great Expectations*—Charles Dickens

  (i) "Magwitch's act of generosity towards Pip has both negative and positive effects on the development of Pip's character throughout the novel."

  Discuss this statement, supporting your answer by reference to the novel.

OR

  (ii) "*Great Expectations* is a masterpiece, full of memorable incidents and bizarre characters."

  Do you agree with this assessment of the novel? Support your answer by reference to the novel.

C *Far from the Madding Crowd*—Thomas Hardy

  (i) What is your view of the decisions Bathsheba makes in matters of romance and affairs of the heart? Support your answer by reference to the novel.

OR

  (ii) "The characters, Oak, Troy and Boldwood, represent different aspects of male behaviour and values."

  Discuss this statement supporting your points by reference to the novel.

D *King Lear*—William Shakespeare

  (i) What, in your view, are the most important changes that take place in the character of Lear during the play, *King Lear*? Support your points by reference to the play.

OR

(ii) "Scenes of great suffering and of great tenderness help to make *King Lear* a very memorable play."

Discuss this statement, supporting your answer by reference to the play, *King Lear*.

E *Hamlet*—William Shakespeare

(i) "The struggle between Hamlet and Claudius is a fascinating one."

Discuss this statement, supporting your answer by reference to the play, *Hamlet*.

OR

(ii) Choose the scene from Shakespeare's *Hamlet* that in your view was the most dramatic. Discuss your choice, supporting your answer by reference to the play. [Textual support may include reference to a particular performance of the play that you have seen.]

F *Antigone*—Sophocles

(i) "*Antigone* is memorable for its ideas and for its dramatic action."

Discuss this statement, supporting your answer by reference to the play.

OR

(ii) How would you judge the attitudes and behaviour of the character of Antigone throughout Sophocles's play? Support your views by reference to the text.

SECTION II
THE COMPARATIVE STUDY (70 MARKS)

Candidates must answer **one** question from **either A** — Theme or Issue **or B** – Literary Genre.

In your answer you may not use the text you have answered on in **SECTION I** — The Single Text.

N.B. The questions use the word **text** to refer to all the different kinds of texts available for study on this course, i.e. novel, play, short story, autobiography, biography, travel and film. The questions use the word **author** to refer to novelists, playwrights, writers in all genre, and film-directors.

A THEME OR ISSUE

1. "Narratives can broaden our understanding of a theme or issue."

   Compare the texts you have studied in your comparative course in the light of the above statement. Support your comparisons by reference to the texts. (70)

   OR

2. "A key moment in a narrative text can illustrate a theme or issue very powerfully."

   (a) Choose **one** of the texts you studied as part of your comparative course and show how an important moment from it illustrates a theme or issue. (30)

   (b) Write a short comparative commentary on **one key moment** from each of the other texts you have studied in the light of your discussion in part (a) above. (40)

B LITERARY GENRE

1. Write an essay on **one or more** of the aspects of literary genre (the way texts tell their stories) which you found most interesting in the texts you studied in your comparative course. Your essay should make clear comparisons between the texts you choose to write about. (70)

   OR

2. "No two texts are exactly the same in the manner in which they tell their stories."

   (a) Compare **two** of the texts you have studied in your comparative course in the light of the above statement. Support the comparisons you make by reference to the texts. (40)

   (b) Write a short comparative commentary on a third text from your comparative study in the light of your discussions in part (a) above. (30)

SECTION III
POETRY (70 MARKS)

Candidates must answer **A** — Unseen Poem **and B** — Prescribed Poetry.

A UNSEEN POEM (20 marks)
Answer questions **1 and 2**.
In this poem by Edna St Vincent Millay the princess recalls a moment that fills her with sadness.

Read this poem at least twice and then answer the questions that follow it.

THE PRINCESS RECALLS HER ONE ADVENTURE

Hard is my pillow
Of down from the duck's breast,
Harsh the linen cover;
I cannot rest.

Fall down, my tears,
Upon the fine hem,
Upon the lonely letters
Of my long name;
Drown the sigh of them.

We stood by the lake
And we neither kissed nor spoke;
We heard how the small waves
Lurched and broke
And chuckled in the rock.

We spoke and turned away.
We never kissed at all.
Fall down, my tears.
I wish that you might fall
On the road by the lake,
Where my cob* went lame,   *a horse
And I stood with the groom
Till the carriage came.

1. (a) What, in your opinion, has made the princess sad? (4)

   (b) Choose two phrases from the poem that show best how she is feeling. Write each one down and say, in each case, why you have chosen it. (6)

2. What kind of life do you imagine the princess lives? Explain your view by referring to words or phrases from the poem. (10)

B PRESCRIBED POETRY (50 marks)

Candidates must answer **one** of the following questions (**1–4**).

1. "Introducing Elizabeth Bishop."

   Write out the text of a short presentation you would make to your friends or class group under the above title. Support your point of view by reference to or quotation from the poetry of Elizabeth Bishop that you have studied.

2. Often we love a poet because of the feelings his/her poems create in us. Write about

the feelings John Keats's poetry creates in you and the aspects of the poems (their content and/or style) that help to create those feelings. Support your points by reference to the poetry by Keats that you have studied.

3. Write an essay in which you outline your reasons for liking and/or not liking the poetry of Philip Larkin. Support your points by reference to the poetry of Larkin that you have studied.

4. What impact did the poetry of Michael Longley make on you as a reader? In shaping your answer you might consider some of the following:

– *Your overall sense of the personality or outlook of the poet*

– *The poet's use of language and imagery*

– *Your favourite poem or poems.*

Acknowledgments (2001 Examination Paper)

For permission to reproduce copyright material in this examination paper, the publishers gratefully acknowledge the following:
Granta Books for an extract from *The Star Factory* by Ciaran Carson;
Elizabeth Barrett, literary executor for 'The Princess Recalls Her One Adventure' by Edna St Vincent Millay.

AN ROINN OIDEACHAIS AGUS EOLAÍOCHTA
LEAVING CERTIFICATE EXAMINATION, 2002

English – Higher Level – Paper 1

Total Marks: 200

Wednesday 5th June — Morning, 9.30–12.20

- This paper is divided into two sections, Section I COMPREHENDING and Section II COMPOSING.
- The paper contains **three** texts on the general theme of FAMILY.
- Candidates should familiarise themselves with each of the texts before beginning their answers.

- Both sections of this paper (COMPREHENDING and COMPOSING) must be attempted.
- Each section carries 100 marks.

SECTION I — COMPREHENDING

- Two Questions, A and B, follow each text.
- Candidates must answer a Question A on one text and a Question B on a different text. Candidates must answer only one Question A and only one Question B.
- **N.B.** Candidates may NOT answer a Question A and a Question B on the same text.

SECTION II — COMPOSING

- Candidates must write on **one** of the compositions 1–7.

SECTION I
COMPREHENDING (100 marks)

TEXT I
THE FAMILY OF MAN

The following text consists of a written and a visual element. The written part of this text is adapted from a preface by the American poet, Carl Sandburg, to a collection of photographs entitled **The Family of Man**. The visual images are taken from the exhibition which was first shown in the Museum of Modern Art, New York, in 1955.

PREFACE by Carl Sandburg

The first cry of a newborn baby in Chicago or Zamboango, in Amsterdam or Rangoon, has the same pitch and key, each saying, "I am! I have come through! I belong! I am a member of the Family."

When you look at these images you see that the wonder of human mind, heart, wit and instinct, is here. You might catch yourself saying, "I'm not a stranger here." People, flung wide and far, born into toil, struggle, blood and dreams, among lovers, eaters, drinkers, workers, loafers, fighters, players, gamblers. Here are ironworkers, bridgemen, musicians, sandhogs, miners, builders of huts and skyscrapers, jungle hunters, landlords and landless, the loved and the unloved, the lonely and the abandoned, the brutal and the compassionate – one big family hugging close to the ball of Earth for its life and being.

Here or there you may witness a startling harmony. In a seething of saints and sinners, winners and losers, in a womb of superstition, faith, genius, crime, sacrifice, here is the People, ever lighted by the reality or the illusion of hope. Hope is a sustaining human gift.

Everywhere is love and love-making, weddings and babies from generation to generation keeping the Family of Man alive and continuing. Everywhere the sun, moon and stars, the climates and weathers, have meanings for people. Though meanings vary, we are alike in all countries and tribes in trying to read what sky, land and sea say to us. Alike and ever alike we are all on continents in the need of love, food, clothing, work, speech, worship, sleep, games, dancing, fun. From tropics to arctics humanity lives with these needs so alike, so inexorably alike.

If the human face is "the masterpiece of God" it is here then in fateful registrations. Often the faces speak what words can never say. Faces of blossom smiles or mouths of hunger are followed by homely faces of majesty carved and worn by love, prayer and hope, along with others light and carefree as thistledown in a late summer wind. They are faces beyond forgetting, written over with faith and dreams of mankind surpassing itself. An alphabet is here and a multiplication table of living breathing human faces. An epic woven of fun, mystery and holiness – here is the Family of Man!

N.B. Candidates may NOT answer Question A and Question B on the same text.

Questions A and B carry 50 marks each.

QUESTION A

(i) What impact do the visual images in this text make upon you? Give reasons for your answer supporting them by reference to the images. (20)

(ii) What, in your opinion, is the most important point that Carl Sandburg makes in his preface to the images in the exhibition? (20)

(iii) Do you think that the written and visual elements of the text go well together? Illustrate your answer by brief reference to the text as a whole. (10)

QUESTION B

Choose **one** of the visual images in this text and, in a **letter** to Carl Sandburg, write your response to its inclusion in the exhibition of photographs entitled *The Family of Man*. [The images have been numbered so that you can indicate your choice clearly.]
(50)

TEXT 2
FAMILY HOME FOR SALE

Novelist, Penelope Lively, remembers her family home through the wealth of little things it contained. This article was published in The Sunday Times *of August 26, 2001.*

A few years ago, the house in which my grandmother had set up home in 1923 had to be sold. It had seen more than seventy years of occupancy by my family, and hardly a hair of its head had been changed during that time. Everything was still as it had always been – the gong-stand by the front door, the photograph albums in the hall chest, the tarnished contents of the silver cupboard, the horsehair mattress on which I slept in the dressing-room during my school holidays.

This country house, tucked away in West Somerset, had seen out the century, and it reflected seven decades of social change. Its furnishings were a secret message, if you knew how to read the code. The place was eloquent; the old sewing machine in the attic, the bell panel in the pantry, the oil-lamps stashed away on the larder shelves, the faded rosettes in the stables – everything spoke of the way we lived then.

Any house tells a story; its furnishings are a shining reference to some aspect of past habitation. They seem to me to be more than just the backdrop of one family's life, and to bear witness to the events of the past. And in this sense our old home was peculiarly well stocked with archival matter. In a large house with cupboards and disused rooms, things are not discarded, they are simply "put away". Seventy years of putting away had created strata from which we retrieved my grandmother's 100-year-old wedding dress, bound volumes of *Punch* from the 1880s onwards, Thermos flasks of the 1950s, a forest of walking sticks, an army of glass jars for fruit bottling, Primus stoves, preserving pans. Granted reincarnation, I would like to be an archaeologist. There is something extraordinarily emotive and exciting about the deductions that can be made about an entire way of life from a few surviving shards, bones, scraps of metal, shadows on the ground.

Through our family homes most of us have an accumulated freight of objects that speak to us of the life history of our own family, all the bits and pieces that we have acquired ourselves along with the things that have filtered down through the generations – an ancestral desk, a grandmother's necklace, a parent's books or pictures. A number of years ago I visited the Soviet Union, as it then was, with a group of British writers; we were entertained one evening in the flat of one of our hosts – two cramped rooms in which all the furnishings were contemporary and utilitarian. I noticed a pretty 19th century coffee cup. Our hostess told me that it had belonged to her mother: "It is all that she had left from her home, after the war." One coffee cup; I thought of the wealth of physical objects that conjure up other times and other people in a country spared such punishment.

N.B. Candidates may NOT answer Question A and Question B on the same text.

Questions A and B carry 50 marks each.

QUESTION A
(i) How, in your opinion, does Penelope Lively feel about her family home? Support your view by detailed reference to the text. (20)

(ii) What features of good descriptive writing are to be found in the above passage? Illustrate the points you make from the text. (20)

(iii) Why, in your view, does the writer include the reference to her visit to the Soviet Union? (10)

QUESTION B
Family Home and Contents for Sale
Drawing on the detail in the above text, and its accompanying illustration, draft the text of an advertisement that offers the home and its contents for sale. (50)

TEXT 3
FAMILIES IN A TIME OF CRISIS

This text is an extract from the novel, The Grapes of Wrath, *by the American writer, John Steinbeck. The novel tells the story of poor farming families who are forced to travel hundreds of miles across America in search of a living. In this extract we learn how the desire of families to support one another leads to the setting up of a society in itself. The novel was first published in 1939.*

The cars of the migrant people crawled out of the side roads on to the great cross-country highway, and they took the migrant way to the West. In the daylight they scuttled like bugs to the westward; and as the dark caught them, they clustered like bugs near to shelter and to water. And because they were lonely and perplexed, because they had all come from a place of sadness and worry and defeat, and because they were all going to a new mysterious place, they huddled together; they talked together; they shared their lives, their food, and the things they hoped for in the new country. Thus it might be that one family camped near a spring, and another camped for the spring and for company, and a third because two families had pioneered the place and found it good. And when the sun went down, perhaps twenty families and twenty cars were there.

In the evening a strange thing happened: the twenty families became one family, the children were the children of all. The loss of home became one loss, and the golden time in the West was one dream. And it might be that a sick child threw despair into the hearts of twenty families, of a hundred people; that a birth there in a tent kept a hundred people quiet and awestruck through the night and filled a hundred people with the birth-joy in the morning. A family which the night before had been lost and fearful might search its goods to find a present for a new baby. In the evening, sitting about the fires, the twenty were one. They grew to the units of the camps, units of the evenings, and the nights. A guitar unwrapped from a blanket and tuned – and the songs, which were all of people, were sung in the nights. Every night relationships that make a world, established; and every morning the world torn down like a circus. At first the families were timid in the building and tumbling worlds, but gradually the technique of building worlds became their technique. Then leaders emerged, then laws were made, then codes came into being. And as the worlds moved westward they were more complete and better furnished, for their builders were more experienced in building them.

The families learned what rights must be observed – the right of privacy in the tent; the right to keep the past hidden in the heart; the right to talk and to listen; the right to refuse help or to accept, to offer or to decline it; the right of son to court daughter and daughter to be courted; the right of the hungry to be fed; the rights of the pregnant and the sick to transcend all other rights. And as the worlds moved westward, the rights became rules, became laws, although no one told the families. And with the laws, the punishments – and there were only two – a quick and murderous fight, or ostracism; and ostracism was the worst. For if one broke the laws his name and face went with him, and he had no place in any world, no matter where created.

There grew up a government in the worlds, with leaders, with elders. A man who was wise found that his wisdom was needed in every camp, and a kind of insurance developed in these nights. A man with food fed a hungry man, and thus insured himself against hunger. And when a baby died a pile of silver coins grew at the door flap of the tent, for a baby must be well buried, since it has had nothing else of life.

N.B. Candidates may NOT answer Question A and Question B on the same text. Questions A and B carry 50 marks each.

QUESTION A
(i) How does the language of the opening paragraph suggest the powerlessness of the migrant people? Support your answer by reference to the text. (20)

(ii) In the remainder of the passage, how does Steinbeck show the bonds between people becoming stronger and more powerful? Support your points by reference to the text. (20)

(iii) "There grew up a government in the worlds . . . " Look again at the final paragraph. What, in your view, is the most important thing it says about people? Explain your answer, illustrating briefly from the text. (10)

QUESTION B
"Rights Must Be Observed"

You have been asked to give a short talk on radio or television about a fundamental human right that you would like to see supported more strongly. Write out the text of the talk you would give. (50)

SECTION II
COMPOSING (100 marks)

Write a composition on **any one** of the following.

Each composition carries 100 marks.

The composition assignments below are intended to reflect language study in the areas of information, argument, persuasion, narration and the aesthetic use of language.

1. ". . . one big family hugging close to the ball of Earth for its life and being . . ." (TEXT 1)

   Write a personal essay in response to the above phrase.

2. "Hope is a sustaining human gift." (TEXT 1)

   You have been asked to deliver a speech on this theme to a group of young people. Write out the speech you would give.

3. ". . . the life history of our own family . . ." (TEXT 2)

   Write an article for a popular magazine or journal in which you explore the aspects of your own family that are special to you. You may, if you wish, write your composition in diary format.
   [N.B. You should not use your own family name.]

4. ". . . after the war." (TEXT 2)

   Write a short story suggested by the above title.

5. ". . . relationships that make a world . . . and . . . the world torn down like a circus . . ." (TEXT 3)

   Write an article (serious or humorous) about the beginning and ending of a relationship in your life.

6. ". . . then laws were made . . ." (TEXT 3)

Write a serious article in which you argue for or against the importance of laws in our society.

7. Write a short story prompted by one or more of the images in TEXT 1.

AN ROINN OIDEACHAIS AGUS EOLAÍOCHTA
LEAVING CERTIFICATE EXAMINATION, 2002

English – Higher Level – Paper 2

Total Marks: 200

Wednesday, 5th June – Afternoon, 1.30 – 4.50

Candidates must attempt the following:
- **ONE** question from SECTION I—The Single Text
- **ONE** question from SECTION II—The Comparative Study
- **THE QUESTIONS** on the Unseen Poem from SECTION III—Poetry
- **ONE** question on Prescribed Poetry from SECTION III—Poetry

N.B. Candidates must answer on Shakespearean Drama.
They may do so in SECTION I, The Single Text (*King Lear, Hamlet*)
Or in SECTION II, The Comparative Study (*Hamlet, Henry V, King Lear, Othello*)

INDEX OF SINGLE TEXTS	
Jane Eyre	—page 2
Great Expectations	—page 2
Far from the Madding Crowd	—page 2
King Lear	—page 3
Hamlet	—page 3
Antigone	—page 3

SECTION I
THE SINGLE TEXT (60 marks)

Candidates must answer **one** question from this section (**A–F**).

A *Jane Eyre*—Charlotte Brontë

   (i) "While many of the situations that Jane finds herself in are sad and pitiful, she responds to them with strength and independence."

   Discuss this statement, supporting your answer by reference to the novel.

OR

   (ii) "In the novel, *Jane Eyre*, we meet characters who show us the best and the worst in human nature."

   Write a response to this statement, supporting your answer by reference to the novel.

B *Great Expectations*—Charles Dickens

   (i) "The course of the relationship between Pip and Estella makes for wonderful reading."

   What is your view of this statement? Refer to the novel in your answer.

OR

   (ii) "In *Great Expectations*, Dickens brilliantly describes a world full of cruelty and inequality."

   Discuss this assessment of *Great Expectations*. Support your answer by reference to the novel.

C *Far From the Madding Crowd*—Thomas Hardy

   (i) "Of all the characters (both male and female) we meet in the novel, Gabriel Oak is the real hero."

   Write a response to this statement supporting it by reference to the novel, *Far From the Madding Crowd*.

OR

   (ii) "In *Far From the Madding Crowd*, Hardy shows he is a superb storyteller who invents fascinating characters and colourful incidents."

   Discuss this statement, supporting the points you make by reference to the novel.

D *King Lear*—William Shakespeare

(i) "Powerful images heighten our experience of the play, *King Lear*".

Write your response to this statement. Textual support may include reference to a particular performance you have seen of the play.

OR

(ii) "Cordelia plays a very important role in the play, *King Lear*."

Discuss this view of Cordelia, supporting your answer by reference to the play.

E *Hamlet*—William Shakespeare

(i) "The appeal of Shakespeare's *Hamlet* lies primarily in the complex nature of the play's central character, Hamlet."

To what extent would you agree with the above statement? Support your view by reference to the play.

OR

(ii) What is your view of the importance of **either** Gertrude **or** Ophelia in Shakespeare's play, *Hamlet*?

Support the points you make by reference to the play.

F *Antigone*—Sophocles

(i) "Creon's unwilling journey from pride and power towards humiliation and weakness leaves him utterly devastated."

Discuss this view of Creon's journey, supporting your points by reference to the play, *Antigone*.

OR

(ii) "The play, *Antigone*, is a tragic struggle between conflicting rights."

Write a response to this statement, supporting your answer by reference to the play, *Antigone*.

SECTION II
THE COMPARATIVE STUDY (70 MARKS)

Candidates must answer **one** question from **either A** — Theme or Issue **or B** – The Cultural Context.

In your answer you may not use the text you have answered on in **SECTION I** — The Single Text.

N.B. The questions use the word **text** to refer to all the different kinds of texts available for study on this course, i.e. novel, play, short story, autobiography, biography, travel and film. The questions use the word **author** to refer to novelists, playwrights, writers in all genre, and film-directors.

A THEME OR ISSUE

1. "A theme or issue explored in a group of narrative texts can offer us valuable insights into life."

    Compare the texts you have studied in your comparative course in the light of the above statement. Your discussion must focus on **one** theme or issue. Support the comparisons you make by reference to the texts. (70)

    OR

2. *(a)* Compare the treatment of a theme or issue in **two** of the texts you have studied as part of your comparative course. Support the comparisons you make by reference to the texts. (40)

    (b) Discuss the treatment of **the same theme or issue** in a third text in the light of your answer to part *(a)* above. (30)

B THE CULTURAL CONTEXT

1. "A narrative text creates its own unique world in which the reader can share."

    Write a response to the above statement in which you compare the texts you have studied as part of your comparative course. Support the comparisons you make by reference to the texts. (70)

    OR

2. *(a)* What is your understanding of the term Cultural Context in relation to any **one** of the texts in your comparative course? Support your view by reference to **at least one** key moment from your chosen text. (30)

    (b) Compare **two other texts** from your comparative course in the light of your understanding of the term Cultural Context as you have discussed it in part *(a)* above. Support the comparisons you make by reference to **at least one** key moment from each of these two texts. (40)

SECTION III
POETRY (70 MARKS)

Candidates must answer **A** — Unseen Poem **and B** — Prescribed Poetry.

A   UNSEEN POEM (20 marks)
Answer questions **1 and 2**.

The poet, Thomas McCarthy, reflects upon the introduction of the euro.

Read the poem at least twice and then answer the questions that follow it.

THE EURO

I've seen the first photograph of the new Euro
in a shop-window in Patrick Street.

Rather than anything that belongs to the future,
it reminds me of the orange ten-shilling note

of my childhood: an orange note
that held the promise of so much happiness.

With a ten-shilling note you could buy
almost anything in Mansfield's shop;

you could take the boat and train to Wembley;
you could secure a bicycle for Christmas
all the way back from the month of September.

I wonder if a boy like myself will think
of a ten-Euro note as something promising –
Though paper money, now, can hardly mean the same

as it did to me, a child of coins.
Somewhere, perhaps in a provincial European city,
in Bologna, maybe, or Antwerp or Nantes,

there is a small boy of ten – a child of coins –
for whom the Euro will come
like a sudden ache of optimism, a sunbeam

to illuminate the cleared path ahead.

I have high hopes for that boy. I honour him.

1. What impact does the first sighting of the new euro make upon the poet? Support your answer by reference to the poem. (10)

2. How well, in your view, does the poem capture the sense of excitement and hope that the introduction of the euro could hold for "a small boy of ten"? Illustrate your answer by reference to the language of the poem. (10)

B **PRESCRIBED POETRY** (50 marks)

Candidates must answer **one** of the following questions (**1–4**).

1. "The poetry of Elizabeth Bishop appeals to the modern reader for many reasons."

    Write an essay in which you outline the reasons why poems by Elizabeth Bishop have this appeal.

2. Write a personal response to the poetry of Eavan Boland.

    Support the points you make by reference to the poetry of Boland that you have studied.

3. Imagine you have invited Michael Longley to give a reading of his poems to your class or group. What poems would you ask him to read and why do you think they would appeal to your fellow students?

4. "Choosing Shakespeare's Sonnets."

    Imagine your task is to make a small collection of sonnets by William Shakespeare from those that are on your course. Write an introduction to the poems that you would choose to include.

Acknowledgments (2002 Examination Paper)

For permission to reproduce copyright material in this examination paper, the publishers gratefully acknowledge the following:
Harcourt Inc. for Carl Sandburg's preface to the collection of photographs entitled *The Family of Man*;
Reed International for an extract from *The Grapes of Wrath* by John Steinbeck;
Anvil Press Poetry Ltd for 'The Euro' by Thomas McCarthy.
The publishers have made every effort to trace copyright holders, but if they have inadvertently overlooked any they will be pleased to make the necessary arrangements at the first opportunity.